Transforming Fate into Destiny

Transforming Fate into Destiny

The Theological Ethics of
Stanley Hauerwas

Samuel Wells

paternoster press

Paternoster Press is an imprint of Paternoster Publishing,
P.O. Box 300, Carlisle, Cumbria, CA3 0QS, U.K.
http://www.paternoster-publishing.com

British Library Cataloguing in Publication Data
A catalogue record for this book is available from the British Library

ISBN 0-85364-906-5

This book is printed using Suffolk New Book paper which is 100% acid free

Cover Design by Mainstream, Lancaster
Typeset by Westkey Ltd, Falmouth, Cornwall
Printed in Great Britain by
Caledonian International Book Manufacturing Ltd, Glasgow

To Ruth Wells
(1930–84)
who knew what
it meant
to be a resident alien

non manentem civitatem

'If you would avoid tragedy (and suffering), avoid love;
if you cannot avoid love, avoid integrity;
if you cannot avoid integrity, avoid the world;
if you cannot avoid the world, destroy it.'

Stanley Covell, *Must We Mean What We Say?*
(Cambridge: Cambridge University Press 1969) p. 349.

Contents

Foreword

I like to think that theology is a communal activity. I say 'like', because such a view may be pure fantasy as theology in modernity cannot help but appear as the product of an individual author. As a result, even theologians like Karl Barth are read as if they are putting forward a 'position' – which, of course, in some ways is undeniable. The irony is that Barth's 'position' was an attempt to defeat other positions in the hope he might say no more than what the Church prayerfully believes.

As a result, the unfinished character of Barth's work at once frustrates some and enthralls others. Massive as the *Dogmatics* are, there is still always something else that needs to be said because of what the Church said through Barth's way of saying. In this respect, as is increasingly recognized in other respects as well, Aquinas and Barth in quite different ways provide a compendium of what the Church thinks through those who have been called across time to the ministry of theology. Compendiums are but a reminder that theology not only depends on a community called Church for intelligibility, but theological work is possible because of those who have gone before as well as those who will come after.

Though I have no pretensions that that little thing called 'my work' can in any way be compared to Barth or Aquinas, I am extremely grateful for the presentation of my work Sam Wells provides in this book. Wells has shown not only that my work is incomplete but that it is necessarily so. Indeed one of the things I so like about this book is the way he shows much of what I try to say only works if supplemented by aspects of what Yoder or Milbank have said. As a result, Wells exposes the communal character of the way I try to work by showing how what I do requires work that others have done better.

Yet Wells' criticism of my work, as well as his own suggestions about the way forward, is equally important for indicating the communal character of theology. This book is not an account of what 'Hauerwas has said', though Wells has certainly provided a wonderfully fair account of what I hope I have said; but rather, Wells has made me say more than I could have said.

I am particularly grateful to Wells for understanding those aspects of my work that I refuse to 'explain'. For example, he sees how an essay like the one I wrote on the suicides at Jonestown was not just about that terror, but was a response to those who think I can provide no way to speak of the truthfulness of Christian convictions. That essay, among others, was, as Wells rightly understands, also meant to give the lie to the accusation I am a relativist. It does no good to mount formal arguments against relativism because such arguments too often simply reproduce the mistakes that created the so-called problem of relativism in the first place. My alternative to such formal responses is, as Wells suggests, to provide in essays like the one on Jonestown a performance in the hope that the truth Christians name about suicide is manifest. Put simply, I believe suicide is a denial of the God Christians know as Father, Son and Holy Spirit.

I am equally grateful to Wells for his account of what he wonderfully calls 'smaller stories', and the role they play in how I try to do theology. Theologians can be perfectly 'orthodox', for example, in their understanding of the relation between creation and redemption, but too often such orthodoxy cannot help but be words that do not work. Wells rightly locates my fundamental conviction that the best way to display the relation of creation and redemption is in relation to everyday matters such as the having and caring for children. Having children is part of God's good gift of creation; yet creation, as well as the having of children, beckons an eschatological future without which creation or children are unintelligible. Christians can and do joyfully have children because we know our very existence is eschatologically constituted.

I confess, however, that Wells' display of the way I try to do theology does raise a question for me: that is, why am I so much better understood in Europe than in America? American readers never seem to be able to get beyond the slogans that allegedly describe my work, for example, that I am a sectarian, and as a result they miss the details without which what I am trying to do is empty. In contrast, Wells sees the adequacy or inadequacy of my work is to be found in the details. Thus slogans like 'the first task of the Church is not to make the world more just, but to make the world the world', are rightly understood in the light of my discussion of the process of judgement and reconciliation found in Matthew 18. My account of such practices, moreover, entails my 'metaphysics', since I believe that such a practice not only describes how Christians must act in relation to one another but reveals the very character of God's creation.

I can only speculate why my work is better appreciated, or at least given a hearing, in Britain than in the United States. Surely part of the reason is the Church in Britain no longer has any pretensions of being 'in control'. As a result some of the things I say that seem 'outrageous' in America must appear rather commonplace in Britain and Europe. I suspect also at work is a quite different intellectual culture. Wells reads me as a theologian not, as is often the case in America, someone who specializes in a disciplinary subdivision called Christian ethics. Accordingly he understands how, for example, my emphasis on the virtues is but part of a much more determinative theological agenda. All of which is to say that I hope Wells' book finds an American audience not simply because through it I will be better understood, but because his wonderful suggestions about how we might do better what I have tried to do will move us beyond battles it matters not who wins.

In conclusion, there is nothing for me to do but praise God that someone as thoughtful and good as Sam Wells has read me and found some use in what he has read. As I suggested at the beginning that theology is a communal practice that requires we help one another, then it is surely a sign what a wonderful God we serve that Sam Wells has found and made connections with me and my work that make us more than we would otherwise be. I hope, therefore, I will not be misunderstood when I say it makes me very happy that a Sam Wells exists who can write a book as hopeful as *Transforming Fate Into Destiny*.

Stanley Hauerwas

Preface

Since my father, grandfather and great-grandfather were all Anglican clergymen, few expressed surprise when I sensed a call to join the family business. As I began to work out the implications of this vocation, I realized that I had lost confidence in the capacity of the Church to follow Christ today.

That loss of confidence was expressed in three ways. First, in an obsession with apologetics: I became one of those whose concern to see all come to faith had, in MacIntyre's phrase, given the world less and less in which to disbelieve. Second, in an uncritical commitment to social action: since the Church was not bringing the kingdom, I sought to join anyone who looked like they might be. Third, in a quest for personal experience: the habits of the Church seemed to hamper as much as help my soul's search for a direct encounter with the living God.

When I read Stanley Hauerwas' *The Peaceable Kingdom* I realized what had happened. Reading Hauerwas made me see that God genuinely intended the Church: and that the resources for its renewal lay in the habits and practices it had neglected. The theology that I hoped would help me change others had succeeded in changing me. I owe a great deal to my teachers, particularly Bruce McCormack, Kevin Vanhoozer and Duncan Forrester, and my fellow students, especially Karl Travis, for helping a bewildered student realize that I was not as wise as the saints. When later I read George Lindbeck's *The Nature of Doctrine* I realized how deeply I had drunk from the well Lindbeck criticizes.

I was privileged to serve my title at St Luke's, Wallsend, a Church that taught me truthfulness and tragedy in equal measure. It was here, with the help of Ann Loades, that I explored the writings of Stanley Hauerwas in detail, in a place where the story he commends was being performed in remarkable ways. I owe a great deal to John Inge and Alec Graham for their vision and virtue. It was during this time that I first met Stanley Hauerwas, and realized that his ethic was an adventure, not a programme. The people of St Andrew's, Cherry Hinton and All Saints, Teversham taught me a great deal about what this adventure meant in suburban and village life, and I am grateful to Christopher Boulton for his part in this. Now I serve the people of St Elizabeth's, north Earlham, a people who know what it means to be resident aliens and a suffering presence, yet long for a future that is golden and new.

I have written this book because I believe that the writings of Stanley Hauerwas offer the Church an invitation to renew its confidence and restore a true sense of its identity. I feel this is particularly so in the more socially deprived areas where I have best understood my calling to lie. Here especially is the need for the story that transforms fate into destiny.

Many people have assisted this study, and I am very grateful to them. Most of all I wish to thank Jo Bailey Wells, who has so courageously and patiently named my silences, and with whom I journey on, exploring what it means to be a community of character.

Norwich
Advent 1997

[1]
From Fate to Destiny

An introduction to Stanley Hauerwas

Over the 25 years of his publishing career, Stanley Hauerwas has acquired a voice in the North American Church and academy which is authentic, legitimate, consistent and distinctive. In this book I display Hauerwas' theological ethics in the form of a story. This story shows how he has arrived at his distinctive convictions, without losing authenticity, legitimacy or consistency on the way.

Stanley Hauerwas was born in 1940 in Texas, the son of a bricklayer. He grew up as a Southern Methodist. He studied at Southwestern University before moving to Yale where he took his PhD in 1968. From 1970 he taught at the Roman Catholic foundation of Notre Dame, Indiana. In 1985 he moved to Duke University, a Methodist foundation in North Carolina.

His characteristic theological style is the occasional essay. He has published nineteen books, and edited five others. Most of these books are collections of essays; altogether he has published more than 250 scholarly articles, including those reproduced in his collections. He is shy of the thorough systematic ordering of theology, since he fears that this kind of disembodied scholarship can become a substitute for living the gospel through the disciplined practices of a particular Christian community.

For it is in such communities that he perceives the heart of Christian ethics to rest. His writing is intended to make clear the way Christian communities are formed by the Christian story, the kinds of practices that this story entails, and the way the Church relates to such issues as arise in community and society. A faithful Church does not dominate the secular agenda: it has no big battalions to win consent and enforce its notion of truth. But it does have a distinctive story to tell, and the task of theological ethics is to show how the distinctive claims of that story shape the life and practices of the Christian community. Hauerwas' considerable ire is directed chiefly against those who suppose the Church's task is to seek the general improvement of society, sharing a broad consensus with all 'people of good will'. In contrast, he insists, the Church's first social ethical task is to be itself: it serves neither God nor society by neglecting its distinctive claims and practices.

The phrase 'from fate to destiny' epitomizes Hauerwas' project. 'Communities formed by a truthful narrative must provide the skills to transform fate into destiny so that the unexpected, especially as it comes in the form of strangers, can be welcomed as a gift.'[1] This one sentence includes many of the themes that run through the course of his work. Communities are formed by narratives; a test of whether the narrative is true lies in whether the community can maintain its integrity without resorting to control or violence. This requires the development of skills through the regular per-formance of practices. Whereas the tradition of ethics Hauerwas inherits is dominated by the competing claims of various 'givens' – sin, human nature, natural law, human rights – Hauerwas himself seeks to change the location of ethics from 'given' to gift – the gift of the stranger, the gift of the son of God, the gift of Scripture, the gift of the Church. The tragic character of human existence, so clear when ethics is perceived to be about unresolvable dilemmas, suggests that human existence lies in the hands of fate. Hauerwas is deeply aware of the attractiveness of this view, since it describes the complexity of the moral life. But it is his achievement to have shown that if the story is told, if it is performed in the practices of the community, if the character of that community develops habits and skills and virtues; if, in short, the community learns how to receive gifts, then human existence may be seen in the thrall of divine destiny. Hauerwas takes ethics from the hubris of supposing one's decisions determine the fate of the world, and transforms it into the humility of realizing one's place in the destiny of creation.

I am in some ways a stranger, and my hope is that Hauerwas, and more importantly the Church, can welcome this particular unexpected stranger as a gift. To understand Hauerwas, one needs to know something of the tradition from which he emerges, something of the position he develops, something of the criticisms that have come his way, and how he has responded, or could respond to them. I offer these things in my first six chapters. I then develop my own criticism in a different way. Rather than dwell in detail on the inconsistencies and implausibilities of Hauerwas' essays, I envisage how the Church, as a community, might welcome Hauerwas, the stranger, as a gift. In my two final chapters I seek to do this by going beyond Hauerwas, in the direction in which he points.

One of the more distinctive features of Hauerwas' work is its combative style. Many of his essays take issue with an opponent with a vehemence that seems, at first glance, overstated. What this degree of engagement shows is that, not only does Hauerwas enjoy a tussle, but that he is, at every step, self-consciously a participant in a much more considerable debate. This 'larger story', within which he has emerged as a protagonist, is the story of twentieth-century North American Christian social ethics. To understand Hauerwas' work, at any stage in his career, one needs an awareness of this larger story. Hauerwas himself seldom explicitly acknowledges this general context for his writing: but that is simply because he takes it for granted. Like a great-grandson, he chafes at the traditions, quarrels with the rules, and distances himself from the grandees; but he can never leave the family.

---

[1] Hauerwas, *A Community of Character: Toward a Constructive Christian Social Ethic* (Notre Dame: University of Notre Dame Press 1981) p. 10.

Christian social ethics in North America

It is helpful to see the last hundred years of North American Christian social ethics as a living tradition – 'an historically extended, socially embodied argument, and an argument precisely about the goods which constitute that tradition'.[2] Hauerwas is part of this tradition, and the longer his quarrel with it continues, the clearer his importance in the tradition becomes. The story I describe in this book becomes much more significant when set against the story of North American Christian social ethics in the twentieth century. This 'larger story' is, it will transpire, but part of a still larger story of Western theology since the Enlightenment: nonetheless, a brief survey of the leading North American writers in Christian social ethics will identify the tradition from which Stanley Hauerwas emerges and with which he quarrels.

The story can be told in four broad stages, all of which are generalized for the purpose of clarity, and the first two of which are heavily influenced by German speakers. The first stage is that of the social gospel, and its best-remembered proponents, Walter Rauschenbusch (1861–1918), Washington Gladden (1836–1918), and Shailer Matthews (1863–1941). The challenge, for Gladden and Rauschenbusch, was the transformation brought to North American city life by the industrial revolution, with its vast inequalities, poverty, and the breakdown of traditional patterns of social relationships. Conventional Protestant individualism had no answer. Where was the Church to turn for a response?

The answer Rauschenbusch found to this question is crucial to understanding the character of North American Christian social ethics. Rauschenbusch looked back to the longstanding values of American civil life: what he, and so many others, saw, was something unique. A new nation, fleeing from the perils of war-torn seventeenth-century Europe; a nation blessed with boundless fertile territory; a nation called to build a new paradigm of human society. This was America. In short, the American project was the testing-ground for the possibilities of the human project: and the ultimate vision was no less than the kingdom of God. The German liberal Protestant Albrecht Ritschl (1860–1944) had already in the 1870s written a whole theology oriented towards the kingdom – a kingdom which Ritschl envisaged being realized within historical time. Ritschl's near-contemporary Adolf von Harnack (1851–1930) summarized this vision as 'the brotherhood of man under the fatherhood of God'. Now Rauschenbusch looked for a fulfilment of this kingdom in contemporary America, through an alliance, between the Church and the working classes,

---

[2] The definition of tradition is that of Alasdair MacIntyre, *After Virtue: A Study in Moral Theory* (London: Duckworth 1984) p. 222. MacIntyre goes on to say that 'Traditions, when vital, embody continuities of conflict' (ibid.). The identification of North American theological ethics as a tradition is that of William Werpehowski, 'Theological Ethics' in *The Modern Theologians* (Oxford: Blackwell 1997[2]) pp. 311–326.

against the evil kingdom of capitalism. The Church's true and long-neglected purpose, as Rauschenbusch saw it, was the transformation of human community into the kingdom.

Jesus Christ has a pivotal role, for Rauschenbusch, in the realization of the kingdom. 'The first step in the salvation of mankind was the achievement of the personality of Jesus.'[3] Yet the actual career of Jesus – his itinerant preaching and healing, his violent death and resurrection – is of only secondary importance. Instead, Rauschenbusch is drawn to the continuities between Jesus and the Old Testament prophets, and to the Jewish Christian community addressed by the letter of James. Following Jesus means embodying his law of love in a genuine earthly kingdom.

Underlying this notion of the kingdom is the largely unquestioned sense of American exceptionalism. America is considered to be uniquely placed to achieve, and be judged by, standards attainable by no other nation. Social ethics thus came, in this period, to rest on a particular reading of American history. Given that America was blessed by political institutions of outstanding democracy and co-operation, the task was to bring economic life into the same exceptional spirit, and save its commerce from competitiveness and inequality. Meanwhile within American exceptionalism lay a further assumption. Not only did America have a special vocation in the world, but mainstream Protestantism had a special status in America. To question this telling of the story is to dig at the roots of twentieth-century North American Christian social ethics. For Hauerwas, the issue is fundamental: is the narrative of America to be treated as either identical with, or more determinative than, the Christian narrative itself? What is the proper subject matter of ethics: Christianity, or America?

The second stage of the story is characterized by the most influential figure in the whole drama – Reinhold Niebuhr (1892–1971). Reinhold Niebuhr's response to the social gospel was based on a deep scepticism about two of the central tenets of Rauschenbusch's programme: the historical Jesus and the positive view of social institutions. Each deserves attention.

Albert Schweitzer's *The Quest for the Historical Jesus* was translated into English in 1910. Rauschenbusch took its emphasis, that Jesus had a radical interim ethic to last until the imminent end of the world, as an indication of its author's bourgeois resistance to the radical demands of the gospel. Reinhold Niebuhr, and the generation that followed him, took Schweitzer's thesis as a revolution in itself – but this time, a revolution not for society but for Christian ethics. Jesus' true character was difficult to decipher through the gospels, as historical criticism was establishing; and what was clear of his teaching was an ethic that had little to say about social relations. Whither therefore Christian social ethics?

---

[3] Walter Rauschenbusch, *A Theology for the Social Gospel* (Nashville: Abingdon Press 1945) p. 151, quoted in Hauerwas, 'On Keeping Theological Ethics Theological' *Against the Nations: War and Survival in a Liberal Society* (Minneapolis: Winston Seabury Press 1985) p. 29.

Certainly not towards the transformation of social and economic institutions by the law of love. This objective of the social gospel was, in Reinhold Niebuhr's view, based on a misunderstanding of Jesus' proclamation. 'The absolutism and perfectionism of Jesus' love ethic . . . does not establish a connection with the horizontal points of a political or social ethic or with the diagonals which a prudential individual ethic draws between the moral ideal and the facts of a given situation. It has only a vertical dimension between the loving will of God and the will of man.'[4] Hence Reinhold Niebuhr sees it as foolish to misdirect Jesus' 'vertical' emphasis on God's transcendence into a practical social or political programme. What Jesus' ethic can still give is, instead, insights and sources of criticism to any social ethic.

This is because Jesus' ethic is radically aware of human beings as *sinners*. Reinhold Niebuhr's writing is pervaded by the recognition of the tragic nature of human history. One can seldom achieve justice without in the process incurring some injustice; one cannot create without destroying, or express oneself without pride. Utopianism ignores human nature. Thus Reinhold Niebuhr's ethics are founded on anthropology. It is not that he has no place for Christ: for only the forgiveness embodied in the ultimate sacrificial love of the cross (the impossible possibility) can undergird social commitment and make despair as misguided as Utopianism. But he does not see the fundamental contours of human history and possibility as changed by Christ.[5] The lordship of Christ is not a lordship within history. Likewise Reinhold Niebuhr's understanding of politics is prior to his understanding of the Church: and his understanding of politics is dominated by the dialectic of his compelling title *Moral Man and Immoral Society*.[6] 'For Niebuhr, there is no mediating possibility, for no alternative community can stand outside this dialectic structure of politics. . . . Niebuhr's argument requires that his conception of politics *define* the place of the church within what is possible in the realm of politics.'[7]

---

[4] Reinhold Niebuhr, *An Interpretation of Christian Ethics* (New York: Meridian Books, Living Age Edition 1956) p. 45, quoted by Michael G. Cartwright, *Practices, Politics and Performance: Toward a Communal Hermeneutic for Christian Ethics* (PhD dissertation, Duke University 1988) p. 34.

[5] John Milbank understands this realism to involve first, the notion that there are non-negotiable limits to human possibilities, second, the doctrine of original sin, and third, an insistence that ethics should be practical. Milbank sees fundamental flaws in such a Christian realism. 'The "realities" to which it appeals are not the realities of history, nor the realities of which Christian theology speaks, but simply things generated by its own assumptions. . . . "Christian realism" has the tendency to become the opposite of what it claims to be . . . its pessimism turns into over-optimism, its pragmatism into idealism, its anti-liberalism into liberalism, its confidence in God into confidence in humanity.' (*The Word Made Strange: Theology, Language, Culture* Oxford: Blackwell 1997 p. 233).

[6] Reinhold Niebuhr, *Moral Man and Immoral Society* (New York and London: Scribner's 1932).

[7] Cartwright, *Practices, Politics and Performance* pp. 43–44. Cartwright sees Reinhold Niebuhr as a 'very modern Augustine', who sees 'prophetic religion' as an instrument to keep Western civilization afloat (p. 56).

It is the insignificance of the Church for Reinhold Niebuhr that exposes the assumptions he shared with Rauschenbusch. Both social gospellers and Christian realists were principally concerned with how Christians were to serve American society. As Hauerwas expresses it, 'For Niebuhr and the social gospelers the subject of Christian ethics was America.... This perhaps explains the oft made observation that Niebuhr paid almost no attention to the social significance of the church – for finally, in spite of all the trenchant criticism he directed at America, America was his church.'[8]

In such a big church, Reinhold Niebuhr exerted a great influence, particularly on the generation of Hauerwas' teachers and peers. This had two substantial dimensions. First, he rehabilitated the pragmatic impulse of the social gospel. The clarity with which he defined the limits of practical social commitment contributed to its reinvigoration. The mainstream Protestant churches henceforth took for granted their role in serving American society. Second,

> His compelling portrayal of our sinfulness, which appeared *contra* liberal optimism, only continued the liberal attempt to demonstrate the intelligibility of theological language through its power to illuminate the human condition. In spite of Niebuhr's personally profound theological convictions, many secular thinkers accepted his anthropology and social theory without accepting his theological presuppositions. And it is not clear that in doing so they were making a mistake, as the relationships between Niebuhr's theological and ethical positions were never clearly demonstrated.[9]

Thus while Reinhold Niebuhr had distanced himself from the optimism of the social gospellers' anthropology, he had only underlined the fact that, for him, anthropology was the crucial issue. One kind of liberalism – the optimistic faith in the transformation of human institutions and the realization of the kingdom – Niebuhr had discredited; but another – the turn to human nature, rather than (as Hauerwas would wish) the Church, as a foundation for ethics – was now the unquestioned master.

Within a generation, a tradition that had begun the century by asserting the revolutionary social implications of the Christian gospel, had developed a rationale not only for why Christians should not make their theological convictions apply directly to their social commitment, but also for how society as a whole could define justice without reference to Christianity. The Church was directed away from theology toward society, and society was directed away from the Church toward anthropology.

As we move from Reinhold Niebuhr to the generation of Hauerwas' teachers and peers, it is important to mention one more name that lies behind Rauschenbusch, Reinhold Niebuhr and the generation which followed. Like Ritschl and Schweitzer, it is a German name: Ernst Troeltsch (1865–1923). One should not underestimate how important it was that the most influential North American Christian social ethicists in the first half of the century were

---

[8]   Hauerwas, 'On Keeping Theological Ethics Theological' *Against the Nations* pp. 31 and 47 n. 22.

[9]   Ibid. p. 31.

German speakers. Even though Troeltsch's *Social Teachings of the Christian Churches* was not translated into English until 1931, already H. Richard Niebuhr (1894–1962) had written his dissertation on Troeltsch and Reinhold Niebuhr was teaching a Troeltschian course in the history of Christian ethics at Union seminary.[10]

To gauge the significance of Troeltsch, one need only recognize two facts: that H. Richard Niebuhr's *Christ and Culture* has been perhaps the most widely-read book of North American Christian social ethics in the whole century; and that H.R. Niebuhr himself describes his book as aiming 'to do no more than to supplement and in part to correct [Troeltsch's] work on *The Social Teachings of the Christian Churches*'.[11] H.R. Niebuhr's power is the power of description. He sets out five types of relationship between Church and world – Christ against culture, Christ of culture, Christ above culture, Christ and culture in paradox and Christ the transformer of culture – in such a way that the last becomes unanswerable. This is developed from Troeltsch's threefold typology of church-type, sect-type, and individual mysticism. Like the work of Reinhold Niebuhr, H. Richard Niebuhr's descriptive ethics implied that social action in support of liberal democracy and society was at the heart of faithful response to the gospel.

It would not be fair to ignore the concern H. Richard Niebuhr had for the Church.[12] Nonetheless the legacy, if not the intent, of the Niebuhrs was to frame the debate in terms of how Christians could best support liberal democracy in North America. When the third generation of the tradition begins, no other purpose for Christian social ethics is seriously entertained. That is the measure of the Niebuhrian achievement.

The third generation of Christian social ethicists in twentieth-century North America can be characterized by two figures, both students of H. Richard Niebuhr: Paul Ramsey (1913–88) and James Gustafson (1925). Ramsey and Gustafson are two of the three figures without whom it is difficult to understand Hauerwas' response to the Niebuhrs: the third is John Howard Yoder (1927–1997). To understand Ramsey's significance one needs to recall the acute discomfort in North American ethical circles in the 1960s exposed by Joseph Fletcher's situation ethics.[13] Paul Ramsey owed a great deal to both

---

[10] H. Richard Niebuhr, *Ernst Troeltsch's Philosophy of Religion* (New Haven: Yale University Dissertation 1924). I owe these observations to Stanley Hauerwas.

[11] H. Richard Niebuhr, *Christ and Culture* (New York: Harper and Row 1951) p. xii.

[12] See especially H. Richard Niebuhr, *The Purpose of the Church and its Ministry* (New York: Harper and Row 1956), and 'The Responsibility of the Church for Society' in K.S. Latourette (ed.), *The Gospel, the Church and the World* (New York: Harper and Row 1946). It should also be said that *The Meaning of Revelation* (New York: Macmillan 1941) is seen by many as a foundation document for narrative theology.

[13] Joseph Fletcher, *Situation Ethics* (Philadelphia: Westminster 1966). As Hauerwas stated on the first page of the first essay of his first book, 'The problem with Fletcher was that in his attempt to state his theory of ethical behaviour ... he came very close to destroying any meaningful ethical discourse'. Hauerwas, *Vision and Virtue: Essays in Christian Ethical Reflection* (Notre Dame: University of Notre Dame Press 1974/1981) p. 11.

Niebuhrs, particularly Reinhold. For example, Ramsey does not naively seek that people stop fighting wars (an aim that simply makes wars more likely), but, given that war will always be with us, he seeks to control violence under the conviction that there are things worse than death.[14] Like Reinhold Niebuhr, Ramsey does not seriously question that Christians have a large stake in upholding liberal democratic society in North America. But what Ramsey sought was a way of maintaining Christian realism that was distinct from consequentialism.[15] He and others among the third generation of the tradition under study faced a host of social changes, particularly involving sexuality and the beginning and end of human life, that the social gospellers had not faced. It was in this environment that Fletcher's situation ethics proved so compelling.[16] To whom was the ethicist to turn to maintain a reasoned deontological stance, and preserve society from thorough-going relativism?[17]

Ramsey turned to Roman Catholic moral theology, recently unleashed by the Second Vatican Council. In doing so, he made a move which would later be significant for Hauerwas. He saw that Roman Catholics had no apparent difficulty standing by a deontological injunction, for example against the taking of human life: and this gave him the theological leverage to support an ethics of principle against the fashionable consequentialism of the day. Ramsey's Niebuhrianism led him to play down the theological convictions behind his deontological stance. The result was similar to the result of Reinhold Niebuhr's wide influence: 'even many of those who are sympathetic with Ramsey's construal of the ethos of medicine in deontological terms see no reason why those deontological commitments require Ramsey's peculiar theological views about the significance of covenant love to sustain that ethos'.[18]

Roman Catholic moral theology brought three further things in which Ramsey was less interested, two of which would help to shape Hauerwas' approach. First, it had a different source; not concerned with making America Christian, or judiciously applying Scripture to life, it arose from the casuistic requirements of penitential discipline.[19] Thus it was intimately bound up with

---

[14] Paul Ramsey, *The Just War: Force and Political Responsibility* (New York: Scribner's 1968).

[15] Consequentialism I define as a moral theory that judges the quality of an action to reside in the likely consequences of that action, rather than being inherent in the action itself.

[16] Situation ethics refers to a variety of consequentialism which seeks the rightness of an action in relation to the situation itself, rather than in prior rules or obligations: the guiding principle, in Fletcher's view, should be that of love.

[17] Deontology I define as a moral theory that sees rightness (and wrongness) as inherent in acts themselves, regardless of consequences and thus stresses duties and obligations rather than motives.

[18] Hauerwas, 'On Keeping Theological Ethics Theological' *Against the Nations* p. 36.

[19] Casuistry is the art of identifying what is right in circumstances where general norms are not sufficiently precise. The intention is to uphold the principle by defining exceptions – for example, someone might argue that killing is wrong but may be permitted during a war.

the practices of the Church in a way that mainstream Protestant ethics was not. This is a crucial point for Hauerwas' ethics. Second, its sense of its own tradition stretched back to Thomas Aquinas and Aristotle, rather than to the social gospel and Augustine as channelled through the Magisterial Reformers. Hauerwas began his career with Aristotle and Aquinas. Third, it had a universal character, since the centre of attention was not and never had been North America. For example, it is arguable that its centre of debate in the 1970s was the Latin American *barrio*, rather than the North American hospital ward or bedroom. Hauerwas has been slower to adapt to this third point: despite his criticism of those who made Christianity American, his audience has continued to be the North American churches.

If Ramsey brought Roman Catholic moral theology into the tradition under discussion, James Gustafson brought the spotlight onto the self. In doing so, he reflects the breadth of H. Richard Niebuhr's scope, for it was the latter who had opened the door to future discussions of character in his *The Responsible Self*.[20] I shall return to the discussion of character in detail in Chapter 2. At this stage it is necessary to observe that Hauerwas' emphasis on character, though developed with the aid of Roman Catholic moral theology in a way that criticizes the Niebuhrian tradition, in fact arises, through Gustafson and H. Richard Niebuhr, as a strand within that same tradition. Both Hauerwas and Gustafson recognize the challenge to the identity of Christian ethics (hence the title of Gustafson's book *Can Ethics Be Christian?*), and it takes Hauerwas several years before he explicitly grounds Christian identity in the scriptural and ecclesial narrative rather than in the qualities of the self.[21] The quarrel between Gustafson and Hauerwas in the 1980s reflects the fact that Hauerwas' notion of character takes him outside the boundaries of the Niebuhrian field, boundaries which Gustafson continues to regard as obligatory.[22] Yet Gustafson, like Hauerwas, regrets the way theology has been sidelined in ethical debate, and he seeks to redress this anthropocentrism with his two-volumed *Ethics from a Theocentric Perspective*.[23]

The work of Ramsey and Gustafson, whom I have called Hauerwas' teachers, makes clear that Hauerwas' dialogue is not directly with the Niebuhrs, but is with the whole tradition of Christian social ethics as it has developed in North America in the twentieth century. Hauerwas' debt to this tradition is as great as his frustration with it; and, as I have shown in reference

---

[20] H.R. Niebuhr, *The Responsible Self* (New York: Harper and Row 1963). Hauerwas points out that Paul Ramsey, being older, studied with H. Richard Niebuhr in an earlier period than James Gustafson, and that the difference can be seen in the influence each received.

[21] James Gustafson, *Can Ethics Be Christian?* (Chicago: University of Chicago Press 1975). For Hauerwas' turn to revealed narrative, see pp. 52–61 below.

[22] See Chapter 5 below.

[23] James Gustafson, *Ethics from a Theocentric Perspective*, Volume I *Theology and Ethics* (Chicago: University of Chicago Press 1981), Volume II *Ethics and Theology* (Chicago: University of Chicago Press 1984).

to Gustafson and Ramsey, the central planks of his alternative approach derive as much from within the tradition as from outside it.

The fourth and last part of this story introduces Hauerwas' colleagues, those who share his anger with the state of Christian social ethics in North America and from whom he has learnt the foundations of a different approach. John Howard Yoder, with whom Hauerwas taught at Notre Dame during the 1970s, draws attention to the way the whole of the tradition outlined thus far simply swallows without question the social strategy of the Magisterial Reformers. But there was another Reformation, which coincided with Luther's, yet did not tailor its theology to the demands of the state. Hence for Yoder, writing in the Mennonite tradition, Christian social ethics is not dazzled by the headlights of America. Its true audience is the Church. The Church has no particular stake in propping up liberal democratic society, but it is committed to following Jesus Christ, and it can hardly do that if Christ is considered to have little or no contemporary significance for social ethics. Yoder thus questions Reinhold Niebuhr's hegemony on two grounds: on hermeneutical grounds he doubts that Jesus can justly be regarded as irrelevant for social ethics; and on ecclesiological grounds he wonders why the Church is ignored in the assumption that all institutions are inherently flawed. Meanwhile Yoder criticizes H. Richard Niebuhr for giving 'culture' a similar unquestioned status to that which his brother bestows upon anthropology. On closer inspection it turns out that H.R. Niebuhr equates culture with political control, thereby automatically making Yoder's notion of Church irrelevant.[24] Hauerwas' decision to pursue, with Yoder, the authenticity and visible *identity* of the Church, and not be dominated by demands for its perpetual *relevance*, is the fundamental watershed in his relationship with Niebuhrianism. It is perhaps largely due to Yoder that Hauerwas can come to see the tradition I have described in this outline as a 'story' at all. What Yoder gives Hauerwas is a perspective from which he can see that the tradition from Rauschenbusch to Gustafson is united by common assumptions that can be seriously questioned.[25]

The story I tell in Chapters 2–5 below rests on the story of this twentieth-century tradition. In the course of these chapters Hauerwas will be found to have several colleagues, notably Alasdair MacIntyre, George

---

[24] See John Howard Yoder, 'Reinhold Niebuhr and Christian Pacifism', *Mennonite Quarterly Review* 29/2 (April 1955) pp. 101–17; *The Politics of Jesus: Vicit Agnus Noster* (Grand Rapids: Eerdmans 1972/1994) Chapter 1; 'How H. Richard Niebuhr Reasons: A Critique of *Christ and Culture*' in Glen H. Stassen, Diane M. Yeager, and John Howard Yoder (eds.), *Authentic Transformation: A New Vision of Christ and Culture* (Nashville: Abingdon 1995); 'Sacrament as Social Process: Christ the Transformer of Culture' in Michael G. Cartwright (ed.), *The Royal Priesthood: Essays Ecclesiological and Ecumenical* (Grand Rapids: Eerdmans 1994) pp. 359–373 (and Michael Cartwright's Introduction to the same volume, pp. 1–49 at pp. 18–21); see also Chapter 5 below.
[25] In this debt to Yoder, and in his pursuit of identity in the shape of the Christian story, Hauerwas is joined by James McClendon. See especially James W. McClendon Jr, *Ethics: Systematic Theology Volume One* (Nashville: Abingdon 1986).

Lindbeck and John Milbank. MacIntyre's work, as we shall see in Chapter 2, exposes the poverty of the Niebuhrian legacy in an era when Christian presuppositions and practices, far from being taken for granted, are in a minority even in North America. MacIntyre contends that implicit in every ethic is a corresponding form of community and practice. Meanwhile Yoder's work encourages Hauerwas to maintain that the distinctive Christian ethic rests on its distinctive community and corresponding practices. In a curious way the philosopher MacIntyre has created the space for Yoder, the unashamed theologian, to be taken seriously on sociological grounds.

MacIntyre goes on to argue that every community rests on a tradition, which in turn requires a narrative. We saw above how Hauerwas discovered character through H. Richard Niebuhr and Gustafson before realizing that character helped to explain what was wrong with Reinhold Niebuhr; now (in Chapter 3) we see how Hauerwas is led to narrative on philosophical grounds but quickly perceives that narrative is crucial to both the revealed nature of God and the character of the Church. George Lindbeck, Hans Frei and John Milbank all, in different ways, direct Hauerwas to the deeply theological and ecclesiological significance of narrative.

The Church emerges (in Chapter 4) as the key to Hauerwas' theological ethics. And yet again, while it was Yoder who first brought to Hauerwas' attention the significance of the visible Church, Hauerwas comes to establish that significance in his own terms. The Church is the place where character and narrative – the two great themes of Hauerwas' early work – meet. The community is shaped by the Christian story, and in turn it shapes the character of its members. It does so particularly by their performance of its story, notably in worship, but also in other distinctive practices, such as peacemaking and disciplined forgiving.

It is not until this point that one can see a genuine alternative to the Niebuhrian tradition emerging. Prior to this, Hauerwas publishes a series of critiques of the tradition he has inherited, but his constructive position tends to be submerged in the weight of his frustration with the way he is defined by Reinhold's anthropology, stereotyped by H. Richard's typology or crudely limited by Joseph Fletcher's (and many of his opponents') decisionism. Not that Hauerwas refrains from continually returning to his complex inheritance (a tendency I have perhaps downplayed in this study, partly because that heritage is no longer so influential in Britain); nonetheless, as I outline in Chapter 5, Hauerwas has described the Church in such a way that one can begin to perceive a relation between Church and wider creation that is unknown to H. Richard Niebuhr and Ernst Troeltsch: a relation that rehabilitates pacifism as a serious theological demand for the first time since Reinhold Niebuhr's critique of Rauschenbusch.

Once this new paradigm is made clear, it is time to pause, as I do in Chapter 6, and review the unappeased protests that Hauerwas' combative style has provoked. Some of these protests, including some of those made by Gustafson, can be traced to Hauerwas' departure from the tradition outlined in this chapter. Others, like Outka and Ogletree, point up the inconsistencies in

Hauerwas' work and the flaws in his logic: some of these Hauerwas has himself addressed and acknowledged. Some, like Lauritzen, follow Hauerwas' logic but seek a surer foundation for its overall justification: these are not to be treated as opponents, for the search for truth is ultimately a shared one. Hauerwas does not assert that he is strong on truth-claims: but few of his critics have constructive alternatives. Finally there are those, like Albrecht, who maintain that, notwithstanding his criticisms of others, Hauerwas himself still belongs to an era that is limited by its provenance among Western white males, whose discipline is selective and which limits as much as it liberates.

Besides addressing each criticism on its own terms, I make two responses to these protests. In the rest of Chapter 6, I give Hauerwas' approach the narrative display that it demands, by telling the story of a community of character, significantly one outside the North American tradition. In Chapters 7 and 8 I explore a more constructive response to these criticisms, not by encouraging Hauerwas to retract his bolder claims, but by showing how he could meet many of them by developing his claims further than he generally does. Both of my proposals relate to the narrative dimension of Christian ecclesiology: the Church's relation to time and to the end of time.

[2]
From Quandary to Character

The shortcomings of conventional ethics

The early part of Stanley Hauerwas' career is dominated by a noisy discomfort with what he perceives to be the way ethics is conventionally approached. He explores two principal lines of criticism. First, conventional ethics is internally flawed, since it rests on an unsustainable account of moral rationality. Second, a distinctively Christian ethic should concentrate on developing the character of the believer, and thus bypass the main focus of most ethical discussion, the decision.

Thus Hauerwas begins in a mode of demolition. What is to be demolished is what he calls 'the standard account of moral rationality'. The most significant feature of the standard account is that it is common ground for almost all of the conventional discussion partners in ethical debate. The heated debates between Kantians and utilitarians, between deontologists and consequentialists, between principle and situation ethics: all these antagonists share an assumption of the standard account.

What exactly is this 'standard account'? Hauerwas never exactly says. It is hard to identify one contemporary moral philosopher who subscribes to the entire range of 'standard' assumptions – though its ancestry is recognizably Kantian. Hauerwas broadly agrees with Jeffrey Stout that Kant's project is best seen in the light of the religious-inspired bloodbath of the seventeenth century: looking back on the catastrophic effects of differences over religion, Kant attempted to ground his ethic on something less irrational.

The principles that guided Kant are alive and well today. Contemporary neo-Kantianism has been helpfully summarized by Gregory Trianosky. His definition includes the following:

1. The most important question in morality is, 'What is it right or obligatory to do?'
2. Basic moral judgements are judgements concerning the rightness of actions.
3. Basic moral judgements take the form of general rules or principles about right action. Particular judgements of the right are always instances of these.
4. Basic moral judgements are universal in form. They contain no essential reference to particular persons or particular relationships in which the agent might stand.

5. Basic moral judgements are not grounded on some account of the human good which is itself independent of morality.
6. Basic moral judgements are categorical imperatives. They have a certain 'automatic reason-giving force' . . . independently of their relation to the desires and/or interests of the agent.[1]

The neo-Kantian reasoning goes like this. People have different genes, different upbringings, different traditions, different dispositions, different temptations, different motives. But they all do much the same actions. By grounding morality in actions, and by chiefly discussing the rightness of actions, a rational debate can continue, and people of all traditions can meet without the constant threat of violence.

Why does Hauerwas begin his project with a series of tirades against this rational form of debate? Put simply, his answer is this: what is the use of discussing the rightness of actions, if two people can do the same 'action' with hugely differing aspirations, purposes, styles, colleagues, antagonists, and with very different descriptions and understandings of what they are doing?[2] Hauerwas rejects all but one of the six tenets listed above. The one he maintains is the fifth one. In doing so, he stands not only against the deontological thrust of the other tenets, but also against utilitarianism and similar consequential theories. These latter theories ground morality on some independent account of the good – such as happiness or the satisfaction of desire or freedom. For Hauerwas there is no foundation to be abstracted from the moral process, no 'still centre'. Thus he rejects the notion of common ground both over what ethics is – the description of ethics – and over what it is for – the prescription of ethics. His criticisms can be arranged under three headings: foundations, decisions, and principles.

Foundations, facts and the observer

In Hauerwas' view, the standard account is wrong because it supposes that there can be an objective, value-free starting-point for morality. Inspired by the scientific ideal of objectivity, the standard account founds moral judge-ments upon the basis of impersonal rationality. Ethics is about the particular only in so far as it translates to the general. The particular point of view of the agent – the agent's history, community, beliefs and character – is distrusted and seen as arbitrary and contingent, subjective and relative: in short, unscientific. Instead, various proposals have been put forward for an imper-sonal starting point – a basic moral principle, procedure, or viewpoint which applies to everyone engaged in moral judgement or action. Such proposals

---

[1] Gregory Trianosky, 'What is Virtue Ethics All About?' *American Philosophical Quarterly* 27/4 (Oct 1990) p. 335. Trianosky has three further tenets, less relevant to the discussion here.

[2] Hauerwas and Alasdair MacIntyre (eds.), *Revisions: Changing Perspectives in Moral Philosophy* (Notre Dame: University of Notre Dame Press 1983) gathers together the most cogent criticisms of the 'standard account'.

include the categorical imperative, the ideal observer, universalizability, or the original position.

The search for some such foundation of ethics seems interminable. These theories make the assumption that what constitutes persons is not any attribute, achievement, relationship, community, role, commitment, belief, or history, but their reason. 'Such theories are not meant to tell us how to be good in relation to some ideal, but rather to ensure that what we owe to others as strangers, not as friends or sharers in a tradition, is non-arbitrary.'[3]

But is even this modest project realizable? The standard account does not fully recognize the value-laden nature of the terms it regards as factual. Notions such as 'murder', 'stealing', and 'abortion' are not simple descriptions whose meaning can be derived from rationality in itself. If they were, why then are moral controversies so hard to resolve?[4] Pro- and anti-abortion activists struggle to discuss issues of right and wrong because they hardly agree on the language they use. Moral notions depend for their display upon examples and histories. No deontological or utilitarian theory can free them from this dependence without sacrificing their rich texture, and thus failing to describe them adequately.

Thus the standard account is misguided on the *what* of morality since it overestimates the ability of moral description to separate fact from value. It is also misguided on the *who* of ethical theory since it privileges the observer's point of view. Participants, it says, cannot see as well as viewers. Morality is seen more truly by the art critic than by the artist. There are two points to criticize here. First, is this form of disinterestedness desirable? Second, is it possible?

Hauerwas argues against the desirability of privileging the observer's point of view. It is largely the contingent nature of a person's projects that makes them valuable to that person. They matter because they express something significant about that person. The distancing implied by the standard account is identified by Hauerwas as alienation.[5] Thus the standard account pictures the self as made up of reason's efforts to control desire – a description which seems to separate pleasure from good altogether. Reason connects us with the universal rules of conduct: desire only with the self's own contingent appetite.

---

[3] Hauerwas and David B. Burrell, 'From System to Story: An Alternative Pattern for Rationality in Ethics' in Stanley Hauerwas, Richard Bondi and David B. Burrell, *Truthfulness and Tragedy: Further Investigations in Christian Ethics* (Notre Dame: University of Notre Dame Press 1977) pp. 15–39 at p. 17.

[4] This is where MacIntyre begins in *After Virtue* (Chapter 2). The examples he cites are war and peace, abortion, and freedom and equality. See also his 'Why is the Search for the Foundation of Ethics so Frustrating?' *Hastings Center Report* 9/4 (1979) pp. 21–22 where he discusses three areas of disagreement between deontologists and consequentialists: 1. causality, predictability, and intentionality, and the relationship of consciousness to the world; 2. law, evil, emotion, and the integrity of the self; 3. the relation of individual identity to social identity and ethics to politics.

[5] Hauerwas, 'From System to Story' *Truthfulness and Tragedy* p. 23.

Having dismissed our passions, the standard account dispenses with our past:

> Morally, the self represents a collection of discontinuous decisions bound together only in the measure they approximate to the moral point of view. Our moral capacity thus depends on our ability to view our past in discontinuity with our present . . . to alienate ourselves from our past in order to be able to grasp the timelessness of the rationality offered by the standard account.[6]

Iris Murdoch points out that it is only the lure of a greater or more beautiful good than we can ourselves will into existence that can occasion genuine disinterest in the self.[7] Thus disinterestedness implies access to a neutral point of view, a neutral story, independent of the past, eternally present. This appears to be the perspective of God. But this discloses Hauerwas' most important, most theological, and most far-reaching contention: *there is no such neutral standpoint, no neutral story. Even God is no neutral observer, for the God of Jews and Christians wills to reveal himself in and through a particular narrative.* The reason of humanity comes face to face with the foolishness of God. If God's actions take the form of a narrative, so should human ones. This is the starting-point for Hauerwas' narrative ethics.

Decisions and actions

By overemphasizing moments of decision the standard account fails to describe adequately the moral life. In the process it reduces moral rationality to one of its parts – and a secondary, dependent part at that – and thus fails to describe the moral experience as it is lived. For this critique, Hauerwas is primarily indebted to a key article in the 'first wave' of virtue literature by Edmund Pincoffs.[8] Pincoffs describes how it is often assumed that ethics concerns problems – dilemmas involving a conflict of choice – and concerns itself with evaluating alternative rational solutions. Such solutions involve judgements that are justified without reference to the particular agent involved in the situation.

What is wrong with 'decisionism'? Hauerwas certainly affirms that decisions are morally significant (and unavoidable). But they are 'in a certain sense . . . morally secondary'.[9] They should not be considered 'the paradigmatic centre of moral reflection'. In Hauerwas' view, the centre of moral reflection is not the development of solutions or principles for decision-making, or

---

[6] Ibid. p. 24. Hauerwas bases this assessment on two quotations from Kant's *Religion Within the Limits of Reason Alone*. See Hauerwas, *Truthfulness and Tragedy* pp. 207–208 note 19.

[7] Iris Murdoch, *The Sovereignty of Good Over Other Concepts* (Cambridge: Cambridge University Press 1967). I shall return to Iris Murdoch in Chapter 5.

[8] Edmund Pincoffs, 'Quandary Ethics' *Mind* 80 (1971) pp. 552–571.

[9] Hauerwas, 'The Virtues and Our Communities: Human Nature as History', in *A Community of Character* p. 114.

rules no decision should break: it is the development of people – people of character. The manner of the actions of such people must display their moral character. It is no use talking about actions apart from the people that do them. There is no such thing as an action that is not done by somebody. The kind of events that ethics is interested in are those that can be done differently. What ethics changes is first of all the person – and only subsequently and consequently the action. A changed (saintly) person can make mistakes; and a bad person can do good. But in Hauerwas' view this risks a misuse of the notion of good: for a good action is one which encourages or reflects the creation of a good person. An overemphasis on decision implies a hard and fast distinction between an action and an agent. For Hauerwas, no such distinction is sustainable (though communities sometimes fasten on one for educative and legal purposes).[10] Even the description of circumstances is a moral event, since our terms and notions presuppose that we are people capable of using them.

Decisionism is thus inadequate in two senses. On the one hand, the vast majority of the things people do in life they do, not because they decide to do them, but because of the kinds of people they are. They do them by habit rather than by choice. An ethic that emphasizes moments of decision ignores the great preponderance of the events of life. Life is not a perpetual crisis of choice:

> Morality is not primarily concerned with quandaries or hard decisions; nor is the moral self simply the collection of such decisions. As persons of moral character we do not confront situations as mud puddles into which we have to step; rather the kind of 'situations' we confront and how we understand them are a function of the kind of people we are.[11]

The convictions a person holds form that person's descriptions of the world and determine the shape of any quandary that presents itself. These convictions 'are like the air we breathe – we never notice them'.[12] The convictions Hauerwas has in mind are, for instance, the duty to provide children and the infirm with care that is not given to the stranger. The force of such convictions is the very fact that they are taken for granted. 'And morally', he adds, 'we must have the kind of character that keeps us from subjecting them to decision'.[13] It is these qualities that make up the substance of the moral life – yet they are so fundamental that they tend to go unnoticed.[14] The examined life dwells more on what is taken for granted than on decisions.

---

[10] Hauerwas, *Character and the Christian Life: A Study in Theological Ethics* (San Antonio: Trinity University Press 1975/1985) pp. xxiii–xxiv.

[11] Hauerwas, 'The Virtues and our Communities' pp. 114–115.

[12] Hauerwas, 'From System to Story' p. 19.

[13] Ibid. p. 20.

[14] 'If fish ever developed intelligence and began to codify and describe their environment, one of the last things they would notice would be the water' (Stanley Hauerwas, 'Community and Diversity: The Tyranny of Normality' in *Suffering Presence: Theological Reflections on Medicine, the Mentally Handicapped, and the Church* Edinburgh: T. & T. Clark 1986 p. 211).

On the other hand, when it seems there *is* in fact a crisis, and a major decision does have to be made, that decision is not, in practice, made in a vacuum: it is dependent on a deeper, prior moral commitment. 'Thus persons of character or virtue may, from the perspective of others, make what appear to have been momentous and even heroic decisions, but feel that in their own lives they "had no choice" if they were to continue to be faithful to their own characters.'[15] Hauerwas stresses that character is not formed by decisions – though decisions may confirm or reveal character: it comes instead from a person's beliefs and dispositions – which the standard account holds to be contingent and non-rational, and thus a retreat from moral objectivity.[16] The issue becomes one of how to reintroduce the 'dreaded first person singular' without moral rationality being reduced to 'because I want to'.

Thus decisionism fails to describe the full complexity of the moral life. Moreover, one could go further than Hauerwas and add that decisionism fails even in its own terms: for rules or principles by themselves cannot tell us how they are to be applied in specific situations, or when they are being applied well.

Principles, violence and the importance of tragedy

Finally, the abstractions made by the standard account have a subtle but real connection with violence. The two are both expressions of alienation.

This connection is implicit first of all in the universalism on which the standard account depends. Within the logic of categorical imperatives and universal laws there lies a powerful justification for violence. Once one has accepted the presuppositions of a universal law, the existence of one who will not act according to it becomes morally objectionable, since such differences should not exist. It is difficult to separate rational failure from moral failure. If someone were to deny the 'universal' laws understood by the standard account, they would seem morally obtuse: it is a short step to forcing them to mend their ways.

In *Against the Nations* Hauerwas quotes Reinhold Niebuhr's indictment of the violence of universalism:

> The logic of the decay of modern culture from universalistic humanism to nationalistic anarchy may be expressed as follows: Men seek a universal standard of human good. After painful effort they define it. The painfulness of their effort convinces them that they have discovered a genuinely universal value. To their sorrow, some of their fellow men refuse to accept the standard. Since they know the standard to be universal the recalcitrance of their fellows is a proof, in their minds, of some defect in the humanity of the non-conformists. Thus a rationalistic

---

[15] Hauerwas, 'The Virtues and Our Communities' p. 114.

[16] Hauerwas 'From System to Story' p. 20. The standard account does not claim that dispositions are irrelevant, but that what counts for moral consideration is the rational, objective and universal.

age creates a new fanaticism. The non-conformists are figuratively expelled from the human community.[17]

The formation of moral principles is the second potentially coercive abstraction. Hauerwas sees a sense of the tragic as that which enables a person to be moral and thus keeps them from violence. He focuses on the practice of medicine to make this clear.[18] It is, in his view, a fallacy that greater techniques of preventing and curing disease will ever free people's lives from tragic dilemmas.[19] The sometimes tragic story of caring can never be thoroughly reconstrued into a comedy of curing. Just as in medicine, so in the rest of moral existence, the right is not always the successful:

> When a culture loses touch with the tragic ... we must redescribe our failures in acceptable terms. Yet to do so *ipso facto* traps us in self-deceiving accounts of what we have done. Thus our stories quickly acquire the characteristics of a policy.... Phrases like 'current medical practice', 'standard hospital policy', or even 'professional ethics', embody exemplary stories.... Since we fail to regard them as stories, however, but must see them as a set of principles, the establishment must set itself to secure them against competing views. If the disadvantaged regard this as a form of institutional violence, they are certainly correct.[20]

Description again appears as Hauerwas' bone of contention with the standard account. Because of the inability to recognize the tragedy implicit in the limits of existence, few can bring themselves to describe an abortion as a death, however unavoidable. Thus people deceive themselves.

Deontological and utilitarian theories seek to overcome the moral divisions of the world by an appeal to an understanding of universal moral rationality. Hauerwas sees in such attempts an inability to face the tragic. The tragic is experienced when a person (perhaps a highly virtuous person) with several responsibilities and obligations, confronted with a single decision having irreversible consequences, finds that these many interests conflict with both his or her own interest and with each other. The lurking temptation is always to avoid the tragic through violence. Hauerwas quotes Stanley Cavell: 'if you would avoid tragedy (and suffering), avoid love; if you cannot avoid love, avoid integrity; if you cannot avoid integrity, avoid the world; if you cannot avoid the world, destroy it'.[21] The world cannot be forced into a premature unity. The standard account is designed to avert violence through

---

[17] Reinhold Niebuhr, *Beyond Tragedy* (New York: Scribners 1965) p. 237. See Hauerwas, *Against the Nations* p. 84 n. 26.

[18] Hauerwas, 'Medicine as a Tragic Profession' in *Truthfulness and Tragedy* pp. 184–202.

[19] Hauerwas, 'From System to Story' p. 37.

[20] Ibid. p. 38. I return to the analysis of violence in Chapter 5 below.

[21] Stanley Cavell, *Must We Mean What We Say?* (Cambridge: Cambridge University Press 1969) p. 349 quoted in Stanley Hauerwas, 'The Church in a Divided World' *A Community of Character* p. 107. I return to the discussion of tragedy in Chapter 8 below.

resolving moral conflicts. Such an ethic of abstract principle based on universal moral rationality is an attempt to resist evil and is not in itself violent; but to the extent that it fails to see the tragic dimension of moral existence it slips into coercion through its own self-deception.

Thus the irony of Kantian ethics is that it is established in order to avert the chaos of religious war; and yet it leads to violence:

> The whole point . . . of the philosophical and political developments since the Enlightenment is to create people incapable of killing other people in the name of God. Ironically, since the Enlightenment, people no longer kill one another in the name of God but in the names of nation-states . . . The ultimate pathos of our times is that we live in societies and polities formed by the assumption that there is literally nothing for which it is worth dying. The irony is that such societies cannot live without war as they seek to hide in war the essential emptiness of their commitments.[22]

As we shall see in Chapter 4, Hauerwas does not set out to abandon principles altogether. His concern is that the focus of ethics should be in the habits and practices of a community. The earthiness and triviality of such a community will bring to light the tragedy of human existence. He is deeply suspicious of attempts to bypass that human community by introducing some supposedly more comprehensive principles. The attempt to do so therefore implicitly undermines the true home of Christian ethics: the Church.

From good actions to good people

The agent's perspective

Hauerwas' early writing is largely about character, virtue and vision. Each of these is implicit in the term 'the agent's perspective'. To see ethics from the agent's perspective means to see their actions in the light of their character, convictions, history and hopes, rather than from the perspective of a neutral observer. Action and agent have a spiralling relationship, in that actions reaffirm the kind of person the agent has been, and shape the kind of person they are becoming. Agents form actions, actions form agents. For Hauerwas, ethical discussion begins with the agent; though as we shall see in Chapter 3, he comes to see that there is a prior action, God's action arising from God's own character.

In establishing the notion of character as the form of human agency, Hauerwas has to distance himself from other descriptions of the self. He does so by stressing the interrelation of character, agent and action.

If one exaggerates the notion of character, one has a self that can do anything it likes, and is influenced by no other factors. This is indeterminism.

---

[22] Hauerwas, *After Christendom: How the Church is to Behave if Freedom, Justice, and a Christian Nation are Bad Ideas* (Nashville: Abingdon 1991) pp. 33, 44.

The indeterminate self is not determined by external forces to act in any particular way. This makes character, that which forms human action, into an uncaused cause. Everything in the world is caused, except the agent's actions. This is absurd, unless the agent is considered to be divine – and it is not clear it makes much sense even then. Besides, how can an indeterminate agent be free and responsible – two conditions which seem integral to the concept of self-agency? Consider the case of a person acting out of will, motives, desires or character: this person is not entirely free, in the sense of being indeterminate. By contrast, if one acts thoroughly indeterminately, without any sufficient cause, how can one be considered responsible? Such a self can hardly be praised or blamed.[23] Indeterminism is therefore to be rejected on two counts, both involving incompatibility with prior assumptions.

Thus the self is not indeterminate. The self *is* determined; but character is *that which ensures that the self is nonetheless not lost in the fact of being determined.* This is made possible by appreciating the interrelation of agent, action and character. The self is determined, but this determination need not take the form of a 'cause'. We do not need to think in terms of a physical, social or mental cause for our behaviour: 'volitions, motives, intentions, reasons do not *cause* or move [persons] to act, but [persons] acting embody them'.[24] Character emerges as that which breaks out of the confusion surrounding the indeterminate-yet-determined self. If we see character in this way we dispense with trying to understand all behaviour in terms of 'causes' visible to an observer. The connections with Hauerwas' critique of the 'standard account' are clear: we have rejected the privileged status of the objective observer.

Indeterminism is thus rejected because it makes an unwarranted separation between action and character. But what of free will – the notion that the true self has an integrity that cannot be affected by actions? This is rejected because it unduly separates action and agent. The notion of free will implies that the self is split between interior action (will) and exterior action (what the agent actually does). How could one begin to demonstrate this interior action? How can one be sure there is not another action (or many in turn) inside it?[25] Does the interior will correlate to the whole of the exterior action or only part of it? Such questions are very difficult to answer. It seems impossible to separate causation entirely from the action itself. How can one describe an act of will except in relation to what it has caused? Hauerwas insists that the will is a property of an action, and not a separate quality.[26]

---

[23] Hauerwas, *Character and the Christian Life* pp. 18–29.

[24] Ibid. p. 21 my italics.

[25] This corresponds to what Timothy O'Connell defends as the 'onion peel view of the self' – moving inward from environment to actions to body to feelings to convictions to the dimensionless pinpoint – the 'I'. See Timothy O'Connell, *Principles for a Catholic Morality* (New York: Seabury 1978), quoted in Hauerwas, *The Peaceable Kingdom: A Primer in Christian Ethics* (Notre Dame: University of Notre Dame Press 1983; London: SCM Press 1984) p. 40.

[26] Hauerwas, *Character and the Christian Life* pp. 23–24.

Hauerwas points out that 'free will' arguments have little time for character. They see character as a limiting factor which the self must transcend if it is to be a free agent. 'Character is but the external and accidental feature of a moral real "internal" and substantive self.'[27] There is no point in developing character: one must overcome it. Again the connections with Hauerwas' description of the standard account are clear: just as indeterminism supposed the observer's point of view, so 'free will' emphasizes moments of decision rather than development of character. For Hauerwas, by contrast, it is character that is the stuff of ethics; it refers to the way our being is determined by our doing: 'Character is not an accidental feature of our lives that can be distinguished from "what we really are"; rather, character is a concept that denotes what makes us determinative moral agents. Our character is not a shadow of some deeper but more hidden real self; it is the form of our agency acquired through our beliefs and actions.'[28] Having rejected indeterminist and 'free will' arguments, Hauerwas is careful to distance himself from behaviourist and determinist models of the self. Hauerwas rejects behaviourism because it has no significant place for character. Behaviourists assume that each person is no more than the product of the interaction of external forces. The observer can therefore perceive the dispositions and actions that go to make up the self. Determinists tend to have a predominantly passive understanding of the self as a being to whom things happen rather than as a self-determining agent. Determinists do not obliterate choice, but understand a set of preconditions that limit the field of choice. Both 'free will' and behaviourist arguments assume the need for a cause for behaviour: the former locate the cause inside the self, the latter outside. Hauerwas steers a path between them by denying the need to search for such a cause beyond the activity itself: 'The self does not cause its activities or have its experiences; it simply is its activities as well as its experience. I *am* rather than *have* both my activities and my involuntary traits and processes. To the extent that I am the latter, I am largely the product of heredity and environment; to the extent that I am my self-activity, I am self-creating and self-determining.'[29]

---

[27] Ibid. p. 23.

[28] Ibid. p. 21. Hauerwas puts this another way when he denies that there is one aspect of our being (such as rationality) that distinguishes us from all other species. He quotes Mary Midgely, *Beast and Man: The Roots of Human Nature* (Ithaca NY: Cornell University Press 1978) p. 207 to point out that what is special about each creature, including humans, 'is not a single, unique quality but a rich and complex arrangement of powers and qualities, some of which it will certainly share with its neighbours. And the more complex the species, the more true this is. To expect a single differentia is absurd. And it is not even effectively flattering to the species, since it obscures our truly characteristic richness and versatility.' See *A Community of Character* pp. 123–124.

Hauerwas' use of Mary Midgely in his later work is significant because it marks a departure from his attention to Iris Murdoch in his earlier *Vision and Virtue*. Midgely's more Aristotelian concentration on the concrete particularity of the moral life coincides with Hauerwas' interest in narrative and counters Murdoch's more Platonic perception of 'the Good'.

[29] Hauerwas, *Character and the Christian Life* p. 26.

Hauerwas insists that if we are looking for an explanation (or an evaluation) of behaviour, we need look no further than the agent. The agent defines and determines the activity. There is no 'event' that can be separated from the action (the determinist mistake) any more than there is a substantive 'self' that can be separated from the agent (the indeterminist mistake). Character refers to the extent and manner of the determination of the agent.

Hauerwas' early critics focus on the sometimes contradictory claims he makes for character. Character, for Hauerwas, appears to be the fundamental way in which the self is oriented to the world in general, and the particular choices that shape this orientation. Thomas Ogletree calls this account intellectualistic, voluntaristic and downright Pelagian, because it exaggerates the role of core convictions and our ability to form our lives by means of them.[30] Gene Outka wrestles with whether Hauerwas is interested in sustaining his early claim that it is better to shape than to be shaped. Outka correctly predicts that Hauerwas will leave this claim behind. The fact that Hauerwas does so weakens the force of most of Outka's and Ogletree's criticisms.[31]

Both Ogletree and Outka concentrate on the underlying conflict between Hauerwas' emerging theme of narrative and his earlier theme of character. Ogletree anticipates that narrative will prove to be the more lasting theme of the two. Outka points out that vision and narrative both incline towards taking the self out of the centre of the picture, in a way that might appear to interfere with the autonomy of the self. In the light of such observations, one may wonder if there is still an abiding place for character within Hauerwas' ethics – at least, if the notion of character involved is to be compatible with the one outlined in *Character and the Christian Life*.

I suggest that Hauerwas' original notion of character still has a place in his overall picture, but that in order for it to do so, we must look into an area that Hauerwas does not explore. That area is causality. In what follows I hope to show that an understanding of causality can restore the place of character in an understanding of Hauerwas' ethics.

The return to Aristotle

Lying behind Hauerwas' discussion of agent, action and character, is an understanding of causality which he does not sufficiently explore. I do not believe it is necessary, possible or desirable to dispense with all talk of causes. Hauerwas excludes discussion of causes in order to deny the privilege of the observer and to explain how the self is inseparable from its experiences and activities. I believe that in rejecting talk of causality, Hauerwas is showing a (justified) suspicion of an overemphasis on one type of causality – final causality.

[30] Thomas Ogletree, 'Character and Narrative: Stanley Hauerwas' Studies of the Christian Life' *Religious Studies Review* 6/1 (January 1980) pp. 25–30.
[31] Gene Outka, 'Character, Vision and Narrative' *Religious Studies Review* 6/2 (April 1980) pp. 110–118.

In the discussion that follows, I develop an understanding of Aristotelian causality that demonstrates the subtleties of what Hauerwas is doing in Christian ethics. I hope to show first that final causality must take its place as one among several forms of causality, and second that final causality is not to be construed individually. I believe that a re-examination of Aristotelian causality will clarify, rather than obscure, Hauerwas' notion of character.[32]

What implications does Hauerwas' understanding of character have for causality? For Aristotle, there are four causes – material, efficient, formal and final. These may be illustrated in relation to a statue:

1. The material cause, out of which the statue is made (bronze).
2. The efficient cause, which brings the statue about (the chisel or sculptor).
3. The formal cause, the shape into which the statue is made.
4. The final cause, the purpose for which the statue is made (the decoration of the courtyard, or the glorification of the model).[33]

Since Aristotle, attention has come to concentrate on what makes things the way they are – and thus on efficient and final causes – meanwhile what things are in themselves – formal and material causes – have come to be seen not as causes at all but as properties of the things themselves.

What Hauerwas is doing should now be easier to explain. Ethics cannot jump straight to *final* causes, as if there were a consensus on the other three areas. One cannot simply discuss whether or not an action should take place without first considering who the person is who is doing it and how a community understands the action that is being considered. This is Hauerwas' constant complaint about 'value-free' ethics, such as the supposedly autonomous disciplines of medical ethics and business ethics. It is therefore a mistake to assume that matter and form are simply the properties of things which can be objectively described by the outside observer. In Hauerwas' hands, the *efficient* cause is king – to the extent that even the 'nature' of things (their matter and form) is not always able to withstand it. In short, things are what

---

[32] John Milbank's argument in *Theology and Social Theory* is that Aristotle understands ethics as rhetorical rather than dialectical; in other words, ethics is not about the proving or testing of virtue, but about the demonstration and thus the description of virtue. In the course of this argument Milbank points out what he describes as 'a key to deconstructing Aristotle'. The key is, that 'at the heart of [Aristotle's] ethics the apparent dominance of final causality, the means/end axis, is subverted by formal causality and a form/matter axis' (John Milbank, *Theology and Social Theory: Beyond Secular Reason* Oxford: Blackwell 1990 p. 350).

Meanwhile, from a very different starting point, Leslie Muray, a process theologian, calls on Hauerwas to provide 'a conceptual elaboration of the relationship between efficient and final causality': Muray himself is anxious not to let go of the latter, which he identifies as the capacity for self-creation and thus freedom (Leslie A. Muray, 'Confessional Postmodernism and the Process-Relational Vision' *Process Studies* 18/2 1989 p. 85.)

[33] Aristotle, *Metaphysics* 1014.

we make of them.[34] There is no objective definition of matter and form to which all agents (efficient causes) must subscribe. Baldly put, the question is not, 'What is this thing for (in itself)?', but 'What can it become in the kingdom of God?'

Once it has been established that final causality is not king, it is easy to see why Hauerwas is so concerned not to place decision-making at the centre of ethical debate. For decision-making is about final causality – the 'means–ends axis', as Milbank calls it. Despite Muray's protestations, freedom does not lie in final causality. The stuff of ethics lies further upstream, in the formation of the agents who are to become the efficient causes. Decisions are still important, but now because they are part of the inescapable form of the self.

The self is not simply matter – that would be the substantialist view. But we can see the force of Muray's criticism that Hauerwas' position 'lends itself to a substantialist interpretation'.[35] Statements such as '[the self] simply is its activities as well as its experience' are designed to get away from a self separate from activity. But the self does develop – it is in some sense a material cause, if not a detachable substance. The self is not, however, just a material cause. If we are self-agents, then the self is also an efficient cause. What enables the self to be both a material and an efficient cause? The answer is, its character. *Character is the formal cause* – 'the form of our self-agency'. It is thus character, the formal cause, that prevents the self from becoming simply matter – the subject of the efficient causes of other agents – and enables the self to be an efficient cause. The self is, of course, not the only efficient cause in the world – there are countless circumstances beyond one's control – but it is because of character that the self is able to be an efficient cause at all. Without character, the self would be simply material at the mercy of circumstance – in short, simply a determined being. Indeterminism, on the other hand, stresses the self as an efficient cause to the exclusion of the self as a material cause: thus the self appears to be an 'uncaused cause'.

Thus when Hauerwas talks about 'active and passive aspects of our existence',[36] on my present interpretation he is talking about how the self is both an efficient (active) cause and a material (largely passive) cause. He points out that 'much of what we are is that which "happens to us" . . . the passive resides at the very core of our agency'. He goes on to say that though a person may conform to a society's expectations, their resulting character is still uniquely their own. This discussion is, I suggest, made clearer by restoring

---

[34] Hauerwas does not altogether deny the existence of 'natural' properties: he simply resists making them the starting-point of ethical enquiry. John Milbank points out that natural laws are laws of *physis,* and thus subject to change, since *physis* is the changeable. 'Aristotle does not really connect the ethical with what is eternally valid' (*Theology and Social Theory* p. 350). This is highly significant for the discussion of 'natural law' or 'creation' ethics.

[35] Muray, 'Confessional Postmodernism' p. 85.

[36] Hauerwas, *Character and the Christian Life* pp. 116–117.

the notions of causality. The material cause is subject to outside forces – notably culture, society, place and time of birth.[37] These are the 'given' aspects of human existence. But one is never just a material cause: one's character is that which 'transforms our fate into our destiny'.[38]

To sum up my argument so far, Hauerwas' causality (if he had developed one) would look like this:

1. The material cause is the self, understood in a passive sense.
2. The efficient cause is the self as an agent, understood in an active sense.
3. The formal cause is the character of the agent, 'the form of our agency'.

The expression 'transforming fate into destiny' gives a clue to the way character ensures human freedom. Freedom is an aspect of character. Character is that which prevents the self from being merely passive, simply a material cause; meanwhile freedom is that which 'protects us from being at the mercy of the moment'.[39] '[Our] choices consist in limiting an indeterminate range of possibilities by ordering them in accordance with [our] intentions. To be free is to set a course through the multitude of possibilities that confront us and so impose order on the world and ourselves.'[40]

Being free means claiming that what was done was one's own, that what took place was not just an event but was one's action. Freedom thus resembles power rather than choice: the 'power of self-possession necessary to avoid the parameters of life that others would impose'.[41] Hauerwas quotes with approval Frithjof Bergmann's compelling argument which begins to show how freedom understood in the light of virtue opens the door to providence and the Christian narrative:

> If it is now understood that the making of a choice gives rise to freedom only if I identify with the agency that does the choosing (i.e. if I regard the thought-process that makes the decision as truly mine, despite its being conditioned, or influenced, or so forth), then it should be clear that freedom can also result from my identifying with an agency other than those processes of thought – and this

---

[37] Hauerwas accuses situation ethics of 'working with a very passive model of the self. The self is always lost amid the contingencies of the particular situation. For men to have autonomy in any meaningful sense, they must be able to meet "the situation" on grounds other than those which the situation itself provides. Such grounds must be based on their character. Situation ethics seem but a secular restatement of the passive view of man associated with the traditional Protestant insistence on justification by faith' (Hauerwas, *Vision and Virtue* p. 54 n. 16).

[38] The phrase 'transform fate into destiny' comes from Hauerwas, *A Community of Character* p. 10.

[39] Hauerwas, *Vision and Virtue* p. 65.

[40] Hauerwas, *Character and the Christian Life* p. 114.

[41] Hauerwas, *A Community of Character* p. 125. Milbank makes a similar claim: 'in the Christian understanding, virtue . . . means a power that constantly generates its own field of operation, which is no longer something to be formed, dominated or inhibited, but instead liberated as a new power and a new freedom' (*Theology and Social Theory* pp. 362–363).

means that I may be free even if the decisive difference between two alternatives was not made by my own choice, as long as I identify with (i.e. regard as *myself*) the agency that did tip the scales.[42]

Hauerwas is not interested in some ideal state in which people might have absolute control over their lives. Freedom means being able to go from saying 'it happened' to 'I did it'. If people are to face their lives without illusion or deception, they need courage. Courage teaches people to face their own death not with denial or illusion but with hope. No ideal freedom could enable them to do this. Virtue is therefore a condition of freedom. ' "Virtue as its own reward" is a reminder that we choose to be virtuous for no other reason than that to be so is the only condition under which we would desire to survive. Only by so embodying the virtues have we the power to make our lives our own.'[43]

If we see character as the formal cause of agency, it becomes easier to see what is meant by saying decisions are part of character. The kinds of decisions people face – the kinds of circumstances in which they sense a decision is required – are the result of the kinds of people they are. One kind of person will face moral difficulties and obstacles of which another kind of person might be unaware. To an observer, such decisions might seem momentous or heroic: to the agent, they might simply seem an inescapable result of being true to his or her own character.

Character emerges as that which provides a proper bridge between one's past and one's future. This is what opens the door for Hauerwas to enter the world of narrative. It does not imply the limiting of actions to a protective routine which escapes the novelty of the unknown. It anticipates responsible reaction to new circumstances. But novelty sometimes denies the good of the past; character therefore does not accept the future unconditionally, it does not passively accommodate to circumstance: it changes circumstance and forms the future. 'The kind of person we are determines the kind of future we will face.'[44]

Where does this leave the final cause? The answer to this question is what takes the discussion away from pure philosophy into theological approaches. A community of character is not a means to an end, it is an end in itself. The final cause is therefore not to be construed individually: it is the production and maintenance of a community made up of people of character – the *communio sanctorum*. This approach is evident in Hauerwas' discussions of matters such as sexual intercourse and *in vitro* fertilization. Whereas the discussion of such issues generally concerns the inherent (and objectively-judged) rightness or wrongness of certain acts, Hauerwas does not discuss these issues in such terms. He is primarily concerned with what will form,

---

[42] Frithjof Bergmann, *On Being Free* (Notre Dame: University of Notre Dame Press 1977) p. 65, quoted in Hauerwas, *A Community of Character* pp. 115–116.
[43] Hauerwas, *A Community of Character* p. 125. Charles Dickens provides a ghastly parody of this notion of virtue in the character of Mr Pecksniff in *Martin Chuzzlewit*.
[44] Hauerwas, *Vision and Virtue* p. 64.

maintain and express the quality of a community of character. This is not narcissistic, because it is a quality of such a people to serve the wider society. Final causes are therefore incomprehensible when separated from the other three causes. There is nothing 'given' about the final cause: its very nature changes by the practices undertaken to shape it. Thus we may add to the summary suggested above:

4. The final cause is the community of character.

I trust that this discussion of Hauerwas' ethics in terms of causality has clarified what is at stake in the debate about the self. I am aware that Hauerwas himself believes that the language of causality can be replaced by the language of description.[45] I hope to have shown why I believe Hauerwas is mistaken in laying causes aside, and how in fact Aristotelian categories clarify various aspects of his conception of character.

To sum up my argument about causality: The 'standard account' assumes one can talk of final causes without concerning oneself with the other three causes. Hauerwas' approach disputes this. I have developed Milbank's claim that Aristotle subverts final causality by his emphasis on formal causality. In Hauerwas' language, this means insisting on character (the formal cause) in place of decision (the final cause). I have pointed to an answer to Muray's inquiry about the relationship between efficient and final causality. These two should not be detached as forcibly from material and formal causes: when all four causes are restored to a place in the understanding of the self, Hauerwas' argument becomes simple and clear: the self is not just a (passive, determined) material cause, or just an (indeterminate, active) efficient cause, but is enabled to be both by its character, the formal cause of its agency and the form of its material. Character is that which enables the self to be both a material cause and an efficient cause. The purpose or final cause of the self is to be in a community of character. It is when all four causes are in harmony that one can talk in terms of the 'unity' of the self. An action is good if it leads to the formation of a good agent; it is bad, not because it is bad in itself, but if it does not lead to the formation of agents of character. 'That certain actions are always wrong is but a way of saying that no virtuous person could ever envision so acting' – because 'such actions injure the practices of the community necessary for sustaining virtuous people'.[46]

---

[45] 'I am not an agent because I can "cause" certain things to happen, but because certain things that happen, whether through the result of my decision or not, can be made mine through my power of attention and intention. The "causation" proper to agents and their actions is not rendered by cause and effect, but by the agent's power of description' (Hauerwas, *The Peaceable Kingdom* p. 42). It is possible that the language of description may be construed causally – that is, description focuses attention on material and formal causes.

[46] Hauerwas, 'Courage Exemplified' *Christians Among the Virtues* p. 206 n. 9. See also MacIntyre, *After Virtue* pp. 149–152.

The communion of saints

This chapter has set out to show the centrality of the Church in Hauerwas' proposal for Christian ethics. First we saw the shortcomings in 'decisionist' ethics. An ethics of character better describes the moral life, moving the emphasis away from final causality – the end in view – toward formal causality – the who and how of the agent. I suggested that if we restore the notions of Aristotle's description of causality, we can identify the self as both the material cause (the 'passive' matter acted upon) and the efficient cause (the 'active' agent). This prevents us from having to see the self as primarily either active or passive.[47] We can go on to see character as the formal cause – 'the form of our agency'. It is a mistake to see the final cause in isolation from the other three causes – this is the error made by the 'standard account'. Yet how are we to think of the final cause?

My suggestion is that the final cause is the Church. If we return to Milbank's criticism of MacIntyre and Hauerwas, we can see that his concern is on exactly this point, the final cause or *telos*. 'What makes an action is *not* the presence of a "human" or "cultural" motive or "internal" reason: all this is still Cartesian and Kantian. What matters is the objective surface presence of a teleological ordering where intention of a goal shows up in visible structure.'[48]

In Christian theology there is often a tension between what might be called a creation/incarnational approach (largely corresponding to 'nature') and an eschatological/soteriological approach (largely corresponding to 'grace'). One can discern a tendency of foundational enterprises toward the former approach, affirming the value of human reason and experience, while nonfoundational enterprises lean toward the latter approach, aware of human shortcomings and the otherness of God. A tendency of Christian ethics of the former kind is to ask of a material, 'What is it for?', while the latter ethics will be more likely to ask, 'What might it become in God's kingdom?'

These are all generalizations, but they help us to see that Hauerwas' approach is largely of the latter kind. As such, it has a central implicit role for eschatology. The world has an End. Hence Hauerwas' view that the moral life be lived not prospectively (the possibilities created by each new choice) but retrospectively. The Church is a body of people whose vision of the world is retrospective from the End. In short, Christian ethics are not teleological but eschatological. The *telos* of the church is the *eschaton*. But the crucial fact in the life of the Church is that unlike the secular *telos*, the *eschaton* has in some sense *already* been achieved in the life, death and resurrection of Jesus Christ. The Church trusts that what it will discover of God at the *eschaton*

---

[47] Milbank still feels he has to make a choice: 'Narrative is our primary mode of inhabiting the world, and it characterizes the way the world happens to us, not, primarily, the cultural world humans happen to make' (*Theology and Social Theory* p. 359).

[48] Ibid.

will be consistent with what has already been revealed in Christ. The Church is therefore delivered from structuring its ethics around an incomplete *telos* which it is obliged somehow to bring about. It need not make the mistake of consequential ethics in assuming a responsibility to make the story end correctly. The story *has* ended correctly. Faithful witness therefore means trusting that this is so – this is the witness of the Church. The Church can therefore be seen in some sense as the proleptic or anticipatory presence of the *eschaton*. It is therefore the final cause of Christian ethics. In its 'visible structure' is what Milbank describes as 'the objective surface presence of a teleological ordering'. The Church's vision of the world from an eschatological point of view is what enables it, through narrative, to form its character by claiming its actions as its own.[49]

Sanctification is a dynamic process, not a static condition. It is a collective movement, not an individual attribute. It concerns the gradual conformity of the community to the description of life offered by Jesus Christ. Christians develop by attending to certain descriptions and forming actions in accordance with them. This attention forms Christian character.[50] Once one has fixed one's attention on these descriptions, one's continuing action reveals surprising and unforeseen new aspects and implications of one's descriptions:

> Thus we may find that we cannot wish to gain as much money as we can and at the same time treat all men fairly. At some point, in relation to a particular situation, we discover that though our agency can be determined by either one of these descriptions, they cannot both be harmonized in the same act. We must choose one or the other, and thereby become as we have chosen.[51]

This illustrates the interrelationship between character, agent and action. For Christians, it is the Church that offers the particular description of the world. Sustained attention to this description informs and forms the life of the Christian. 'Sanctification is thus the formation of the Christian's character that is the result of his [or her] intention to see the world as redeemed in Jesus Christ.'[52]

In the Introduction to the third printing of *Character and the Christian Life* Hauerwas adopts the metaphor of the moral life as a journey.[53] He is concerned that sanctification should not be descriptive of a status: it is in danger of becoming an abstract condition.[54] He therefore retains the meaning

---

[49] For an extended discussion of eschatological ethics, see Chapter 7 below.

[50] See Hauerwas, *Vision and Virtue* p. 58.

[51] Ibid. p. 63.

[52] Ibid. p. 67.

[53] Hauerwas, *Character and the Christian Life* p. xxvii. He derives the metaphor from Meilaender, who distinguishes between dialogue (a continual back-and-forth between law and gospel) and journey ('becoming . . . the sort of person God wants us to be'). See G. Meilaender, 'The Place of Ethics in the Theological Task' *Currents in Theology and Mission* 6 (1979) p. 199.

[54] For this reason it drops out of his more recent work almost entirely, and is replaced by particular narratives of individuals and communities.

of the term but plays down its significance: sanctification simply reminds Christians of the kind of journey they must undertake if they adopt and attend to the Church's description of the world.[55]

Part of the problem is that sanctification seems to imply a normative description of the virtues of the Christian life. But a glance at the diversity of virtues recommended by different societies and thinkers reveals a disarming lack of consensus, even upon a principle for determining the key virtues. This leaves the notion of sanctification vulnerable to historical disputes and inquiry: hence the temptation toward abstraction. Hauerwas is anxious to maintain the historical character of virtue, and therefore begins to steer away from the term sanctification toward language that speaks more concretely about participation in the Church. Nonetheless sanctification as a theme remains crucial to Hauerwas, as we shall see elsewhere, because it concerns performance and is thus crucial to assessing the truth of Christian convictions. It is also a collective thing: the communion of saints, just as much as the community of character, represents the final cause of Christian ethics.[56]

Virtue

Virtue and the virtues

While the development of the notion of character in Christian ethics is particularly associated with Stanley Hauerwas, the rediscovery of the significance of virtue is a much wider field. The symbolic centre of this field is Alasdair MacIntyre's *After Virtue*, published in 1981.

MacIntyre tells the story of how the contemporary fragmented Western ethical world came to be. The current Western ethical condition is a chaos of incompatible fragments of past ethical systems. The prevailing modern view concentrates on a particular understanding of freedom. As an individual, one is free to determine one's own good: it is not a question of there being one united good end for human life. Such an end tends, if at all, to be expressed as freedom or happiness. These are inadequate as ends since they are quiet on method and empty of content. They neither offer practical guidance for the conduct of a life oriented to such an end, nor describe what an end might be like were one to arrive at it. What has been rejected in the process is the teleological understanding of ethics – the idea that ethics is designed for a certain end, that is, the good for humankind. This

---

[55] See Hauerwas, *The Peaceable Kingdom* p. 94.

[56] Hauerwas would no doubt heartily concur with Karl Barth's discussion of whether *communio sanctorum* refers to sacred things (*sancta*) or sacred people (*sancti*). Barth commends both. 'Sancti means not specially fine people, but, for example, people like "the saints of Corinth", who were very queer saints. But these queer folk, to whom we too may belong, are *sancti*, that is, men set apart – for holy gifts and works, for *sancta*' (Karl Barth, *Dogmatics in Outline* translated by G.T. Thomson, London: SCM Press 1949).

teleological understanding is central to the way ethics was understood in the classical period, and is assumed by Plato and Aristotle. It sees the purpose of ethics as the production of good people. In the medieval period the understanding of the good was redefined in more theological terms and the means to the end, the virtues, were expanded to include faith, hope and love, lest they otherwise seem to imply some form of merit. The end of ethics was the production of good character, understood as the possession of the virtues. Today, however, there is no such consensus on the good. Even if there were perceived to be a single good to seek, the quest would be considered purely a matter of personal choice. Thus there is not so much an ethical vacuum as a cacophony of voices with little agreement on the method, possibility or desirability of adjudicating between them. MacIntyre recommends a return to the classical-medieval approach: the development of human character through the practice of the virtues.

He and Hauerwas are both aware that in this fragmented condition, a renewal of interest in human community, and the virtues that community entails, is unsurprising. Yet it is significant that this approach to ethics is still a minority pursuit. Few share the view that the barbarians are waiting beyond the frontiers – let alone that they have been ruling over us for some time.[57] The mainstream of ethicists remains committed to articulating an ethic of principle which can resolve conflicts in a manner that avoids arbitrariness. 'Virtue ethics' in this light seems subjective and relative, and thus of no more than limited usefulness for the ethical project. And of those who do share MacIntyre's general diagnosis, there is no consensus over the cure. 'Virtue ethics' is an umbrella term covering those who see themselves as standing in the same tradition as MacIntyre. Their diversity is shown by the number who would not describe MacIntyre as either a leader or even a highly significant member. The reason for this is that 'virtue ethics' has subscribers in several fields – theology, philosophy and public philosophy, with interested parties among educational-ists, psychologists and sociologists. MacIntyre's book is less easy to classify.[58]

---

[57] Alasdair MacIntyre, *After Virtue* p. 263.

[58] Lee Yearley, 'Recent Work on Virtue' *Religious Studies Review* 16/1 (1990) pp. 1–9. Yearley identifies three types of philosophical work on virtue. Philippa Foot, Bernard Williams, Edmund Pincoffs and others consider the relation of virtue to deontologi-cal or contractarian theories of morality, investigating whether virtue can replace or at least supplement such theories. Amelie Rorty and others discuss philosophies of mind and action and the way character affects action and the relationship of practical judgments, emotions, and dispositions. Hauerwas engages with some of these issues in *Character and the Christian Life*. See also Thomas Tracy, *God, Action and Embodiment* (Grand Rapids: Eerdmans 1984). Finally the third group are among those concerned with axiological questions of whether one can justify one kind of life that manifests the good more thoroughly than other kinds.

The debate in public philosophy largely surrounds R. Bellah et al. (eds.), *Habits of the Heart* (Berkeley: University of California Press 1985), R. Bellah et al. (eds.), *The Good Society* (New York: Knopf 1991), and further discussions in Richard Neuhaus (ed.), *Virtue – Public and Private* (Grand Rapids: Eerdmans 1986).

In theological ethics, one can distinguish three broad approaches to 'virtue ethics'.[59] The first sees virtue and character as being nurtured in particular communities which witness to the larger community but stand in some sense apart from it. They inherit from MacIntyre ideas surrounding narrative, community and tradition, and consider the vision of their tradition through history, symbol and story. This approach encompasses Hauerwas, McClendon and Meilaender.[60] The second group are anxious to avoid forming particular communities, being more concerned to converse with the larger, secular culture. By using philosophic and social scientific approaches, as well as the prominent place of virtue in Christian tradition, they can critique the types of character and world-view of contemporary society. This group includes Gustafson, Herms, Adams and Sokolowski.[61] The third approach is more interested in theories of human development as discussed in debates surrounding Piaget, Erikson and Kohlberg. This involves rather more consideration of education and psychology than of theology. Dykstra and Capps have been the most significant contributors in this area.[62]

Hauerwas is committed to a view of human existence as historical, bounded by creation and *eschaton*, embedded in particularities and contingencies, far removed from ideals and abstractions. He goes back to the pre-Christian era and finds that Aristotle's account of the virtues is well suited to the temporal character of life. It is as if Aristotle is all dressed up for a strenuous journey yet requires the medieval theologians to provide somewhere to go. What Aristotle lacked was a narrative context for the development of virtues. His account 'begs for a narrative display'. Here Hauerwas sees through the eyes of MacIntyre:

> The medieval vision is historical in a way that Aristotle's could not be. It situates our aiming at the good not just in specific contexts . . . but in contexts which themselves have a history. To move towards the good is to move in time and that movement may itself involve new understandings of what it is to move towards the good.[63]

---

[59] Yearley, 'Recent Work on Virtue', p. 3.

[60] James McClendon, *Ethics: Systematic Theology Volume One* (Nashville: Abingdon Press 1986). Gilbert Meilaender, *The Theory and Practice of Virtue* (Notre Dame: University of Notre Dame Press 1984).

[61] Gustafson, *Ethics from a Theocentric Perspective*; Eilert Herms, 'Virtue: A Neglected Concept in Protestant Ethics' *Scottish Journal of Theology* 35/6 (1982) pp. 481–495; Robert Adams, *The Virtue of Faith and Other Issues in Philosophical Theology* (Oxford: Oxford University Press 1987); Robert Sokolowski, *The God of Faith and Reason: Foundations of Christian Theology* (Notre Dame: University of Notre Dame Press 1982).

[62] Craig Dykstra, *Vision and Character* (New York: Paulist Press 1981) Donald Capps, *Deadly Sins and Saving Virtues* (Philadelphia: Fortress Press 1987). Hauerwas discusses this approach in 'Character, Narrative and Growth in the Christian Life' *A Community of Character* pp. 129–154.

[63] MacIntyre, *After Virtue* p. 176. See also Hauerwas and Pinches, 'The Virtues of Happiness' *Christians Among the Virtues* pp. 17–30.

Hauerwas confesses that Aristotle's list of the virtues is chaotic and arbitrary. But underlying Aristotle's account is a sense of unity expressed in terms of self-possession. This is the notion of integrity, constancy, steadfastness of character – the kind of character necessary to be able to feel the right things rightly as well as act at the right time, in the right way and toward the right people.[64] Both Hauerwas and MacIntyre identify the importance of the novel in portraying constancy. Constancy unites commitments and obligations, past and future, and demands narrative display.[65] In Jane Austen's *Mansfield Park* Fanny Price refuses marriage to Henry Crawford and thereby 'places the danger of losing her soul before the reward of gaining what for her would be a whole world. She pursues virtue for the sake of a certain kind of happiness and not for its utility.'[66]

If constancy is one aspect of the historical character of virtue, perhaps the definitive aspect is habit. Hauerwas sees habit as the key, and he identifies this as a difference between foundational and non-foundational accounts of ethics. Both Plato and Kant try to establish a foundation for morality that makes habits and their acquisition secondary. Aristotle's insistence that morality begins with the acquisition of habits indicates that there is no foundation for morality apart from historic communities.[67]

The discussion of habit concerns the way character is developed through behaviour. Training and repetition enable people to learn simple habits early in life. The actions which people perform in turn shape the performer. The vast majority of actions are performed not by rational decision but by habit. The implications of this are not fully worked out in *Character and the Christian Life*, where the fact that habit appears to describe automatic or mechanical response causes Hauerwas some anxiety.[68] At this stage Hauerwas is concerned to protect the agent as decision-maker, and is concerned lest habit make virtue seem mechanical. In later works – particularly after his contact with people with a mental handicap has qualified his understanding of moral rationality – habit comes increasingly to take the role in Hauerwas' thought

---

[64] Hauerwas, 'The Virtues of Happiness' p. 23. See Aristotle, *Nicomachean Ethics* 1105a pp. 26–35 and 1105b pp. 7–9.

[65] 'The virtues and the harms and evils which the virtues alone will overcome provide the structure both of a life in which the *telos* can be achieved and of a narrative in which the story of such a life can be unfolded' (MacIntyre, *After Virtue* p. 243).

[66] MacIntyre, *After Virtue* p. 242. If Austen is MacIntyre's (and Gilbert Ryle's) heroine, Hauerwas' hero is Trollope – to whom none is the equal for characterization. Reading novels is moral training: 'we are stretched through a narrative world that gives us the skills to make something of our own lives.' See Hauerwas, 'Constancy and Forgiveness: The Novel as a School for Virtue' *Dispatches From the Front: Theological Engagements with the Secular* (Durham, North Carolina: Duke University Press 1994) p. 56, and pp. 48–51 below. See also Hauerwas' admiration for the Aristotelian Martha Nussbaum in his 'Can Aristotle be a Liberal? Nussbaum on Luck' *Soundings* 72/4 (Winter 1989) pp. 675–691.

[67] Hauerwas, *A Community of Character* p. 273 n. 20.

[68] Hauerwas, *Character and the Christian Life* pp. 69–70.

that MacIntyre reserves for practice.[69] Habit offers a dimension that the term 'practice' lacks: the dimension of non-cognitive yet learned behaviour – a level open to people with a mental handicap. It is habit that preserves Hauerwas' ethic of virtue from charges of élitism.

More important than the specific virtues commended by Hauerwas is where he goes looking for them. The key to understanding how his concept of character develops into a call for specific virtues lies within his gradual perception of the significance of narrative. For the twin aspects of virtue correspond to the twin aspects of narrative. On the one hand narrative conveys the particular, historical, temporal, contingent nature of human existence, and thus virtue correspondingly engages with the questions of the unity of human lives and the extent to which one can be held accountable for one's character. Constancy is among Hauerwas' concerns in this broad understanding of virtue. On the other hand every story has an End, and the virtues particularly commended by Hauerwas – especially faithfulness, hope, patience, peacemaking and courage – are those appropriate to an eschato-logical view of the world. In *The Peaceable Kingdom* he identifies patience and hope as the central Christian virtues, and he emphasizes that love should not be separated from hope and patience, lest the eschatological and political aspects of Christian existence be neglected.[70]

We may continue the distinction between the broad notion of *telos* and the specifically Christian anticipation of *eschaton*, and extend this distinction into the area of virtue. For the cardinal virtues are those suited to the notion of *telos*, and the theological virtues – to which Hauerwas adds a few of his own, notably peacemaking – are those which anticipate the *eschaton*. This accords with the thrust of the most significant criticism of the way Hauerwas adapts Aristotle's discussion of virtue and the virtues, which comes from John Milbank. It is the most significant because its concern is one even closer to Hauerwas' heart than virtue – nonviolence. Hauerwas himself describes how in the absence of virtues sufficient to structure self-possession we seek security through power and violence.[71] Milbank questions whether any notion of virtue can be founded on antiquity. Just as Augustine charged the Romans with having no real virtue, because they had no real peace, so Milbank extends this charge, on both a practical and an ontological level, to the whole of antiquity. Antique virtue, says Milbank, assumed violence, and thus was concerned with control – of self, soul or city. Milbank considers that the ontological priority of peace is more important than virtue.[72] A distinction between *telos* and *eschaton*, and its extension into a distinction between theological and antique virtue, would enable Hauerwas to withstand Milbank's criticisms on this point.

---

[69] Hauerwas acknowledges in *Character and the Christian Life* that some have come to understand habit as involving imagination, intellect and will (p. 69).

[70] See Hauerwas, *A Community of Character* p. 268 n. 66.

[71] See ibid. pp. 126 and 267 n. 58.

[72] Milbank, *Theology and Social Theory* Chapter 11 especially pp. 363–364.

Virtue and medicine

Hauerwas' writings on medicine are worth considering in detail, because they demonstrate what he means by an ethic of virtue, and they illustrate his frustrations with the way ethics is often discussed.

Hauerwas wryly observes that the quandaries of medicine have saved many ethicists from severe self-doubt about the plausibility of their profession. He disputes the supposition that it is the technological power of modern medicine that has brought ethics to the fore by raising a host of pressing questions. Instead, technology, in Hauerwas' view, is a result of moral confusion rather than a cause of it. For in the absence of a consensus on what constitutes a well-lived life, slogans such as 'right to life', 'right to choose', and 'right to die' replace consideration of the when to fight and when to accept death. It seems almost easier to develop the technology to keep blood flowing around the body than establish what might be a good death. So physicians are expected to treat death as the ultimate enemy to be resisted by every available means.

The ethics of medicine that interest Hauerwas are not the dilemmas connected with technology, but the underlying morality of the physician's art. It is taken for granted in Western societies that some people are set apart to care for the sick. Illness is not regarded as a reason why a person should be neglected or excluded from human community. This is a highly significant tenet of these societies, the more remarkable for the fact that it generally goes unnoticed.

However, recent debates in medical ethics threaten this core principle. When freedom is exalted above all other qualities, it begins to jeopardize the moral foundation of medicine. In the name of freedom, humans are perceived to be most 'natural' when they are intervening to transcend the 'natural' constraints on life. Biological destiny comes to be seen as a matter of choice. This view of individual freedom pervades the whole of life. Hauerwas observes that physicians will become like bureaucrats, respecting freedom without imposing particular views, or like a newspaper-deliverer who distributes serious journals to some clients and soft pornography to others, according to taste.[73]

This notion of freedom will not succeed, in Hauerwas' view, in securing the first principles of medicine, the protection and care of each person's life. For example, it is hard to see how an ethic of freedom will see the mentally handicapped as anything other than an anomaly. Indeed, Hauerwas exposes the way such approaches, in the name of eliminating suffering, sometimes tend towards eliminating the sufferer.[74] One should not be too quick, he says, to assume that suffering is a threat to human autonomy. Instead, one gains autonomy when one finds or perceives a story by which suffering can become one's own. If medicine attempts to deny suffering, it can turn out in a curious way to be a threat to autonomy.

---

[73] Hauerwas, *Suffering Presence* p. 9.
[74] Ibid. p. 24.

Hauerwas is suspicious of attempts to eliminate suffering altogether. Suffering is something with which one must learn how to live. 'No account of the moral life which is worthy of our serious consideration can avoid asking us to endure suffering. Indeed, the morally interesting question is not whether we are asked to suffer, but how and for what we are asked to suffer.'[75] The danger comes when medicine encourages the view of suffering as pointless, thus suggesting a mechanical model. Then medicine becomes the overarching power for meaning in human life. Hauerwas describes this kind of threat as 'the modern analogue to the Gnostic heresy'. By this he means that medicine is seen as a form of salvation, is chiefly concerned in freeing humans from the limits of their bodies, and resides in an esoteric knowledge of the specially trained.[76]

In their desire to be socially relevant, theologians working in ethics have frequently underwritten the kinds of suppositions which Hauerwas finds so dubious. In their doing so, theological ethics when applied to medicine has tended to become another form of the quandary ethics that Hauerwas has so thoroughly challenged. By subordinating religious convictions to the ethos of freedom, theologians have reached a wider audience, but in the process they have been digging their own grave and undermining the principles of medicine as a moral discipline. In the interests of cultural consensus, theologians have tended to downplay the distinctiveness of their convictions. But this only reinforces the view that theological claims have little significance in understanding issues in medicine or for medicine as a whole.

So what does the Church have to offer to medicine? How can theological convictions be significant in medical ethics? The answer, for Hauerwas, is to return to the remarkable agreement that society does not give up on a person just because they are ill. This means that medicine is about caring, even when no cure is possible – indeed, especially when no cure is possible. 'The physician's basic pledge is not to cure, but to care through being present to the one in pain.'[77] The constant temptation for the physician is to see medicine as the elimination of suffering (hence the dependence on technology) rather than the care of the sufferer. The task of the physician is to be a bridge between the world of the sick and the world of the healthy, teaching the healthy about the frailty of our reason and control, while caring for the sick, thus binding the suffering and the non-suffering into the same community.

This task is immensely difficult, for how can one confront pain day after day, without becoming hardened to it? One hardens one part of one's heart in order to retain some sense of feeling in the rest. It is hard to continue to see the fullness of humanity in the suffering person, if one regularly encounters the demeaning nature of exposure to pain. The helplessness of the other can lead to hate if it reminds the carers of their own helplessness. This is where medicine becomes a matter of character; this is where the

---

[75] Ibid. p. 25.
[76] Ibid. p. 51.
[77] Ibid. pp. 78–79.

Church speaks to the physician: and this is where all the concerns of this chapter draw together.

Hauerwas considers Job's comforters: 'They sat with him on the ground seven days and seven nights, and no one spoke a word to him, for they saw that his suffering was very great' (Job 2:13). Medicine looks to the Church for the habits and practices required for the care of those in chronic pain. Through prayer, Christians believe that God can be present whether or not medical skill proves capable of curing. By being a community with the skills of presence, the Church helps to keep together the world of the sick, the world of the carer, and the wider world. This is based on the Church's commitment not to fear the stranger. 'The hospital is ... a house of hospitality along the way of our journey with finitude', rather than a means of isolating those who are ill from everybody else.[78] By the way it is present to the sick and dying, the Church points to the presence of God, and affirms the necessity and role of virtue and character in medicine.

Summary

Hauerwas began his career by exposing the flaws in the conventional way of doing ethics. This chapter has explained these shortcomings, notably the emphasis on the neutral observer and on decisions; there is also an underlying suspicion that conventional ethics presupposes violence. In place of the 'standard account of moral rationality', Hauerwas proposes an ethic of character and an attention to particular narratives. Character is Hauerwas' way of explaining how people are not simply passive beings at the mercy of circumstance, yet neither are they entirely independent.

Hauerwas' account of character is incomplete. By restoring Aristotle's notion of causality I explained that what Hauerwas is doing in asserting character over decision is to say that ethics is about how things are done and who does them, rather than solely about the anticipated end-products of these actions. Actions only have significance because of who is doing them and how they are being done.

There is no intention of doing away with principles altogether. The emphasis on virtue is simply an attempt to describe the moral life more thoroughly. The reduction of ethics to principles alone is a method which implies a story of its own – and a sinister one at that. My discussion of tragedy and violence makes this point.

The next chapter will show how narrative discloses the formation of character, particularly in its historical and contingent nature. A truthful narrative lies not with the agent or the observer, but with the community – the Church. It would be true to Hauerwas' themes to suggest that the end (or conclusion) of all action, the *eschaton*, has its character revealed by the life, death and resurrection of Jesus Christ. Therefore any other intended

---

[78] Ibid. p. 82.

end (or *telos*) of action is secondary to the building-up of the Church, which is the true final cause of Christian ethics. This communion of saints unites Hauerwas' notions of character, narrative and virtue.

In conclusion, the discussion of virtue and medicine has shown how the presence of the Church in the face of human suffering is a both a profound witness to its faith and an example of how it can contribute to the moral foundations of the society in which it shares.

[3]
From Character to Story

In Chapter 2 I outlined how Hauerwas began his career by identifying the shortcomings of conventional ethics. He proposes that the emphasis in ethics should shift from the nature of the action to the character of the person performing the action. He illustrates this shift with particular reference to medicine. The movement from action to agent, deed to doer, as the chief focus of ethics, has three implications which form the substance of this third chapter. Hauerwas does not proceed with these implications in a systematic way: he stumbles upon them as he explores the agent's perspective.[1] In his work from the early 1980s, one can see these implications emerging. It is this exploratory character that gives this work a more pioneering quality than the more robust, but less substantial, work of the early 1990s.

The first implication of the agent's perspective is that because agents differ, ethics differs when it concerns differing agents. Hence Hauerwas' insistence that one cannot do 'ethics for anyone': all ethics must have an epithet. There can be Christian ethics, Marxist ethics, Buddhist ethics; Protestant ethics, Roman Catholic ethics, Mennonite ethics; but not business ethics or medical ethics, since these refer to spheres of *activity*, not kinds of *people*. Hauerwas has little time for the quest – almost a given since Immanuel Kant – to ground ethics in some universal faculty of humankind.[2]

---

[1] Hauerwas acknowledges this in *The Peaceable Kingdom* xxv.

[2] At first glance, this may look similar to situation ethics. Situation ethics, associated with Joseph Fletcher's book of the same title, was a rebellion which arose in the 1960s against conventional ethics. Fletcher pointed out that in many cases, particularly in extreme situations, conventional ethics contravened the law of love. Fletcher advocated that in such situations one should do the most loving thing, even if it broke an ethical law. This view had already been much criticized before Hauerwas started his writing career. Hauerwas himself points out that situation ethics takes no more account than conventional ethics of the *character* of the people involved in the situation. To extract love from the Christian gospel as its normative principle is to rob love of its content and make it an abstract ideal. Thus both Hauerwas and Fletcher disagree with conventional ethics, but Fletcher has not yet seen the need to move from action to agent: he thus still sees ethics as primarily about quandaries. See *Vision and Virtue* pp. 11–29, 93–126.

The second implication of the shift from deed to doer is the logical connection between character and narrative. Once one has stopped asking, 'What should I do?' and started asking, 'What kind of a person should I want to be?' one has opened up a series of other questions – questions which point towards story. To assess how the quandary arose in the first place, and to understand the issues at stake in whatever decision the agent might make, is to begin to tell a story about that person which provides the indispensable context for the decision. Then to look into the future and the kind of character the agent aspires to develop through the proposed course of action, and to describe other persons whose lives shape the agent in question, is to appreciate that the story is a much more significant focus for ethical discussion than merely the decision itself. The question becomes, 'Of what stories do I find myself to be a part?' The language of change, growth and development is the language of story. Stories are ways of giving coherence to a jumble of events: both what people have done, and what has happened to them. They are a thread which ties together a series of situations, and gives them a collective character. Thus narrative is where Hauerwas turns when he strives to tie character to event.

The third, more subtle, implication arises out of the shortcomings in Hauerwas' new proposal of the agent's perspective. As we saw in Chapter 2, Hauerwas arrives at the agent's perspective by rejecting action as the locus of ethics. What is important in an action is *what the neutral observer cannot know*, that is, all the reasons why *this* action matters to *this* person – in short, the person's story. But Hauerwas has another commitment: while he sees the intention of the action as crucial, he refuses to see that intention as 'prior' to the action. To do so would take him back to the Cartesian ('substantial') model of the self that he is setting out to avoid.[3] It is this kind of tangle that leads to Hauerwas dropping 'the agent's perspective' from the vocabulary of his later work. *Character and the Christian Life* is concerned largely with the individual self. The category of narrative emerges as Hauerwas considers the unresolved issues arising from that book. In the process, the agent's community replaces the agent as the centre of ethics: for it is the community that turns convictions into practices. What matters is not how the agent sees their own actions, but what significance those actions have in the narrative of their community. In the context of community, narrative is a way of describing agents and their actions that is at the same time publicly accessible and privately significant.

Thus in this chapter I show how narrative arises out of character but remains inadequate without community. In Chapter 4 I shall outline the way Hauerwas unites the notion of community with that of narrative to form his mature position on ethics and hermeneutics. In this chapter I look at the building-blocks from which his understanding of narrative is constructed. I shall review what these perspectives offer, where they can be criticized,

---

[3] See pp. 20–23 above.

whether they can be adapted, and how they are related to Hauerwas' work as a whole.

'Narrative from below'

During what I have called the 'exploratory' phase of Hauerwas' writings on narrative (roughly 1977–84) he works with several different notions of narrative. He acknowledges this in *The Peaceable Kingdom* (p. 28), where he articulates three claims involved in his understanding of narrative.

The first concerns the contingent, created character of the self. The self does not exist by necessity: there was when it was not. It came from somewhere and shares its existence with other beings. Simply to ask, in the moment, 'What should I do?', may well miss the more far-reaching, 'Who (or what) am I?', and thus the more obviously narrative-based, 'How have I come to be here?'

The second claim expands on the first by considering the self in its setting. Existence in society is historical. A person who can thread together separate events and realities in his or her life has established an identity; a community which can do the same has established a tradition. Without formation by the tradition of a community, the self is unlikely to establish a coherent identity. 'Objective' ethics, ethics without historical community, therefore consider the self outside its setting. One might as well consider fish outside the sea.

The third claim is of a very different kind. Narrative is the form of God's salvation. The heart of revelation is the story of the covenant with Israel, its recapitulation first in the life, death and resurrection of Jesus, and over again in the history of the Church. Narrative is thus the shape of the Christian life which seeks to conform to the character of God's salvation.

There is a discontinuity here. The first and second claims are formal ones. Hauerwas is not here talking about Christian ethics, but about ethics in a wider sense. He is describing human experience in general, rather than Christian experience in particular. Though he points out the story-formed nature of human existence, he offers no prescriptive or metaphysical considerations. This I shall describe as 'narrative from below' – that is, from an anthropological perspective. It is an experiential and descriptive category.

By contrast, the third claim is revelatory and prescriptive. It is not grounded in general human experience. It is not anthropological, but theological. It is concerned to show that the biblical narrative manifests God's character. Because narratives display character in the way they link intentional action, the Christian community's tradition of stories shapes the character of Christians. This I shall call 'narrative from above', because it is a claim about the character of God, rather than about the nature of human life.

In his later work, Hauerwas distances himself from the formal claims for story that were such a prominent part of the period prior to 1984. He becomes more interested in narrative as the manner of God's revelation, and less interested in any abiding narrative character of human existence. In *A Community of Character* he sees the two claims as readily compatible, indeed flowing into one another. Before looking at the issues of 'narrative from above' therefore, I shall review Hauerwas' use of 'narrative from below'.

Life as a story

A number of theologians and ethicists have embraced the bolder claims of narrative to describe human existence.[4] Perhaps the most significant such author for Hauerwas (though the significance is not extensively made explicit in Hauerwas' work) is the moral philosopher Alasdair MacIntyre. Hauerwas had begun to write about story before the publication in 1981 of MacIntyre's influential *After Virtue*; nonetheless it is worth describing MacIntyre's understanding of narrative because it broadly represents Hauerwas' position in 'narrative from below' vein.[5]

MacIntyre sees narrative as a claim for intelligibility. Human action, to be intelligible, needs a setting, which has a history. All actions are disjointed parts of a possible narrative. Life is experienced as a story: people live in stories with beginnings and endings – births and deaths. All people find that they are characters in one another's stories. They experience the unpredictability of lived narratives, and they form their actions by conceptions of a shared future (teleology). Because they are story-telling beings, humans can only answer the question, 'What am I to do?' by addressing the question, 'Of what stories do I find myself to be a part?' They learn about virtues and roles through myths and legends. They inherit a moral starting-point from the tradition of their community: even rebellion is an expression of that community's character. A good, living, tradition embodies these conflicts and conversations about the ends it pursues: it is a not-yet-completed narrative.

MacIntyre follows Aristotle in maintaining that the moral life gains its unity from the systematic asking and answering of what is the good life for the self and for humanity. But behind these questions lies a larger story. Great traditions all have narrative canons. And it is significant that these canons claim to be true: the difference between fiction and non-fiction lies in the fact that in history, the characters are never more than co-authors of their own stories.

---

[4] This 'narrative from below' position is well expressed by Stephen Crites. See 'The Narrative Quality of Experience' *Journal of the American Academy of Religion* 39/3 (1971) pp. 291–311, and 'Myth, Story, History' in Tony Stoneburger (ed.), *Parable, Myth and Language* (Cambridge, Mass: Church Society for College Work 1968).

[5] MacIntyre, *After Virtue*. The outline in this section follows Chapter 15 of MacIntyre's book. For Hauerwas' early work on story, see *Vision and Virtue* pp. 68–89, *Truthfulness and Tragedy* pp. 15–39, 71–81, and *A Community of Character* pp. 99–152.

Hauerwas' early perspective is very much like that of MacIntyre. This is largely because of his frustrations with the failure of conventional (Kantian) ethics to describe the moral life. The moral life looks much more like the way MacIntyre describes it. The questions MacIntyre asks ('Of what stories do I find myself to be a part?') need to be answered before the interminable quandaries of life can be faced. At times Hauerwas can make somewhat sweeping affirmations of this perspective. 'All significant moral claims are historically derived and require narrative display . . . Appeal to the narrative dependence and structure of moral rationality is . . . an attempt to illuminate, in a formal manner, the character of our moral existence as historic beings.'[6] In Hauerwas' later work, such statements are seldom found. It becomes less certain that this is the way all people experience life: but it remains clear that Christians should be taught to do so.

Character and narrative

We have established that to understand a moral context, one must be aware of the agent's tradition and community. Such a context presupposes a story. There is a second sense in which narrative is helpful. It offers a way of describing how an agent can change and develop. Ethics vary because agents vary; meanwhile agents themselves change and grow in the course of their lives, while remaining the same person. Thus narrative is helpful both in establishing the tradition that unites various agents, and in conveying the identity of a person whose character has developed in the course of their life.

Protestant ethics have tended to be reluctant to talk about moral development. The emphasis since Luther has been that the human being before God is always a sinner, totally dependent on God's grace. To seek moral progress seems, against this background, to be a way of seeking justification before God through one's own good works, rather than through dependence solely on his grace. Hauerwas points out the political implications of this position: it has left Protestants open to whatever has been the prevailing morality in their culture. This has frequently resulted in identifying being Christian with simply being decent.

Hauerwas, by contrast, is interested in how agents change, grow and develop over time. The Christian life is a journey, in which patterns and character can be developed and discerned. Hauerwas began his career by establishing the significance of character for theological ethics. But how can people be said to retain the same character if they change? It is the attempt to answer this question that leads Hauerwas from character to narrative.

People change in good ways and in bad ways. What the Christian story offers to an ethics of character is a way of incorporating both positive and

---

[6] Hauerwas, *A Community of Character* p. 99.

negative developments in the moral life. Christianity's story covers both human growth and human failure.

To start with the negative, a pressing question is, 'How can it be that those who have grown morally are yet prone to exceptional moral failure?' The Christian story answers this by showing that moral development is not an adequate description of what is required. Sin is pervasive and subtle. It cannot be 'grown out of': on the contrary, the more faithful a Christian becomes, the more their awareness of sin increases. The nearer one draws to God, the more one understands the depth of one's estrangement. Agents must therefore abandon false accounts of themselves. They must incorporate all dimensions of what they have been and what they have done and what has happened to them, including the shameful elements. They must transform their vision of the past, learning to see even these shameful elements, now forgiven and transformed, as part of an ongoing grace. They must commit themselves to be constantly vigilant in maintaining a truthful account of themselves. Development is an inadequate term to describe this process. The Christian term is conversion. Thus the response to moral weakness is through an understanding of narrative.

These theoretical observations thirst for particular illustration. It is perhaps surprising that Stanley Hauerwas has not explored biography at greater length, since it seems an ideal way of expressing an ethics of character.[7] One exception is an important essay on self-deception.

Hauerwas discusses self-deception through the autobiography of Hitler's minister of armaments, Albert Speer.[8] Hauerwas identifies self-deception as arising from the desire to be consistent: when the range of experience and behaviour becomes so wide and diverse that it threatens to expose that consistency as an illusion, the agent seeks increasingly deceptive methods of sustaining a sense of unity. The parts of the agent's life that he or she is reluctant to spell out are those which break this consistency: these are the parts where the agent is vulnerable to self-deception. The irony is that the agent who makes little effort to lead a consistent life is less prone to such self-deception.

Albert Speer was an outstanding administrator who maintained a characteristic German distrust of politics. He sought the establishment of Berlin and Nuremburg as magnificent cities. For ten years he saw and perceived and even despised what was going on around him, yet failed to realize the consequences of sharing government with madmen. Speer was a man who

---

[7] Biography was one of the first areas to be explored during the early wave of narrative theology. The most influential work has been *Biography as Theology* (Philadelphia: Trinity Press 1990²), in which James McClendon explores the reconciling work of Christ through the lives of Dag Hammarskjold, Martin Luther King, Clarence Jordan and Charles Ives. McClendon continues this approach in his *Ethics: Systematic Theology Volume One* (Nashville: Abingdon 1986) where he considers Dietrich Bonhoeffer, Jonathan and Sarah Edwards, and Dorothy Day.

[8] Hauerwas, *Truthfulness and Tragedy* pp. 82–98.

thought he needed no story beyond his own administrative skill: he was manipulated by those who offered an intensely compelling, but false, story.

From the horror of Speer's autobiography, Hauerwas illustrates how essential is the need for a truthful narrative which can check the agent's propensity to self-deception. This story must enable the agent first to recognize the evil that he or she has brought about, and second to accept responsibility for it and not shroud it in illusion. At the same time they must, thirdly, find the courage to continue to act. The truthful narrative, the gospel, trains Christians to acknowledge their self-deceptions before (like Speer) they are forced to.

Moving to the positive, how does moral growth take place? This question comes more and more to the fore in Hauerwas' writing, and I shall return to it in Chapter 5. The way he sets about his answer demonstrates how he gradually moves from 'narrative from below' to 'narrative from above'. Moral formation is something that is primarily received rather than attained. (Thus is any taint of justification by works avoided.) The self is a gift; so is the story of salvation. One is not one's own person – one's story is not simply one's own story. One does not know oneself, but discovers oneself as one learns to place oneself in the Christian story. Crucial to doing this is the development of particular habits. The formation of these habits is the chief purpose of Christian nurture. To be a Christian one must be a disciple: and a disciple is an apprentice to a skilled artisan. By imitating such a person, the disciple learns to take the right things for granted and thus grows in the moral life.

Thus 'narrative from below' is concerned with finding that one's life and moral experience are best understood as a narrative. This narrative is always formed in the context of one's tradition and community, which likewise are best expressed as a narrative. The journey to 'narrative from above' is the identification of a normative story into which all other stories need to be grafted if they are to be truthful and faithful. 'Narrative from below' is chiefly concerned with expressing the character of the agent: by using narrative one can give a much more adequate description of the agent than is allowed for in most moral thinking. 'Narrative from above' is more concerned with prescription than description: it points towards how the agent's character can be formed and trained.

It would not be entirely accurate to suggest that Hauerwas' interest in narrative evolved organically out of a concern for character. To some extent narrative has enabled Hauerwas to acknowledge the flaws in his early work while retaining its principal themes. As he himself says, 'it is a mistake to assume that my emphasis on narrative is the central focus of my position ... Narrative is but a concept that helps clarify the various themes I have sought to develop ...'[9] 'Narrative from below' can be seen as Hauerwas' attempt to

---

[9] Hauerwas, *The Peaceable Kingdom* p. xxv. Hauerwas is really criticizing his own earlier work when he complains of 'the general tendency of action theory to isolate and abstract "action" from the narrative contexts that make an action intelligible' (*A Community of Character* p. 262 n. 11).

save the agent's perspective from death by a thousand qualifications. It arises chiefly from Hauerwas' concern to avoid a substantialist understanding of the self.[10] In his stress on the agent's perspective, he is in danger of implying a new internality – that of intention – to replace old and rejected internalities such as 'free will'. In Milbank's more radical view, the problem begins in trying to separate a discrete sphere of 'action':

> To hang on to 'action' as a special ethical sphere is still to cling to certain notions of internality. Hence many current proponents of an 'ethics of virtue' began by insisting on 'the agent's perspective' to distinguish intentionally informed action (although not a Cartesian intention posited 'before' an action) from mere natural causation, which can be fully comprehended from 'outside'. However, they have quickly realized that post-Wittgensteinian considerations force one to see that if an intention is situated within an action, then it is also constituted through language, and so is in principle as comprehensible to an outside observer as to the agent herself.[11]

Hauerwas himself acknowledges the importance of Wittgenstein: 'Wittgenstein ended forever any attempt on my part to anchor theology in some general account of "human experience"' and taught him to look instead to 'the grammar of the language used by believers'.[12] He also clarifies the agent's perspective by invoking the agent's community in the role that he previously (in *Character and the Christian Life*) assigned to the agent and Milbank earmarks for the 'observer'. In doing so, he remains consistent with the second ('historical') claim for narrative as discussed above. He is concerned to find 'an account of how my way of appropriating the convictions of my community contributes to the story of that people. . . . It is useful to think of such an account as a narrative that is more basic than either the agent's or observer's standpoint.'[13]

This clarification of the agent's perspective ensures that Hauerwas avoids criticisms of a substantialist view of the internal self. What replaces the internal self is the 'internal' community. To talk of an internal community simply means that the community is ethically prior to the individual self. This has implications for the way the community is perceived to relate to the outside world: for a substantialist view of community is intolerable to many, who assume it implies sectarianism.

What really saves Hauerwas from charges of internality is his identification of one particular narrative as normative for ethics: 'Narrative provides the conceptual means to suggest how the stories of Israel and Jesus are a "morality" for the formation of the Christian community and character.'[14] It

---

[10] See pp. 20–23 above.

[11] Milbank, *Theology and Social Theory* p. 358. Milbank believes, against Aristotle, that 'there is no universal, special sphere of "action", and therefore no distinct subject called "ethics". Questions of "the moral" rather intrude everywhere.'

[12] Hauerwas, *The Peaceable Kingdom* p. xxi.

[13] Hauerwas, *A Community of Character* p. 135.

[14] Ibid. p. 95.

is his non-foundational assertion that narrative is the form of God's salvation that resolves his earlier foundational claims. 'We are "storied people" because the God that sustains us is a "storied God" whom we come to know only by having our character formed appropriate to God's character. The formation of such character is not an isolated event but requires the existence of a corresponding society – a "storied society".'[15]

What emerges is the unique importance and pivotal role of the Church. It is the Church that enables Hauerwas to hold onto all three claims about narrative made in *The Peaceable Kingdom*. For the Church concerns the character of the individual ('that community where we as individuals continue to test and are tested by the particular way those stories live through us'[16]) as well as the character of God ('the earnest of God's kingdom',[17] the 'recapitulation' of the life of Jesus[18]) and the character of the world ('the . . . space for us to . . . understand the disobedient, sinful, but still God-created character of the world'[19]). It is Hauerwas' concept of Church, absent from *Character and the Christian Life*, and derived from his understanding of the ongoing nature of God's story, that finally saves ethics from the clutches of agent or observer, and demonstrates the compatibility of contingent, historical, and community-dependent ethics with anti-foundational claims about the nature of revelation.

The novel

For Hauerwas, the novel is the perfect form for the display of character. By its detailed description of the particulars of existence, it affirms the way character is revealed over time. In its narrative, the novel demonstrates how character can incorporate change. By placing its characters against the backdrop of other lives, it shows the inter-connectedness of moral existence. By seeing the story through to its end, the novel shows the implications of a character's convictions. The novel mirrors life by placing the agent in relation to other characters, luck and accident, with foreseen and unforeseen consequences. It finds meaning and pleasure by telling a story.

Hauerwas refers to several novelists in the course of his work.[20] Four authors in particular illustrate the role of the novel in Hauerwas' understanding of narrative. I shall refer in turn to Anthony Trollope, Anne Tyler, Peter DeVries and Richard Adams.

The virtues described by Aristotle, Aquinas and others are highly commended. If, however, they are to be understood and learned, they require

---

[15] Ibid. p. 91.

[16] Ibid. p. 96.

[17] Ibid. p. 92.

[18] Hauerwas, *The Peaceable Kingdom* p. 29.

[19] Hauerwas, *A Community of Character* p. 92.

[20] Considering his early interest in Iris Murdoch, it is perhaps surprising that he nowhere discusses her novels in detail.

narrative display. The gift of Anthony Trollope is that of telling stories which demonstrate the significance of virtue in the culture of his time. Hauerwas discusses this ability in two essays, 'Constancy and Forgiveness: The Novel as a School for Virtue', and 'On Honor: By Way of a Comparison of Karl Barth and Trollope'.[21] For example, it is difficult to define a gentleman without telling a story: only through such illustration can one display the appropriate qualities of judgement, diffidence, courage and honesty. And these are not static qualities. It is in the complex detail of plot and character that a man like Dr Wortle of *Dr Wortle's School* must learn how to be a gentleman in trying circumstances. Only in the novel can one see how a man of such aggression, ambition and passion can emerge with such loyalty and honour.

Constancy and forgiveness are typical of the kinds of qualities that narrative is uniquely able to display: for as I have discussed (pp. 44–48), they combine the elements of continuity and change that are so difficult to incorporate in the notion of character. Hauerwas shows how in *The Vicar of Bullhampton*, the prostitute Carry Brattle is eventually forgiven by her father Jacob, the miller, through the agency of the vicar, Mr Fenwick. In the person of Jacob Brattle is seen a man whose constancy makes it hard for him to forgive, but a man who finally realizes the necessity as well as the cost of forgiveness. Trollope presents this, the central theme of his book, only in a sub-plot, emphasizing that a person such as Carry Brattle will invariably find herself a minor character in others' stories.

Anne Tyler's *Saint Maybe* likewise demonstrates the complex and lengthy journey of forgiveness.[22] The novel rests on the shock of discovering that, 'You can't just say "I'm sorry, God" '. . . . You have to offer reparation' – even when appropriate reparation is hard to find. Ian Bedloe's life changes dramatically when he asks for forgiveness and is told that it will not be forthcoming unless he takes practical steps to undo the harm he has done. These steps involve dropping out of college and spending the next 20 years bringing up the three children left by the death of his brother Danny and sister-in-law Lucy. In the detail of this nurture, Ian finds a richer life that teaches him to forgive as well as be forgiven. Only in making reparation does Ian understand what he has done wrong. Thus he claims his life as his own.

Peter DeVries' novel *The Blood of the Lamb* is used extensively by Hauerwas in *Naming the Silences*. The novel details the journey of the appropriately-named Don Wanderhope through a life pitted with tragedy – his brother's death, his father's madness, his girlfriend's death, his wife's suicide. The climax is his young daughter's death from leukaemia. DeVries' narrative displays several themes. The underlying comparison of Don's story is between his struggle for belief and the struggle for the child's life. Set against this is the sudden recovery of the significance of the everyday, which Don experiences when his daughter is in temporary remission. Whilst Hauerwas discusses the vital role of ordinary behaviour in many essays, there is, in terms of Hauerwas'

---

[21] Hauerwas, *Dispatches from the Front* pp. 31–57 and 58–79.

[22] Ibid. pp. 80–88.

wider claims for narrative, a more far-reaching point.[23] Adults cope with tragedy by trying to tell the story of a whole life, with beginning, middle and end. But a child's death undermines that strategy, for a child has only a beginning. Faced with the horror of having no story, Don totally immerses himself in the power of medicine, a power that replaces his family's Dutch Calvinism. The novel shows how absurd it is that Don condones his daughter's suffering at the hands of doctors while he continues to abhor any suffering at the hands of God. Thus DeVries' novel displays many themes that connect character to narrative.

Hauerwas is concerned with the moral value of narrative. He reserves his particular criticism for the liberal 'story that there is no story'. The following sums up the situation that frustrates Hauerwas so much:

> Liberalism, in its many forms and versions, presupposes that society can be organized without any narrative that is commonly held to be true. As a result it tempts us to believe that freedom and rationality are independent of narrative – i.e. we are free to the extent we have no story. Liberalism is, therefore, particularly pernicious to the extent it prevents us from understanding how deeply we are captured by its account of our existence.[24]

Of all Hauerwas' assaults on liberalism, one of the most impressive is his use of the work of Richard Adams in 'A Story-Formed Community: Reflections on *Watership Down*'.[25] In *Watership Down*, a small group of rabbits escape from a warren when one has a premonition of its destruction. After a series of adventures, they form a new home on Watership Down, withstanding an attack from a regimented warren whose does they have stolen. At the start of their journey, the rabbits are a collection of individuals who have in common only the stories of the prince of rabbits, El-ahrairah. By the end, they are transformed, sharing a history of adventures interpreted through the traditions of El-ahrairah.

Of the three warrens encountered by the rabbits, the first resembles a traditional class society, the second the modern welfare state, the third a totalitarian regime. Watership Down itself is presented as an ideal society. The respective societies are judged by whether in their environment the stories of El-ahrairah, the prince of rabbits, can be authentically retold. In the traditional warren, stories had become a means of entertainment only: security and stability could not be disturbed. The liberal warren had ceased to tell stories, and forgotten how to tell them: nothing must disturb the terrible secret that each rabbit would one day fall victim to the man who apparently protected and fed them. The totalitarian warren was so dominated by its fearsome leader that rabbits had ceased to be able to make decisions for themselves. The

---

[23] See especially Hauerwas, 'Taking Time for Peace: The Ethical Significance of the Trivial' *Christian Existence Today: Essays on Church, World, and Living in Between* (Durham, North Carolina: Labyrinth Press 1988) pp. 253–266.

[24] Hauerwas, *A Community of Character* p. 12.

[25] Ibid. pp. 9–35.

Watership Down warren prevailed because of both its leader and his followers. The leader was prepared to learn from all the others and use the gifts of all of them. The other rabbits were able to accept their leader in spite of his mistakes, and be formed by stories of El-ahrairah and inspired by them in times of trouble. These are the lessons taught by the narrative.

The 'ten theses'

Hauerwas' essay on *Watership Down* impressively illustrates his 'Ten Theses Toward the Reform of Christian Social Ethics', which he lists at the beginning of the essay. The 'Ten Theses' are the high water mark of his 'narrative from below' period. A list of these ten theses here will show how each one relates to the themes discussed in my present chapter:

1. The social significance of the Gospel requires the recognition of the narrative structure of Christian convictions for the life of the church.
2. Every social ethic involves a narrative, whether it is concerned with the formulation of basic principles of social organization and/or concrete policy alternatives.
3. The ability to provide an adequate account of our existence is the primary test of the truthfulness of a social ethic.
4. Communities formed by a truthful narrative must provide the skills necessary to transform fate into destiny so that the unexpected, especially as it comes in the form of strangers, can be welcomed as a gift.
5. The primary social task of the church is to be itself – that is, a people who have been formed by a story that provides them with the skills for negotiating the danger of this existence, trusting in God's promise of redemption.
6. Christian social ethics can only be done from the perspective of those who do not seek to control national or world history but who are content to live 'out of control'.
7. Christian social ethics depends on the development of leadership in the church that can trust and depend on the diversity of gifts in the community.
8. For the church to be, rather than to have, a social ethic means we must recapture the social significance of common behaviour, such as kindness, friendship, and the formation of families.
9. In our attempt to control our society Christians in America have too readily accepted liberalism as a social strategy appropriate to the Christian story.
10. The church does not exist to provide an ethos for democracy or any other form of social organization, but stands as a political alternative to every nation, witnessing to the kind of social life possible for those that have been formed by the story of Christ.[26]

---

[26] Ibid. pp. 10–12.

I have already shown (pp. 42–52 above) some of the tensions in Hauerwas' early writing between 'narrative from above' and 'narrative from below'. Thesis 2 makes a 'narrative from below' claim which it is very difficult to defend, because of its foundational nature.[27] Hauerwas increasingly comes to recognize that such sweeping claims are unnecessary and detract from his more sustained development of the way the Christian narrative forms the Church. Thesis 1 shows Hauerwas starting to make the journey from the descriptive 'narrative as the form of human life' to the prescriptive 'narrative as the form of Christian convictions'. Thesis 3, the need for truthfulness, is amply displayed in Hauerwas work on 'narrative from below', as I have already shown in discussing Albert Speer and the warrens of *Watership Down*. In this sense novels, though fiction, can be truthful, since they account for our existence. Novels also fulfil the criteria of Thesis 8. Theses 4, 6 and 7 are thoroughly borne out by *Watership Down*. The dangers of Thesis 9 have been mentioned above in relation to *The Blood of the Lamb*, where Don is vulnerable to the power of medicine because he has no story to make sense of his life.

From the mid-1980s onwards, Theses 5 and 10 become the principal themes of Hauerwas' writing. In *A Community of Character* he writes: 'All significant moral claims are historically derived and require narrative display'.[28] Without explicitly distancing himself from larger claims of this kind, Hauerwas allows them quietly to disappear from his later work. In their place comes more detailed discussion of how the Christian narrative forms Christian character.

The bridge between the two eras comes in Thesis 3, on the issue of truthfulness. A social ethic is of no value if it is not true: effectiveness is no substitute, as the encounter with the liberal warren in *Watership Down* makes clear. Truth is difficult to assess, but it must include the ability to describe our existence adequately. For Hauerwas, only the Christian story does this. Having the right story is crucial. For it is not just a question of describing the world, but of going further and forming character. A truthful story forms a truthful community and truthful people. Thus 'narrative from below', the sense that the moral life requires narrative display, is but a preliminary to the formation of a people by the Christian story – 'narrative from above'.

'Narrative from above'

Hauerwas starts to talk about narrative because of the way narrative fills out what remains unsaid by decisionist ethics. Narrative is thus a *descriptive* category – descriptive of the moral life of the agent. But Hauerwas comes to see narrative as a *prescriptive* category when he settles on the Christian

---

[27] For a discussion of some of the difficulties involved in such claims, see L. Gregory Jones, 'Alasdair MacIntyre on Narrative, Community and the Moral Life' *Modern Theology* 4/1 (1987) pp. 53–69.

[28] Hauerwas, *A Community of Character* p. 99.

narrative as the truthful narrative which shapes a truthful people. Because Hauerwas does not explicitly acknowledge this development, nor distinguish between the two understandings of narrative, nor withdraw his earlier, more formal, claims for narrative, his work contains no programmatic essay that sets out his stall for the Christian narrative in the way that 'A Story-Formed Community' does for 'narrative from below'. In this chapter I therefore need to discuss what is at stake in his understanding of the revealed narrative in a way that he does not fully do himself. To do this I refer to two figures with whom Hauerwas has often been linked, and whose perception of what I am calling 'narrative from above' largely corresponds to Hauerwas' own. This excursus from the main body of Hauerwas' writing is essential if one is to understand the pressing issue of whether Hauerwas neglects the truth of Christianity in his pursuit of the truthfulness of Christians' lives. When Hauerwas does write in detail about 'narrative from above', he does so in order to link narrative to community. This emphasis I discuss in Chapter 4.

Hauerwas consistently pays tribute to the way his work has evolved in conversation with colleagues and friends. For each area of his work it is possible to perceive at least one such dialogue partner, and in this study I highlight these figures – Murdoch for vision, Aristotle and Aquinas for virtue, MacIntyre for 'narrative from below', Yoder for nonviolence, and so on. As we have seen, Hauerwas gradually recognized in the early 1980s that his stress on the Christian narrative no longer rested on formal claims for narrative in general. In this journey his most significant fellow-traveller is George Lindbeck. Lindbeck's book *The Nature of Doctrine* put him at the centre of a group of 'postliberal' theologians. Hauerwas' interest in this world is perhaps the closest he comes to being a member of a theological 'school'. Many of the criticisms of this 'school' of 'postliberal' theologians have been applied to Hauerwas himself. The interests of postliberals broadly correspond with what I have so far termed 'narrative from above'.

In the rest of this chapter I shall examine the distinctive features of postliberalism, particularly as represented by George Lindbeck and Hans Frei. It is important to remember that what took Hauerwas into the postliberal world was his insistence that the story should be true. Truth emerges as the central issue in narrative from above, and it is around the question of truth-claims that most of the criticisms arise. In my next chapter I shall show how Hauerwas' awareness of these criticisms leads him to expand on his notion of community.

Postliberalism

Postliberalism is primarily a statement about revelation. It is a rejection of the Enlightenment assumption that reality can be discovered empirically, and that the 'world' disclosed in the Bible – revelation – is true only to the extent that it coincides with this given empirical world. Instead, postliberals start theological reflection with God's self-revelation. They adopt no *a priori* philosophical understanding of the nature of existence – no 'foundation'. For this reason they are sometimes known as 'non-foundationalists' or 'antifoundationalists'. They see the theologian's task as primarily to describe the way the faith works. In this they differ from those who seek to explain or to justify the faith.[29]

In introducing *Against the Nations*, Hauerwas allies himself with those referred to by George Lindbeck as concerned to 'renew in a post-traditional and post-liberal mode the ancient practice of absorbing the universe into the biblical world'.[30] He thus recognizes both his place alongside such theologians as Hans Frei, George Lindbeck and David Kelsey, and his debt to Karl Barth. It is a loose grouping, regarded as a theological school less by themselves than by others. They have been called 'the New Yale Theologians', since they all have a connection with Yale as opposed to Chicago or Berkeley, the other chief centres of narrative theology.[31]

The publication of George Lindbeck's *The Nature of Doctrine* identified postliberalism by placing it in relation to two rival approaches to doctrine. The three approaches correspond to three eras: preliberal (pre-Enlightenment), liberal (Enlightenment), and postliberal (post-Enlightenment). The preliberal approach sees a clear correspondence between the language of the Bible and the world it describes. It apprehends relatively little difficulty in taking the Bible as a factual account of the way things are. Lindbeck calls this approach 'cognitive–propositional', because it understands doctrine as a body of truth-claims about objective realities. The liberal approach sees religion as primarily concerned with particular experiences and the expression of particular inner feelings. Public, outer features of religion are objectifications of a fundamentally personal experience: thus, in theory, a Buddhist and a Christian might have basically the same faith. This has often been the way Christianity since Schleiermacher has responded to Kant's turn to the subject. Hence this second approach Lindbeck call 'experiential–expressive'. What Lindbeck proposes is a third, postliberal approach. This sees doctrines as like the rules of a language, guiding what 'fits' and what does not. The primary location of Christianity is not so much deep within the self of the believer, but in the worship and practice of the believing community. This community's view of the world is formed by the scriptural narrative. Lindbeck calls this approach 'cultural–linguistic', and it is the most thorough description of what is meant by postliberalism.

Although Hauerwas is always likely to play truant from any theological school, he shares many of the presuppositions of the postliberals. Hauerwas

---

[29] The best introductory and classificatory article in the field is Gary L. Comstock, 'Two Types of Narrative Theology' *Journal of the American Academy of Religion* 55/4 (Winter 1987) pp. 687–717.

[30] George Lindbeck, *The Nature of Doctrine: Religion and Theology in a Postliberal Age* (Philadelphia: Westminster 1984) p. 135.

[31] The phrase is first used by Brevard Childs in 'The Canonical Approach and the "New Yale Theology" 'in *The New Testament as Canon: An Introduction* (Philadelphia: Fortress Press 1984) pp. 541–546, and is used extensively by Mark I. Wallace, *The Second Naïveté: Barth, Ricoeur and the New Yale Theology* (Macon GA: Mercer University Press 1990).

has frequently been accused of proposing belief in God without offering any rational grounds, and this is such a pressing criticism that it needs to be investigated thoroughly. The best way to do this is to see the shape of this criticism as it affects postliberalism as a whole, and this requires a proper introduction to the postliberal project.

Hauerwas, together with the other theologians associated with narrative from above, is concerned to identify the Christian community with the distinctive vision of the world narrated in the Bible. This vision includes a sense of time as bounded by creation and *eschaton*; the sense of life as a contingent gift; the sense of God's purpose in calling Israel, sending Jesus and empowering the Church; the sense that Christ's passion has definitively overcome evil and displayed God's sovereignty. I shall examine the postliberal approach, and especially the key issue of truth, under three headings: hermeneutics, doctrine and apologetics.

Hermeneutics

The first common area between Hauerwas and the postliberals is an intratextual hermeneutical method. For postliberal theologians, theology reflects on the Biblical narratives primarily as *narratives*, rather than sources for historical investigation, or expressions of common human experience, or truths which could equally well (or better) be expressed non-narratively. This form of hermeneutics is described as intratextual.

Extratextual theology reinterprets the scriptural world according to a variety of concepts and approaches from other disciplines in order to 'help' the Bible speak to contemporary concerns and clarify its 'message'. By contrast, intratextual theology

> does not make scriptural contents into metaphors for extra-scriptural realities, but the other way around. It does not suggest . . . that believers find their stories in the Bible, but rather that they make the story of the Bible their story. . . . It is the religion instantiated in scripture which defines being, truth, goodness, and beauty, and the non-scriptural exemplifications of those realities need to be transformed into figures . . . of the scriptural ones. Intratextual theology redescribes theology within the scriptural framework rather than translating scripture into extrascriptural categories. It is the text, so to speak, which absorbs the world, rather than the world the text.[32]

This quotation summarizes Lindbeck's understanding of hermeneutics. The question to be explored is, what does it mean for the text to 'absorb the world'?

The intratextual method is developed by Hans Frei in his book *The Eclipse of Biblical Narrative*. Frei describes how theologians of the early Church and the Reformation period derived their theological method from the narrated world of the Scripture. The great change came in the seventeenth and

---

[32] Lindbeck, *The Nature of Doctrine* p. 118.

eighteenth centuries. Since the Enlightenment, Frei argues, biblical scholars have looked to general, extratextual categories to determine the validity of the theological claims of Scripture. In other words, the rules of interpretation were set not by the text itself, or even by the worshipping community formed by the text, but by the historian, social scientist or philosopher. This change is what Frei calls 'the great reversal': 'interpretation was a matter of fitting the biblical story into another world with another story rather than incorporating that world into the biblical story'.[33]

Thereafter the touchstone was human experience: the truth of the biblical narrative could, it seemed, only be preserved by reinterpreting its meaning so that it conveyed a moral lesson or a way of being-in-the-world. Deism, historical criticism and Hume's scepticism about historical claims undermined confidence in the veracity of the biblical narratives. The result was the separation of the meaning of the text (what it literally says) from its reference (what historical events it describes). For Frei, the Bible is 'literally', though not always 'historically', true.

We move on to Frei's concept of narrative. Like Hauerwas, Frei is fascinated by the novel. Frei draws on the description by the French literary critic Erich Auerbach of the method of the 'realistic novel'.[34] The interplay of plot and character in a realistic novel renders its vision of reality. Theologians, in Frei's view, should cease to be distracted by the 'failure' of the Bible to refer to objective history, and recognize that it is history*like* – that is, that the genre of narrative is indispensable for grasping the meaning of the greater part of Scripture. What Frei intends by the term 'narrative' here is that we understand the story's meaning not as '*illustrated* (as though it were an intellectually pre-subsisting or preconceived archetype or ideal essence), but *constituted* through the mutual, specific determination of agents, speech, social context and circumstances that form the indispensable narrative web'.[35] In *The Identity of Jesus Christ* Frei develops this intratextual method of interpretation. He traces how the gospels provide normative patterns of Jesus' identity and thus offer a way of redescribing the reality of Jesus within the world of the Bible, rather than translating this reality into abstraction or timeless typological or mythological universals.

Despite using an extratheological source – Erich Auerbach – Frei is anxious to stress that narrative is important because it is what we find in the Bible, and not vice versa. This is what makes his approach 'narrative from above', not 'narrative from below':

> I am not proposing or arguing a general anthropology. I am precisely *not* claiming that narrative sequence is the built-in constitution of human being phenomenologically uncovered. That may or may not be the case.... If there is a 'narrative

---

[33] Hans Frei, *The Eclipse of Biblical Narrative: A Study in Eighteenth and Nineteenth Century Hermeneutics* (New Haven and London: Yale University Press 1974) p. 130.

[34] Erich Auerbach, *Mimesis: The Representation of Reality in Western Literature* (Princeton: Princeton University Press 1953).

[35] Frei, *The Eclipse of Biblical Narrative* p. 280.

theology', the meaning of that term in the context of the self-description of the Christian community is that we are specified by relation to its particular narrative and by our conceptual redescription of it in belief and life, not by a quality of 'narrativity' inherent in our picture of self and world at large.[36]

Frei's belief in the perspicuity of Scripture – the transparency and accessibility of the 'literal sense' – seems to be in conflict with other concerns of postliberal theology. It seems inconsistent with Lindbeck's emphasis on the alienness of the text to the modern mind and the need for catechesis. It is also out of step with the whole thrust of Hauerwas' book *Unleashing the Scripture*, which denies that 'America knows how to read the Bible'.[37] Frei talks of the 'plain sense' and the 'literal sense': but his assumption that there is one such sense and that it is the one he identifies seems to put him on the supposedly neutral high ground that Lindbeck – in common with several schools of suspicion from Marx onwards – disavows. Frei amends his position in a later article, where he recognizes that the reader is part of an interpretative community, and that the 'literal' reading is specific to this community.[38] This turn to the 'hermeneutical community' corresponds to the way Hauerwas comes to deal with hermeneutical questions, as we shall see in the next chapter.

Doctrine

A second common area between Hauerwas and the postliberals is his antifoundationalism. Foundationalism, in this sense, is the principle that it is possible to step outside a tradition (a culture and language) and express doctrine in a universalizable way. It is this view that the postliberals reject. In Chapter 2 we saw how Hauerwas rejects foundationalism in ethics – the idea that a neutral observer is best placed to adjudicate objectively on the basis of impersonal rationality. Hauerwas argues that this exaggerates the distinction between fact and value; but the crucial point is that not even God is a neutral observer, because God is revealed through a particular narrative. This argument takes Hauerwas into the area of theological antifoundationalism. Hauerwas bases his *Against the Nations* on the premise that 'theological convictions have lost their intelligibility' (p. 6). That is to say, the universal rational principles, that are the *sine qua non* of foundationalism, simply no longer exist – if they ever did. There must therefore be another criterion for judging the truth or falsity of Christian convictions. For George Lindbeck this criterion is internal coherence, measured by performance.

---

[36] Quoted by Paul Nelson, *Narrative and Morality: A Theological Enquiry* (Philadelphia: Pennsylvania State Press 1987) p. 77.

[37] Hauerwas, *Unleashing the Scripture: Freeing the Bible from Captivity to America* (Nashville: Abingdon 1993).

[38] Frei, 'The "Literal Reading" of Biblical Narrative in the Christian Tradition: Does it Stretch or Will it Break?' in Frank McConnell (ed.), *The Bible and the Narrative Tradition* (New York: Oxford University Press 1986) pp. 36–77.

Preliberals (whom Lindbeck also calls 'cognitive-propositionalists') have a very different method for judging truth-claims. Using Frei's analysis, Lindbeck identifies how preliberals separate the reference of the biblical text from its meaning, and take religious utterances to refer to objective facts conveying information, after the manner of empirical science. Thus some positions are true and others are false. In this preliberal view there is a permanent and simple correspondence between what is known and the way it is known – between proposition and reality. There is an assumption here of the universalizability of certain facts and information. As Frei also shows, the onslaught made by Hume, Lessing and their contemporaries against religious truth-claims left this precritical method in retreat.

The issue between foundationalists and antifoundationalists is primarily one of rationality. The foundational task in religion is committed to showing that particularistic convictions are the surface beneath which lie universal principles or structures. Intelligibility and credibility – for believer and unbeliever alike – rest on such universals. The problem is this: 'If there are no universal or foundational structures and standards of judgement by which one can decide between different religious and non-religious options, the choice of any one of them becomes, it would seem, purely irrational, a matter of arbitrary whim or blind faith.'[39]

Thus the key problem for the intelligibility of Lindbeck's project – and for Hauerwas – is of how to tell that Christianity is true. Antifoundationalism seems to be purely irrational, since it undermines the acceptance of universal foundations of reasonableness. It thereby gives itself no visible means of support. Lindbeck's response is as follows:

> Anti-foundationalism . . . is not to be equated with irrationalism. The issue is not whether there are universal norms of reasonableness, but whether these can be formulated in some neutral, framework-independent language. Increasing awareness of how standards of rationality vary from field to field and age to age makes the discovery of such a language more and more unlikely and the possibility of foundational disciplines doubtful.[40]

This sounds to many foundationalists like a surrender to postmodernism and a counsel of despair. It puts the whole foundational project at risk. How then is it possible for Lindbeck's project to be rational and intelligible, when criteria for judgement are not available?

Lindbeck meets this need for reasonableness by appealing to Aristotle's notion of rationality as a matter more of skill than of universal principle. In Aristotle's view, rationality is not innate but acquired; it lies not in the mind but in intelligible practices, which must be learnt. 'Reasonableness in religion and theology, as in other domains, has something of that aesthetic character, that quality of unformalizable skill, which we usually associate with the artist or the linguistically competent. . . . Intelligibility comes from skill, not theory,

---

[39] Lindbeck, *The Nature of Doctrine* p. 130.
[40] Ibid.

and credibility comes from good performance, not adherence to independently formulated criteria.'[41]

Since there is no neutral high ground from which to adjudicate truth, the only criteria for assessment come from within theology itself. A sentence has truth within its appropriate context; but abstracted from that context it is neither true nor untrue. It is simply meaningless:

> The sentence 'this car is red'... cannot be a proposition, for it specifies no particular auto and no particular time before or after which the vehicle might be of a different color: it can be neither true nor false. The same point holds *mutatis mutandis* for religious sentences: they acquire enough referential specificity to have first-order or ontological truth or falsity only in determinate settings, and this rarely if ever happens on the pages of theological treatises or in the course of doctrinal discussions.[42]

The point is not that there is no such thing as propositional truth.[43] The point instead is that theological truth demands response and participation, and its merits cannot be investigated any other way. For Lindbeck, the proposition 'Jesus is Lord' is true, but the only way to assert its truth is to act accordingly. Lindbeck cites St Paul and Luther as two theologians who believed in the objective reality of the lordship of Christ – but both insisted 'that the only way to assert this truth is to do something about it, i.e. to commit oneself to a way of life; and this concern, it would seem, is wholly congruent with the suggestion that it is only through the performatory use of religious utterances that they acquire propositional force'.[44] The sentence 'Christ is Lord' becomes, for Lindbeck, a proposition capable of making ontological truth-claims only when it is used by individuals and communities acting in accordance with the truth of such a statement – that is, in 'the activities of adoration, proclamation, promise-hearing, and promise-keeping', activities which affirm Christ's lordship.[45]

The result of Lindbeck's understanding of truth-claims is a new hierarchy of disciplines. Whereas the preliberal approach to truth is in danger of ceding decisive authority to history and science, Lindbeck's 'first division' comprises liturgy, preaching and ethics. It is in these latter activities that one aligns oneself performatively with what one takes to be most important in the universe – and thus claims the truth. It is easy to see how Hauerwas' theological agenda brings him close to the postliberals.

---

[41] Ibid. pp. 130, 131.

[42] Ibid. p. 68. This has a significant bearing on Hauerwas' exchange with Gloria Albrecht. See pp. 68–73 below.

[43] Note especially 'There is nothing in the cultural-linguistic approach that requires the rejection (or the acceptance) of the epistemological realism and correspondence theory of truth' (Lindbeck, *The Nature of Doctrine* pp. 68–69). Several critics of Lindbeck choose to ignore his abiding realism.

[44] Ibid. p. 66.

[45] Ibid. p. 68.

Apologetics

Lindbeck's new hierarchy of disciplines apparently leaves metaphysics and ontology in the second division. He never disavows these disciplines: it is simply that the cultural–linguistic model he advocates leave them an open question. Justification of Christianity for Lindbeck lies primarily with narrative description accompanied by performance of the implications of the story. Wittgenstein offers a discussion of the difficulty of recognizing this kind of justification for what it is:

> The difficulty . . . is not that of finding the solution but of recognizing as the solution something that looks as if it were only a preliminary to it. 'We have already said everything – Not anything that follows from this, no *this* itself is the solution!' This is connected, I believe, with our wrongly expecting an explanation, whereas the solution of the difficulty is a description, if we give it the right place in our considerations. If we dwell upon it and do not try to get beyond it. The difficulty here is: to stop.[46]

If the temptation to move from description to explanation is one that should, in general, be resisted, what form of apologetics is permissable? Lindbeck looks back to Aquinas and Luther, and perceives that for both, 'revelation dominates all aspects of the theological enterprise, but without excluding a subsidiary use of philosophical and experiential considerations in the explication and defense of the faith. Similarly, a postliberal approach need not exclude an *ad hoc* apologetics, but only one that is systematically prior and controlling in the fashion of post-Cartesian natural theology and of later liberalism.'[47]

Reason is not used to shore up faith with general non-theological foundations: its role is to advance the intelligibility of non-foundational claims that have already been made. Argument is something that one engages in within the 'language of faith': it does not lead one to faith. Thus postliberal theologians all derive insights from extratheological sources to make their own claims more intelligible. Frei employs Auerbach, Lindbeck makes considerable use of Wittgenstein, Geertz and Kuhn, and Hauerwas often cites MacIntyre, Bernard Williams and Iris Murdoch. The important point is that this is done in an *ad hoc* manner: what postliberals are anxious to avoid is the extratheological models *materially framing* the theology, in the way one might see the relation between, for example, Heidegger and Bultmann.

---

[46] This passage is quoted by D.Z. Phillips, 'Wittgenstein's Full Stop' in Irving Block (ed.), *Perspectives on the Philosophy of Wittgenstein* (Cambridge, Mass: MIT Press 1983) pp. 179–200 and subsequently highlighted by Comstock, 'Two Types of Narrative Theology' p. 705.

[47] Lindbeck, *The Nature of Doctrine* pp. 131–132.

Summary

This chapter has charted the way Hauerwas' journey moves from character to narrative, and from a formal claim for narrative to a prescriptive demand for the Christian narrative. Narrative arose as the most helpful way of describing the particularity of the moral agent. Narrative has the ability to show what is unique about this agent in such a way that this uniqueness can be comprehended by others. Hauerwas explores the way narrative displays character at some length, particularly in his discussion of the novel. Increasingly he values the ability to sustain a truthful story in the face of self-deception and moral failure. This desire for truthfulness leads him to recognize the unique status of the Christian story, and its ability to enable people to face the truth about themselves.

Once Hauerwas has arrived at the significance of the Christian story, he finds himself in the company of those, like Lindbeck, who have come to a similar place for other reasons. Hauerwas is seeking to make truthful people by forming them around a truthful story. Does Christianity provide a single story, and is this story truthful? Hauerwas finds it impossible to answer these questions without introducing the community of faith. For he is concerned with the holy story primarily in so far as it forms a people to be holy. The relationship between holy story and holy people is the subject of my next chapter.

The journey from character to community (via narrative) is part of a longer journey from quandary to the Church (via character, narrative and community). This latter journey sums up Hauerwas' whole project. His overall concern is to shift the focus of ethical reflection from the individual in a crisis to the Church in its faithfulness. The purpose of theological ethics, for him, is not to make quandaries easier, but to build up the Church.

Narrative is at the centre of both the smaller journey, character to community, and the larger journey, individual to Church. It is the stage at which Hauerwas' ethics become truly theological. Narrative starts as a helpful way of displaying the character of an individual: and ends by revealing the character of God.

4

From Story to Community

In Chapters 2 and 3 I have demonstrated how Stanley Hauerwas comes to regard narrative as so significant to theological ethics. He points out how the emphasis on decision presupposes an agreement over the other elements in human life – an agreement which does not exist. This makes conventional ethics implicitly coercive. A more thorough rendering of ethics should take into account the story of the agent under consideration, and be aware of how the agent's character is both reflected in and formed by the matters in question. Liberal democracies have tended to discourage these particular stories, believing them to jeopardize an ethical consensus. The particular story must be a true one, and Hauerwas believes that only the Christian narrative enables agents to face the truth about themselves and yet go on. Because the Christian story is about God entering the narrative, and thus ceasing to be detached, one cannot continue to prize the neutral observer as the stronghold of ethical discussion.

The theologians that have been described as postliberals have described what it might mean for the Church to 'live in the Christian story'. They have started from the demise of neutral language, and have shown how abandoning a philosophical foundation does not make the Christian narrative wholly irrational. This is what I have called 'narrative from above'. This approach attracts two kinds of criticism. One is, 'How can one talk of *the* Christian story, when there seem to be so many rival versions of it? What about all the versions that have been suppressed over the centuries?' The other is, 'How can one know the story is true? How does one know it is not "just a story"?'

It is in the need to address these issues that we can see Hauerwas making the journey from story to community. As this chapter shows, Hauerwas sees the community as that which embodies and performs the story. By doing so, the community offers the only form of truth that can be found.

Is there just one story?

A number of commentators have criticized Hauerwas on his discussion of narrative and the way it forms community. It is often said that the path from story to community does not run as straight as Hauerwas seems to suppose. For all the criticisms, Hauerwas has not altered his position significantly. The brushes that tar him invariably tar a great part of the Christian tradition at the same time – so he seldom stands alone: this perhaps helps to explain his reluctance to reformulate his understanding of narrative. The general issue is whether Hauerwas is in touch with the Church as it is or as it ever has been; whether the tradition he values coincides with genuine history; whether the lines he appears to draw can ever be so clearly defined. I shall offer a brief introductory survey of the hermeneutical questions raised, before looking at three in detail: plurality, social location and relativism.

Hermeneutics

Is there such a thing as 'the Christian story'? Does the Bible tell one continuous narrative, from Eden to the new heaven and new earth, or does it contain a collection of stories? To what extent can one say that the story (or stories) of the Church are continuous with the story (or stories) of the Bible? How comfortably do the non-narrative sections of the Bible dovetail into the story? Is the whole notion of a single story inevitably a means of suppressing sub-narratives?

As one can see from these questions, the issue of whether there is one story or many is a highly significant one for Hauerwas and the postliberals. Central to the postliberal emphasis on narrative is the intratextual insistence that the Bible sees itself as a story, and demands to be read as such.

Is there not much in Scripture that is not narrative in character? Hauerwas replies to this question in terms of the community's memory. The term 'narrative' incorporates the Church as well as Israel and Jesus. 'Narrative' does not simply refer to the literary genre of the text: it is in many ways a shorthand term to denote the ethical method of a tradition that tries to regulate its character according to the character of God as found in Scripture. It is not necessary to claim that all of Scripture is narrative. Narrative is not simply the form of Scripture or that which constitutes the Christian tradition or that which presupposes the Church. Narrative is the Christian understanding of God:

> Scripture contains much material that is not narrative in character. But such material . . . gains its intelligibility by being a product of and contribution to a community that lives through remembering. The narrative of scripture not only 'renders a character' but renders a community capable of ordering its existence appropriate to such stories. Jews and Christians believe this narrative does nothing less than render the character of God and in doing so renders us to be the kind of people appropriate to that character. . . . Our understanding of God is not inferred from the stories but is the stories.[1]

As Hauerwas' own work has developed, these comments apply more and more to him too. His non-narrative work relies for its power on the concrete display of character in the stories he tells and the story he recalls.[2]

---

[1] Hauerwas, *A Community of Character* p. 67.
[2] The doctrine of the Holy Spirit should be at the heart of understanding the continuity between the scriptural story and the story of the Church, and this is undoubtedly a neglected area in postliberal theology. See pp. 97–98 below for further discussion of the role of the Holy Spirit.

Does the Bible tell one story or several? Hauerwas is critical of efforts to render the theology of Old or New Testaments in terms of a handful of abstract nouns such as law, covenant or promise. He commends David Kelsey's view of the Bible as a long 'loosely structured non-fiction novel'.[3] The Bible abounds in sub-plots and minor characters, representing the potential for a host of different ways of telling the story. It is important that the Church retains an awareness of these sub-plots, and countless others in the subsequent tradition, so that it understands the narrative not as a single story that tyrannizes minor stories, but as a continuing conversation. Perhaps the most significant of the sub-plots is the continuing history of the Jews: the relationship of Church to Jews is analogous to the relationship of the two testaments. It is a sub-tradition with which Hauerwas is anxious to maintain a conversation. The issue of sub-plots is significant, for it relates to the issues discussed earlier under the heading of elitism. It is important to note that sub-plots are less a matter of differing conceptions of truth than of the continuing conversation – between evangelists, legislators, prophets, exiles, kings, prisoners and generations of hearers – about what kind of a community the Church should be to follow this kind of a God.

Are some texts more significant than others? There can be no question, despite Hauerwas' enjoyment of Christian diversity, that he has something of a 'canon within the canon'. There is a backbone of doctrine that seems to focus on the synoptic gospels as central to his scriptural understanding.[4] Though he talks of faithfulness to the story of Israel, it is to the story of Jesus, especially his passion, death and resurrection, and the Sermon on the Mount, that he constantly turns. His justification for this seems to lie with the practice of the early Church – the Christian community who took their Jewishness for granted, did not dwell so much on more abstract doctrines such as revelation and prevenience, but concentrated on the concrete – discipleship, faithfulness, memory, community. This accords with Hauerwas' insistence that ethics and theology are but two sides of the same coin.

Who tells the story? Several generations of the hermeneutics of suspicion have increased the awareness of many modern hearers that the Bible was written by dead Jewish males. The question of who tells the story is related to that of whether there is one story or several – especially if one assumes that many have been suppressed. Hauerwas again turns to the conversational character of the tradition, the incorporation of Church history into the narrative, and the variety of the kinds of literature in the Bible to assert that no conspiracy theory is sustainable: 'One reason the church has had to be

---

[3] David Kelsey, *The Uses of Scripture in Recent Theology* (Philadelphia: Fortress 1975) p. 48. See Hauerwas, *A Community of Character* p. 67.
[4] Frei focuses on Mark, as does McClendon, and Thiemann concentrates on Matthew. Hans Frei, *The Identity of Jesus Christ,* James McClendon, *Ethics: Systematic Theology* Chapter 12, Ronald Thiemann, *Revelation and Theology.* Hauerwas to some extent redresses the imbalance by his publication of several sermons – see especially *Unleashing the Scripture.*

content with the notion of canon rather than some more intellectually satisfying summary of the content of scripture is that only through the means of a canon can the church adequately manifest the kind of tension with which it must live.[5] The canon makes no attempt to resolve the diversity of the texts it draws within itself. Diversity and disagreement are therefore an integral part of the tradition.

Perhaps Hauerwas' weakest hermeneutical question is again one of justification, namely, 'Why *these* texts?' Having established a method that understands the role of narrative in the community's continuing discussion of what and how it should be, it is difficult for Hauerwas to answer this last question satisfactorily. The tendency is either to revert to foundationalism ('these texts ... alone satisfy ... our craving for a perfect story which we feel to be true') or simply to maintain a circularity ('Faith is Christian because it relates itself to classically-expressed models').[6] The only consistent way Hauerwas can answer this question is to say once again that Christians do not find themselves on neutral territory, adjudicating over a plurality of competing truths. Instead they are in mid-stream, in a tradition that has taken this canon as authoritative. The questions therefore are rather, 'Are these texts treated as authoritative in the community?' (the descriptive question) and, 'Should they continue to be?' (the 'what kind of community?' question). The fact that these texts are considered authoritative is indeed an implied judgement on other texts and on practices which contradict these texts: but that judgement is not made from a supposed neutral standpoint.

Plurality

The question of plurality is a two-dimensional one. The first dimension is that of belief: can one genuinely say that all Christians in all ages have believed the same story? The second is that of practice: if Christians have indeed believed the same story, how has it been that they have responded to it in such contradictory ways?

I begin with the first dimension, that of heterodoxy. Given the importance Hauerwas places on the biblical text, it is difficult to see how he reconciles the fact that Catholics, Protestants and Jews do not recognize the same Scriptures. Do the identity-descriptions 'render' different identities (to use Frei's terminology)?[7] Take a concept such as that of divine providence – a notion that is highly significant to the way one understands the story: the term appears only in the Apocrypha. A true intratextualist must therefore either recognize a larger canon, or recognize that extra-biblical texts *have* partially determined the 'grammar of God'; the only alternatives are to reduce providence to references in the Hebrew Bible and the New Testament, or to

---

[5] Hauerwas, *A Community of Character* p. 66.

[6] Ibid., for both quotations.

[7] See Michael Goldberg, 'God, Action and Narrative: *Which* Narrative? *Which* Action? *Which* God?' *Journal of Religion* 68/1 (January 1988) pp. 39–56.

read providence into those texts.[8] Thus does intratextuality appear neither possible nor desirable, nor true to the practice of the Church through the centuries.

This is a serious criticism, and highlights the strengths and the weaknesses of Hauerwas' curious ecclesial position, with his Methodist, Roman Catholic and Mennonite influences. While it is possible for him to glean the best fruits from each tradition, it is less straightforward for the whole Church to do so, as Tilley's account demonstrates. It is no coincidence that Lindbeck's book arose from an ecumenical concern.

Anxious to avoid systems, the postliberals are in danger of being caught in another system, and one that is difficult to break out of, since postliberals are adept at denying validity to opposing proposals. Again, Lindbeck is accused of the ironic step of breaking one of his own principles. John Milbank accuses Lindbeck of abstracting narrative from history. Despite his attention to the context of concepts, Lindbeck's narratives are 'hypostasized', atemporal, and 'dangerously ahistorical', functioning with an 'essentially unproblematic code' which 'has artificially insulated the Christian narrative from its historical genesis'. Milbank calls Lindbeck's metanarrative realism 'a new narratological foundationalism' which is 'more rigid, and less open to revision' than the doctrine it replaces. Thus narrative has lost its temporal, historical character, and become a rigid system.[9] Milbank's suggestion is to extend the narrative to embrace the Church – and this is exactly Hauerwas' approach.

Hauerwas seeks to resolve most of these questions by turning attention from the text to the community that reads the text. For example, to prevent the Christian story from being a single-line narrative that suppresses sub-plots, requires a people who are capable of reading in a way that listens to the cry of the oppressed. Such a people is of course formed by the narrative, and thus a hermeneutical spiral develops. But Hauerwas' *Unleashing the Scripture* is written as a warning not to assume that that spiral can casually be entered from contemporary American liberal culture. The Bible does not suppress characters or sub-plots that challenge, or qualify, the main story-line, because it would not be truthful to do so. To read the Bible faithfully, the community must be similarly open to the truth encountered in the stranger.[10] Thus Hauerwas addresses some of Tilley's criticisms concerning what is meant by a cultural-linguistic world; yet Tilley's call to face the realities of the controversial canon still carries weight.

The second dimension of the plurality question is that of heteropraxis. Given Stanley Hauerwas' emphasis on performance as a crucial and indispensable element in scriptural hermeneutics and the assessment of Christian truth, one of the biggest problems for him lies in coming to terms with the

---

[8] Terrence W. Tilley, 'Incommensurability, Intertextuality and Fideism' *Modern Theology* 5/2 (January 1989), p. 102.

[9] Milbank, *Theology and Social Theory* pp. 386–387. Milbank even calls Lindbeck Kantian on this point.

[10] See Hauerwas, *A Community of Character* pp. 64–69.

plurality and variety of responses to the gospel. The problem is this: if the performance of the Christian story requires specific forms of behaviour, how can one account for the fact that neither today nor at any time in its history has the Christian Church been united in most of the controversial areas of behaviour? If on the other hand no specific forms of behaviour are entailed, in what sense can communities be said to be performing the story? Is there one tradition, or are there simply a plurality of traditions?

This is, I believe, Hauerwas' weakest point, for it exposes Hauerwas' uncertainty over whether he is describing or prescribing, whether his call for Church renewal has any genuine authority in the history of the Church. Paul Lauritzen demonstrates how Hauerwas and Johannes Metz, for example, broadly concur in three respects in their understanding of narrative.[11] Both see the self as located within the narratives of his or her community; both see practice and theory as inseparable; and both have a functional or pragmatic approach to justifying Christian convictions. Both connect narrative and community; both draw out the implications of the memory of Jesus' crucifixion and resurrection; both talk of Christian social action in terms of the imitation of Christ. But Metz believes in revolutionary social action, while Hauerwas is a pacifist. Metz is committed to liberation from economic and social inequality, while Hauerwas maintains that Christians need fear not even their oppressors since it is the cross which determines the meaning of history and helps us *understand* (rather than necessarily change) our life difficulties.

When it comes to practical consequences, therefore, Hauerwas and Metz are some way apart. But both appeal to narrative and both appeal to pragmatic tests for the truthfulness of Christian convictions. There are two problems here. In the first place, do Hauerwas and Metz share a common story? Coming from different denominations, they hold to different texts, and may frequently read the same text in a different way. Hauerwas' ambivalence about his own denomination is an illustration of this problem. The nature of the sacraments and the status of the saints are among the issues at stake. Here, as elsewhere, we see Hauerwas straining at the boundaries of his own Methodist denomination. We have already seen the central place of the *communio sanctorum* in his theology. It seems that his natural home lies within the Catholic Church, yet, as we shall see in Chapter 5, its sheer scale and resistance to pacifism seems a perpetual barrier. Lindbeck's *The Nature of Doctrine* starts with a concern for ecumenical dialogue, and it is clear that a greater understanding between the churches is a necessary ingredient of Hauerwas' theology too.

In the second place, even if Christians share a common story they need not share a common praxis. And this undermines the truth of Christian convictions if they are to be assessed pragmatically. Hauerwas does say that, 'The church, the whole body of believers, ... cannot be limited to any one

---

[11] Paul Lauritzen, 'Is "Narrative" Really a Panacea? The Use of "Narrative" in Metz and Hauerwas' *Journal of Religion* 67, (1987) pp. 322–339.

historical paradigm or contained by any one institutional form. Rather the very character of the stories of God requires a people who are willing to have their understanding of the story constantly challenged by what others have discovered in their attempt to live faithful to that tradition.[12] The question is, what is the extent of the variety of understandings that the tradition can absorb before becoming incoherent? Hauerwas may well be right that non-pragmatic criteria of truthfulness tend to try to bypass the Church – but pragmatic criteria have here been shown to be difficult to assess.

Hauerwas acknowledges that Christians can often be found on nearly every side of any issue.[13] But he denies that this undermines the truth of their convictions. His job as a theological ethicist is to elicit what Christians ought to think given their basic convictions and practices, to enhance the 'political' process through which disagreement is adjudicated, and remember that Christian convictions are represented as much by the *manner* of the confrontation as by its resolution.

Where Hauerwas is correct is in showing the significance of the context in which the narrative is read and how the story forms communities capable, in turn, of understanding the story. He is correct in demonstrating how a person or community attempting to live out the story will read the story in a different way from a person scouring it for supposedly objective truth. He is correct in showing how close attention to the Christian story can deliver persons and communities from the self-deception that arises from adopting a false story in times of anxiety and fear. But the principle that pragmatic justification is the only way to assess the truth of the narrative is very difficult to sustain, not least because of the variety of Christian responses within similar contexts evidenced by the tradition. For example, Hauerwas owes a substantial debt to Thomas Aquinas, who was writing during a period of Church history with which the Radical Reformation tradition is deeply uncomfortable: and yet Hauerwas owes perhaps as much to John Howard Yoder, a prominent contemporary exponent of that tradition.

Who tells the story?

Perhaps the most detailed criticism of Hauerwas comes from the feminist ethicist Gloria Albrecht. Rather like Hauerwas' anger with the Niebuhrian inheritance, Albrecht's complaints against Hauerwas have all the intensity of a family quarrel. I take this to be because Albrecht is attracted to the communitarian flavour of Hauerwas' writing, but finds herself at odds with the character of the story and the descriptions of virtuous practices she finds in his work. Her five lines of criticism centre around the way Hauerwas' ethics disclose his social location.

The first complaint is with the class (and national) location of Hauerwas' community. It is a luxury to sit as loosely to democracy as Hauerwas claims

---

[12] Hauerwas, *A Community of Character* p. 92.
[13] Ibid. p. 108.

to do: for Albrecht reminds him that '. . . Christians do not all live in democratic societies, that not all Christians are being tainted by liberty and individualism, and, most important, that a theological ethics shaped by (and in response to) liberal Western society cannot be for "all" Christians'.[14] What Hauerwas is talking about is the North American middle-classes, says Albrecht, and the spirituality of patience in the face of tragedy is, in fact, a prescription for a paralysis of cynicism and despair.

What makes this worse, she goes on, is the economic location of Hauerwas' community. She mentions Hauerwas' suggestion that Christians declare to their own congregations their level of income, but she notes that more generally he neglects the social significance of how Christians earn a living. More particularly, she says, he fails to address the economic power of the white middle-class male. Violence is so implicit in the economic power-relations of the workplace that it surely needs to be addressed here before one can consider nonviolence elsewhere.

Most painful to Albrecht, Hauerwas reveals the gender location of his community. The real resident aliens of Hauerwas' writing are women: 'women's lives expose the church's consistent embeddedness in culturally particular, patriarchal views of women'.[15] The area of predominantly male influence, the public economic sphere, is left largely untouched, whereas the personal sphere, of reproduction and the family, is the centre of the Church's witness. This only enhances the way women's lives are controlled by men: '*Her* personal is *his* politics.'[16]

Two further weaknesses compound the shortcomings of Hauerwas' social location. Hauerwas does not define violence. This is not necessarily a shortcoming in itself: but because he fails to name experiences such as the centuries of male violence against women, Albrecht argues that his limited notion of nonviolence is in fact a concealed form of violence. 'Only from the view of those denied adequate education, housing, health care, employment, and nutrition due to the colour of their skin, or their gender, or their residence in a nation of the two-thirds world or an abandoned centre-city of the US, can such a socially located gospel of nonviolence and nonresistance be exposed as violent.'[17] Hauerwas' nonviolence is very different to the more commendable views of those such as Martin Luther King and Oscar Romero.

Albrecht's final criticism, one which pervades her argument, is that Hauerwas has a monolithic, Augustinian notion of the Christian story and Christian truth, one which has no room for the diversities of Christian life as marginalized peoples, in particular, experience them:

---

[14] Gloria Albrecht, *The Character of our Communities: Toward an Ethic of Liberation for the Church* (Nashville: Abingdon 1995) p. 107.

[15] Gloria Albrecht, 'Review, *In Good Company: The Church as Polis*', *Scottish Journal of Theology* 50/2 (1997) pp. 218–227 at p. 224.

[16] Albrecht, *The Character of our Communities* p. 129.

[17] Ibid. p. 117.

An Augustinian theology of absolute divine control and absolute human fallenness justifies, for Hauerwas, ... the refusal to enter with others into a world of ambiguity and complexity that does not respond to the desire for absolute control that originates in the myth of one truth. In the face of problems that will not yield to the desire for total control, moral perfection, or absolute victories, nonresistance is Hauerwas' only alternative to the use of coercion.[18]

The result of these five flaws in Hauerwas' writing is that the errors of liberalism are not corrected but repeated: 'Positing a new universal theological ethics results in a defence of white male social privilege against the stirrings of subjugated voices.'[19]

To what extent is Albrecht's criticism justified, and can her criticisms be accommodated without wholesale revision of Hauerwas' approach?

Albrecht greatly, and in some places almost absurdly, overstates her case. It is not fair to identify Hauerwas with the cult of patriarchal marriage structures when he makes it so clear that singleness is the norm of eschato-logical ethics. It is not altogether fair to suggest that an awareness of the significance on having children implies a narrow understanding of the vocation of women, when two of the stories Hauerwas discusses at greatest length, Peter DeVries' *The Blood of the Lamb* and Anne Tyler's *Saint Maybe*, both concern children brought up solely by men.[20] It is extraordinary to confuse Hauerwas' sense of the way feelings can strengthen self-deception in relationships with a parallel assumption that Hauerwas shares with the men's movement a difficulty in coping with emotions. It is particularly unfortunate for Albrecht to criticize Hauerwas for claiming to describe Christian tradition while herself speaking unselfconsciously of 'women's experience'.

More important is the way Albrecht talks of Hauerwas' heavily Augustinian theology of absolute truth and absolute divine control. This, I believe, is the heart of the issue. It is a dispute about who controls the story. What this quarrel reveals is the need for an understanding of the story I narrated in Chapter 1. Hauerwas has spent his career reacting against what might be called the 'Augustinianism' of Reinhold Niebuhr. He makes no claim to speak to (or for) all America. He is therefore likely to find references to 'women's experience' infuriating. Yet he has accepted much of Reinhold Niebuhr's scepticism about the transformation of human institutions. This makes him quiet on the economic sphere, and, in the context of the tradition I described in Chapter 1, Albrecht's emphasis on this area reads, to someone steeped in the tradition, like a throwback to Walter Rauschenbusch. Put in a different way, when Hauerwas' work is set in the Radical Reformation context of John Howard Yoder, as it will be in Chapter 5, it becomes hard to talk of his having an oppressive notion of 'absolute truth'.

What Hauerwas dislikes about Reinhold Niebuhr, as we saw in Chapter 1, is that Niebuhr's definition of human nature is prior to his notion of the

---

[18] Ibid. p. 115.

[19] Ibid. p. 137.

[20] See pp. 49–50 above for a discussion of these stories.

Church. This leads us to the criticism that Hauerwas does not define violence. He does not do so for the same reason that he objects to Niebuhr. In this sense it would be fair to call Hauerwas Augustinian, since violence, like sin, cannot be defined. God, and, through Jesus, the Church, positively exist: humans are creatures and exist contingently. One can come to know them as one tells a story, a story about creation and sin, a story in which violence has a painful place. Violence – like sin in general – does not have an existence independent of or prior to that story.

Hauerwas' scepticism about treating the nation as if it were the Church leads him to concentrate on redefining politics in terms of ecclesiology. The Church is political by understanding truly what it means to be holy. Hauerwas' emphasis on holiness has brought about its own criticisms, as I discussed in the previous section. He finds himself accused of Donatism by Wallace and Augustinianism by Albrecht – an extraordinary paradox.[21] My suspicion is that this has arisen because he has been so conscious of the master narrative he opposes, and has been less aware of the (largely unintended) implications of his own language.

For example, Albrecht is quite right to point out that Hauerwas is not at all consistent in his use of 'we'.[22] It is not at all clear when Hauerwas says 'we', whether he is talking about 'we Americans', 'we Christians' or 'we self-conscious resident aliens'. I would suggest that he generally means 'we inheritors of the tradition of North American Christian social ethics, particularly in the Methodist, Episcopalian and Presbyterian churches of the United States of America', but if Albrecht detects a more sinister 'we', then Hauerwas has only himself to blame for being misunderstood. Hauerwas would make himself much clearer if he stopped altogether using the word 'we' in such phrases as 'why do we have children?'

But for Albrecht to move from a timely criticism of Hauerwas' use of 'we' to an identification of his theology as concerned with absolute control is a thorough misreading of his ecclesiology. For Hauerwas, the Church is God's principal way of working in the world: for sure, it is constantly in need of repentance and renewal, and Albrecht offers many far-reaching instances of where that is necessary; but the resources for both criticism and renewal come from within its own story, not from prior epistemologies from elsewhere. For example, as Hauerwas points out, the Roman Catholic Church, whose 'personal' ethics Albrecht so deeply opposes, is nonetheless the true church of the poor in Latin America.[23] If the Christian community fails in the way Albrecht describes, it fails by its own standards. Albrecht simply underestimates the importance of ecclesiology to Hauerwas: it *is* his epistemology; it *is* his politics.

When all this is said, Albrecht's critique of Hauerwas is still an important one. She relentlessly points out the ways in which Hauerwas' approach

---

[21] For Wallace's criticism see pp. 83–85 below.

[22] Albrecht, *The Character of Our Communities* pp. 109–110.

[23] Hauerwas, 'Failure of Communication or A Case of Uncomprehending Feminism' *Scottish Journal of Theology* 50/2 (1997) pp. 228–239 at pp. 237–238.

needs yet further narrative display if it is not to be limited by its own examples. There is no use proposing virtue if the virtues one advocates are not genuinely true to salvation. There is a healthy dialogue to be had, for example, about what this means for church discipline; and about the relationship of child-rearing in a community that is trying to shed patriarchy. Unlike Albrecht, I do not think Hauerwas inherently excludes such issues. His distrust of feminism arises from the degree to which it has been defended by what he sees as the liberal philosophical project. His differences from Albrecht do not genuinely lie in her diagnosis of pervasive violence. They lie more in his confidence in orthodox theology, particularly ecclesiology, to renew practices which address violence faithfully and truthfully, and in his misgivings about the proposals to be made once Albrecht's diagnosis is finished.

Perhaps the central point at which Hauerwas and Albrecht clash is in the way the practices of communities shape the character of their members. Albrecht agrees with the theory of this, but points out that many such Church practices involve the abuse of power. Referring to Hauerwas' essay 'What Could It Mean for the Church to be Christ's Body? A Question without a Clear Answer', Albrecht protests as follows:

> In Sneem, Ireland, little boys in white suits and little girls in white dresses, adorned as the brides of Christ, celebrate their first communion. According to Hauerwas, these are the sorts of practices that make the church the embodiment of Christ in the world, that answer who God is and what God is doing in the world. What he does not see is that these are the sorts of practices that embody a long Christian history of men's domination of women. . . . Dressing little girls in white as brides of Christ in a church where only males represent Christ is a traditioned practice that sustains sexist hegemonic power and betrays the sacred.[24]

I can only answer: sometimes, but not always. I would like to take Hauerwas' argument at its strongest and support it by relating a story which shows how traditioned practices do exactly what Hauerwas says they do.

The background to the story is the sixth-century struggle for Arabia between Judaism and Monophysite Christianity before the rise of Islam. The king of southern Arabia (now Yemen) settled on Judaism and set about persecuting Christians. One Christian widow called Ruhayma was told that if she did not deny Christ she would die. She went to the market to clothe herself and her daughters for the confrontation, and spoke these words to those gathered there:

> Look at me, for twice you have seen my face: at my first wedding, and now at this second one also. With unveiled face before all of you I went over to my first spouse, and now again with unveiled face I am going to Christ my Lord and my God . . . just as he came to us. . . . If I denied Christ, I should die, but if I did not deny

---

[24] Albrecht, 'Review, *In Good Company*' pp. 226–227, commenting on Hauerwas, *In Good Company* pp. 19–31.

Christ, I should live. . . . Behold how with unveiled face I am going out of your city in which I have lived as if in a temporary dwelling, so that I may journey, I and my daughters, to the other city, because it is to that place that I have betrothed them.

The account goes on: 'After this she went out of the city, head uncovered, with her daughters, and came and stood before the king with her face unveiled, unabashed, and holding with her hand her daughters who were adorned as though for a wedding.' Then, true to his pledge, the king slew Ruhayma, her daughter Umma, and her granddaughter Ruhayma, who refused to spit on the cross and spat at the king instead.[25]

What this story shows is the way the practice of 'dressing little girls in white as brides of Christ' can be a profound witness in the resistance to oppression, not just in its imposition. Stories like this constitute the tradition that enables the Church to continue its nonviolent witness in every age. The irony of the story is that the women's courage is recalled to this day, while the king's name is not recorded.[26]

For a full response to the question of social location, more attention could be paid to the historical, rather than social, location of the Christian community. I take up the eschatological dimensions of the community's historical location in Chapter 7. There is lacking in Albrecht a sense of the ironic role of the Church and the reign of God, and this I develop in Chapter 8.

Embodying the story

More important to Hauerwas than the holy story is the holiness of the community that reads and performs it. Anxiety about the hermeneutical issues involved in the story only distracts from the necessity of a community, and the way a community has to learn how to read the story. How should a community read the story?

Hauerwas develops his understanding of the role of Scripture in forming Christian doctrine and life in three key essays, 'The Moral Authority of Scripture: The Politics and Ethics of Remembering', 'The Church in a Divided World: The Interpretative Power of the Christian Story' and 'The Church as God's New Language'.[27] In these essays, particularly the last of them, Hauerwas clarifies the relationship between narrative as a formal claim and narrative as the definitive form of Christian understanding:

The emphasis on narrative, therefore, is not first a claim about the narrative quality of experience from some unspecified standpoint, but rather is an attempt

---

[25] I am grateful to Kenneth Bailey, from who I heard this story. It can be found in Irfan Shahid, *The Martyrs of Najran: New Documents* (Brussels: Société des Bollandistes 1971) pp. 54–60.

[26] For further such reflections on irony, see Chapter 8 below.

[27] Hauerwas, *A Community of Character* pp. 53–71 and 89–110, *Christian Existence Today* pp. 47–66, respectively.

to draw our attention to where the story is told, namely, in the church; how the story is told, namely, in faithfulness to Scripture; and who tells the story, namely, the whole church through the office of the preacher. For ... the story is not self-referential but creates a people capable of being the continuation of the narrative by witnessing to the world that all creation is ordered to God's good end.... The church is ... at once the storyteller as well as a character in the story.[28]

What Hauerwas is doing develops from the general thrust of Hans Frei's thought. Hauerwas is moving the emphasis from text to people: in his view it is the people, rather than the text, that are the bearers of the narrative.[29] In Hauerwas' words, 'the text does not refer, people do'.[30] The point is well expressed by Nicholas Lash:

> The *poles* of Christian interpretation are not ... written texts ... but patterns of human action: what was said and done and suffered, then, by Jesus and his disciples, and what is said and done and suffered, now, by those who seek to share his obedience and his hope. We talk of 'holy' scripture, and for good reason. And yet it is not, in fact, the *script* that is 'holy', but the people: the company who perform the script.... The fundamental form of the Christian interpretation of scripture is the life, activity and organization of the believing community.[31]

This makes clear how Christian ethics, for Hauerwas, is inseparable from narrative, and inseparable from the Church. Each is the context for the other two. Hauerwas is making a claim for the epistemological priority of Christian community. Hauerwas underlines this understanding by describing the authority of Scripture as a political claim. In 'The Church in a Divided World', Hauerwas argues that Scripture shapes a community of people who respond to it. Without such a community, the idea of a canon of Scripture makes no sense. For a canon is the collection of texts that a people have come to regard as authoritative. This community aims, through its hearing and performance of Scripture, to be true to the character of God. 'Christian social ethics should begin ... with the formation of a society shaped and informed by the truthful character of the God we find revealed in the stories of Israel and Jesus. The remarkable richness of these stories of God requires that the church be a community of discourse and interpretation that endeavours to tell these stories and form its life in accordance with them.'[32]

---

[28] Hauerwas, 'The Church as God's New Language' *Christian Existence Today* p. 61.
[29] Hauerwas is, nonetheless, anxious to point out that Frei occasionally refers to the hermeneutical indispensability of the Church. See 'The Church as God's New Language' *Christian Existence Today* p. 59 and Hans Frei, *The Identity of Jesus Christ* p. 157.
[30] Hauerwas, 'The Church as God's New Language' *Christian Existence Today* p. 59.
[31] Nicholas Lash, *Theology on the Way to Emmaus* (London: SCM Press 1986) pp. 42–43.
[32] Hauerwas, *A Community of Character* p. 92.

Hauerwas denies that one can understand the character of God and the authority of Scripture without beginning with the social, or 'political' community. Hauerwas is making a hermeneutical point: there is a spiralling relationship (though Hauerwas does not use the term) between the text and the extent to which a community puts it into practice. Since the text creates a world and demands that the readers inhabit that world, one cannot step out of that world in an effort to read the text 'truthfully'. Inhabiting the world that the text demands constitutes accepting scriptural authority. The meaning of the text is established by the forms of life which issue from it; reading theoretically, outside the context of the practising community, is not reading 'objectively' but reading unfaithfully.

Ronald Grimes makes a suggestion in accord with Hauerwas' understanding of narrative and community when he asks, 'What would happen if the road from narrative to ethics passed through ritual?' Ritual is a highly significant way in which a community embodies its texts in specific practices. It is not the only such way, but is certainly one that is neglected by Hauerwas. Grimes says, in a manner reminiscent of Hauerwas' discussion of the ethical value of the novel:

> Ritual can contain rich dramatic possibilities that allow us trial runs and explorations not possible in the ethically framed world. . . . Without a ritual-dramatic stage between the narrative experience and the ethical judgement we are extremely subject to self-deception [one of Hauerwas' emphases] concerning the degree to which we have embodied our ethics. Without a keenly developed ritual-dramatic sense our narratives are at best intellectual ideals and at worst sources of heteronomously imposed, introjected images.[33]

Grimes also helpfully points out the difference, underestimated by most theological treatments of narrative, between reading (or hearing) for the first time and re-reading (or hearing again).[34] This perhaps, along with preaching, provides a bridge between narrative and ritual. The activity of worship is the place where in word and sacrament, through hearing and ritual, text is converted to deed and deed is informed and challenged by text. The practice of reading and reinterpreting the same stories constitutes Christian tradition: and tradition, which Hauerwas describes as 'the memory sustained over time by ritual and habit', involves the incorporation of the history of the Church into the narrative of Israel and Jesus.[35]

---

[33] Ronald Grimes, 'Of Words the Speaker, of Deeds the Doer' *Journal of Religion* 67 (1986) pp. 1–17. On the novel, see Hauerwas, *A Community of Character* pp. 9–35, and *Dispatches from the Front* pp. 31–79. On self-deception, see Hauerwas, *Truthfulness and Tragedy* pp. 82–98, and pp. 44–48 above.

[34] Grimes, 'Of Words the Speaker, of Deeds the Doer' p. 16.

[35] For Hauerwas' definition of tradition, see *A Community of Character* p. 92. For Hauerwas' view of the place of the sermon, see *Christian Existence Today* pp. 47–65, as well as Stanley Hauerwas and William Willimon, *Preaching to Strangers: Evangelism in Today's World* (Louisville: Westminster/John Knox 1992) and *Unleashing the Scripture*.

So important is this regular practice of relating to Scripture that it leads Hauerwas to suggest that only certain kinds of communities are capable of reading the story. This is the substance of his response to hermeneutical criticisms. One of his most polemical works is *Unleashing the Scripture*. In the introductory chapters (the body of the book is made up of twelve sermons) Hauerwas works through with uncompromising logic the implications of his view that the Church is the source and location of Christian ethics. He makes the highly provocative assertion that the Church should take the Bible out of the hands of individual North American Christians.

The background to this extraordinary plea comes in the story he tells of how the Bible became the possession of the individual citizen. In line with the North American distrust of authority came the notion that the sense of the Bible is both single and plain. This frees the Bible from the Church and its clergy and places it squarely with the individual conscience. However the result is that the Bible becomes 'the possession of nationalistic ideologies. America becomes a Christian nation sanctified by God.'[36]

This central assumption, that the biblical text has an objective meaning which is immediately accessible to any reader, is shared by the otherwise contrasting views of fundamentalism and historical criticism. Both of these movements bypass the Church by stressing the individual interpreter. But, in the process, both approaches give unchecked power to certain interpreters of Scripture – a power no person ought logically to have. Thus, in the case of historical criticism, a small body of German scholars have determined the boundaries of a new science. At no stage does either movement acknowledge the political dimension of what they are doing. While one dogmatism has been loudly shouted down, another dogmatism – with a corresponding polity – has been quietly ushered in. Hauerwas is characteristically quick to point this out, in an argument closely related to his denial of the objectivity of 'objective ethics'.

> Fundamentalism and biblical criticism are Enlightenment ideologies in the service of the fictive agent of the Enlightenment – namely, the rational individual – who believes that truth in general (and particularly the truth of the Christian faith) can be known without initiation into a community that requires transformation of the self. . . . Both camps assume an objectivity of the text in order to make the Bible available to anyone, and that 'anyone' is assumed to be the citizen of democratic polities.[37]

Hauerwas rejects the assumption that the text has a 'real meaning'. Instead, texts exist in 'a web of interpretative practices'. The fact that Paul's letters to the Corinthians have become Scripture means that their meaning now relates to the books that are placed alongside them and to the history of their interpretation over the centuries since they were written. 'There is simply no "real meaning" of Paul's letters to the Corinthians once we

---

[36] Hauerwas, *Unleashing the Scripture* p. 32.
[37] Ibid. pp. 35–36.

understand that they are no longer Paul's letters but rather the Church's Scripture.'[38]

This view of Scripture derives from an understanding of the Church as more determinative than the written text. Roman Catholics are able to enjoy the diversity of readings of Scripture that arise in different cultural contexts because they are all rooted in one union with Christ in the eucharist. It was the Church that wrote the New Testament and decided on a Christological reading of the Old Testament. Scripture and tradition witness to the Church, rather than vice versa. It is the Church that enables the Scripture to be read as a narrative, rather than as a collection of tales, instructions and aphorisms. Scripture exists, not for itself, but for the formation of the Christian community, that it may better discern the Spirit and reflect its pattern. The practice of preaching, year after year, on the same texts, embodies the fact that the text has no fixed meaning, but is instead employed in the building up of the Christian community.

It is therefore within the Church, and more particularly in the context of worship, that Scripture should be read. One cannot understand Scripture unless one is open to having one's life changed by it. A life that is seeking virtue and imitating the saints is a life that is open to hearing the Scriptures. This is a point Hauerwas takes up in relation to Will Willimon's sermons: 'as important as what and how the preacher says what he or she has to say are the habits that constitute the "ears" that will hear what is said. In a decisive sense, preaching can be only as good as those ears make possible.'[39]

Is the story true?

Truth in community

Having considered what Hauerwas means by the Christian story, and what is at stake in the hermeneutical issues surrounding the story, it is time to consider the second pressing issue concerning 'narrative from above': is the story true? Hauerwas appears to have a pragmatic approach to truth, but because he refuses to outline a philosophical foundation for his theology, he (together with others classed as postliberals) is accused of fideism – belief without reason – and relativism – belief which makes no more claim to truth than other beliefs.

The logic of 'narrative from above' appears to lead to a relativist notion of truth. It is not that Hauerwas believes all religions to be equally true, but that he is sceptical about attempts to compare them. If one dispenses with any framework to argue the truth of one religion over another, can one still maintain a realist approach to truth? Realism refers to the notion that there is some sort of objective order that theological claims conform to, whether one recognizes these claims as true or not. Hauerwas never disallows realism,

---

[38] Ibid. p. 20.
[39] Hauerwas, *Preaching to Strangers* p. 9.

but neither does he specifically include it as a necessity, and this is where the problem lies. Since realism is not built into Hauerwas' approach, his desire to hang onto realism looks like fideism, that is, belief without rational grounds.

So which is Hauerwas, a realist or a relativist fideist? To answer this question, I suggest we review Hauerwas' relation to Karl Barth. His acknowledged debt to Barth would suggest that realist assumptions lie not too far beneath the surface. On the one hand Barth is committed to intratextualism. One of his chief concerns is to render Christian theology in scriptural language. On the other hand he is a thoroughgoing realist. For Barth, theological language does make assertions, and not just descriptions, since God, by disclosing reality in Christ, has given his people the language to render his word. Theology addresses 'the very definite order of being which Holy Scripture makes manifest, when in its witness to God's revelation it confronts and relates God and man, divine facts and human attitudes, [which] enforces an order of knowing conforming to it'.[40] Thus Christian religious language, for Barth, does more than describe the internal relationships between doctrines. It conforms to a revealed reality.

George Hunsinger provides a most helpful way out of the confusion that tends to cloud the truth-claims debate at this point. He distinguishes four different dimensions of validity claims – intelligibility, truth, rightness and truthfulness – which represent different media of reality – linguistic, external, social and internal respectively:

1. Claims of *intelligibility* . . . relate to the domain of language; they would pertain to formal matters of logic, internal consistency, and sense.
2. Claims of *truth* relate to the domain of external reality; they would pertain to matters of cognitive content, predication, and reference.
3. Claims of *rightness* relate to the domain of social reality; they would pertain to performative content, patterns of behaviour, and communal norms and values.
4. Claims of *truthfulness* relate to the domain of internal reality; they would pertain to matters of intention, sincerity, and aptness of emotive expression.[41]

For Hauerwas, the hierarchy runs roughly as follows:

rightness
intelligibility
truthfulness
truth

---

[40] Karl Barth, *Church Dogmatics* 1:2,5 quoted in Mark I. Wallace, *The Second Naïveté* p. 109.

[41] George Hunsinger, *How to Read Karl Barth: The Shape of his Theology* (New York: Oxford University Press 1991) p. 167. It is very important to note that Hunsinger uses the term 'truthfulness' in a different sense to that used by Hauerwas, for example in Hauerwas' debate with Julian Hartt and Stephen Crites (recorded in Hauerwas and L. Gregory Jones (eds.), *Why Narrative? Readings in Narrative Theology* Grand Rapids: Eerdmans 1989 pp. 279–319). Hauerwas' use of the term 'truthfulness' corresponds more to Hunsinger's term 'rightness'.

This is because Hauerwas places social reality at the head of understanding. Social reality mediates linguistic reality, and subsequently the two together mediate internal and external reality. One consequence of this is that rightness (social performance) becomes a necessary condition for the possibility of truth.[42] As I suggested in Chapter 2 (pp. 29–31), it is the social reality (rightness), or Church, that is the primary form of reality for Hauerwas. It is this emphasis on the 'internal' community that enables Hauerwas to avoid criticisms of having a 'substantialist' view of the internal self.[43] One can see how Hauerwas' sense of the priority of the social reality is borne out in his writing on medicine, where his greatest concern is for virtuous practices and discourse – which he regards as prior to 'right' actions. In this light the sense of the Church as the final cause – as an end in itself – becomes a different way of seeing that without community, a shared notion of truth becomes highly problematic.

Hunsinger's four dimensions of validity and reality demonstrate why there is a conflict between Hauerwas and his critics over truth, and why some see Hauerwas as a fideist while Hauerwas resists the charge. The question resolves into this: 'To what extent is there a *logical* and *sequential* relation between these four domains of truth?' If there is little or no logical connection between the four, it is quite reasonable to wonder why Hauerwas should apparently fail to address one of them, external reality, while addressing the other three. If on the other hand there *is* a logic connecting and a hierarchy between them, it becomes easier to see why Hauerwas concentrates on social, internal and linguistic reality and is sceptical of any attempts to jump straight to external reality without proceeding through the three necessary hoops.

Who is right? Hauerwas, who believes one gets to external reality only through social, linguistic and internal reality, or his 'cultured despisers', who sense a more direct route is possible and desirable? This question leads us into the area of revelation.

Revelation is significant because Hauerwas' main problem in reaching external reality through social, linguistic and internal reality is a tendency to anthropocentrism. Hauerwas' emphasis on narrative concentrates on the way God chooses to reveal himself through the story of Israel, Jesus and subsequently the Church. To a large extent the controversy over revelation resolves itself into a matter of emphasis. Those who, like Hauerwas, stress narrative as the definitive form of revelation are analogous to those who in

---

[42] Lindbeck illustrates this by referring to the nadir of Christian performance in the Crusades. 'The crusader's battle cry "*Christus est Dominus*," for example, is false when used to authorize cleaving the skull of the infidel (even though the same words in other contexts may be a true utterance)' (Lindbeck, *The Nature of Doctrine* p. 64).

[43] For Barth, truth and intelligibility never depend as fully as for Hauerwas on rightness and truthfulness – in fact external reality and language are logically independent of social and internal reality. Frei retains this strain in Barth's thought when he claims that the 'plain sense' of Scripture is intelligible to any reader, regardless of the social reality. This is why Frei seems to conflict with Hauerwas and Lindbeck on this point.

other debates have concentrated on the particularity and humanity of Christ; meanwhile those who stress God's sovereign ability to communicate in a variety of ways are analogous to those who in other debates have concentrated on the universality and divinity of Christ.

Hunsinger insists that the total context of truth is determined by God, rather than by culture or language. In his view the postliberals seem to underestimate the 'miracle of grace'. Meanwhile Hauerwas' understanding of revelation corresponds with his antifoundationalist epistemology – what Hauerwas would call his ecclesiology. Resisting all temptation to found revelation on a prior phenomenology of existence, Hauerwas understands that the role of revelation is defined by Scripture and the Church (and is therefore narrative in character) rather than vice versa. The danger of this is that it retains God's prevenience as its starting point, but thereafter appears anthropocentric, since it concentrates on human language and society.

The ironic conclusion is that both foundationalist and antifoundationalist epistemologies involve anthropocentrism: the former in (philosophical, ex-periential) theory, the latter in (cultural-linguistic) practice. To Hauerwas, an effort to reassert God's grace and prevenience (and meanwhile bypass human culture and language en route to external truth) will fall into the hands of liberal foundationalism. However, in an effort to avoid foundationalism, Hauerwas can get so involved in the social and linguistic media of revelation that the sovereign power of the Revealer is neglected.[44] I shall now look at how his social, pragmatic, anthropocentric understanding of truth leads him to his stress on the nonviolent witness of the Christian Church.

Relativism

If a religion is to be judged by its practical consequences, and a great variety of religions appear to have very agreeable consequences, are a great number of religions equally true? If a sacred story leads believers into lives without deception, lives of selflessness and sacrifice, an awareness of tragedy and a spirituality of peace, is it thereby a story about God? If it were, it would be hard to sustain the uniqueness of the Christian story or the exclusivist claims the Bible makes for itself.

In response to this there are two clear options. The first is the one unequivocally adopted by John Milbank. In his book *Theology and Social Theory* he recognizes that the chief candidates to fill the role as judge over

---

[44] Brueggemann points towards one way Hauerwas might develop his understanding: "Barth has made clear that the God of the Bible is 'Wholly Other'. In conventional interpretation, the accent has been on 'wholly', stressing the contrast and discontinuity. When, however, accent is placed on 'other', dramatic interpretation can pay attention to the dialectical, dialogical interaction in which each 'other' impinges upon its partner in transformative ways. That is, 'otherness' need not mean distance and severity, but can also mean dialectical, transformative engagement with." (Walter Brueggemann, *The Bible and the Postmodern Imagination: Texts under Negotiation* London: SCM Press 1993 p. 106 n. 19)

the plurality of stories are the social sciences. But Christianity is not content to be just one story amongst many, one path to virtue alongside several others. Milbank insists on the 'metanarrative realism' of Christianity, its ability to out-narrate all other stories: and he insists that this applies in the social field as much as the ontological and historical. Like Hauerwas, he holds up the social practice of the Church as the visible test of the truth of its story:

> A gigantic claim to be able to read, criticize, say what is going on in other human societies, is absolutely integral to the Christian Church, which itself claims to exhibit the exemplary form of human community. . . . The *logic* of Christianity involves the claim that the 'interruption' of history by Christ and his bride, the Church, is the most fundamental of events, interpreting all other events. And it is *most especially* a social event, able to interpret other social formations, because it compares them with its own new social practice.[45]

By the metanarrative Milbank means not just the scriptural narrative, but the continuing story of the Church, 'already realized in a finally exemplary way by Christ, yet still to be realized universally, in harmony with Christ, and yet *differently*, by all generations of Christians'.[46]

To what extent does Hauerwas subscribe to Milbank's 'metanarrative realism'? In his earlier work it would seem he does not: he says, 'There is no story of stories, i.e. an account that is literal and that thus provides a criterion to say which stories are true or false. All we can do is compare stories to see what they ask of us and the world we inhabit.'[47] However, in his later work Hauerwas moves nearer to Milbank's Augustinian approach, particularly on the question of the performance of good deeds by bad people. Hauerwas concurs with the view that to say a bad person has done a good action is a misuse of the notion of good.[48] This is because Hauerwas subscribes to a teleological, rather than consequential, notion of ethics. What the bad person did might have had some good results, but if it did not put them on the path towards being good, it cannot be called a good action. For fundamentally, it is people that are good or bad, not actions. This argument can be extended to the discussion of whether there can be more than one truthful story. Hauerwas might say that a story might *appear* good and true if people who believed in it performed good actions; but this would be only a semblance of virtue, since teleologically their actions would not be good unless they contributed to the final cause: the upbuilding of the Church.[49]

The alternative to Milbank, a second response to the problem of relativism, involves a less ambitious but more nuanced attempt to show how the Christian community lives alongside other stories. In an early essay, Hauerwas proposes four working criteria for the evaluation of stories. These involve an

---

45 Milbank, *Theology and Social Theory* p. 388, italics original.
46 Ibid. p. 387, italics original.
47 Hauerwas, *Truthfulness and Tragedy* pp. 78–79.
48 Hauerwas, *Character and the Christian Life* p. xxiii.
49 The teleological notion is best seen as an eschatological one, as I argue in Chapter 7.

emphasis on avoiding self-deception, violence and false notions of power.[50] However, Hauerwas is not innocent when it comes to the use of heavily value-laden language, and there can be no question that the terminology of these criteria – 'destructive', 'violence', 'tragic' – is governed by the particular narrative he is representing. It is better to look to his 'Ten theses for the reform of Christian social ethics' for a thoroughly contextual approach.[51] The third thesis runs: 'The ability to provide an adequate account of our existence is the primary test of the truthfulness of a social ethic.' There is no neutral ground for adjudicating this, of course, but Christians believe that the cross and resurrection of Christ describe the world, its history and future most adequately. The fourth thesis runs: 'Communities formed by a truthful narrative must provide the skills for transforming fate into destiny so that the unexpected, especially as it comes in the form of strangers, can be welcomed as a gift.'

Hauerwas explores the implications of this fourth thesis in a discussion that resembles the *ad hoc* apologetics characteristic of Frei, Lindbeck, Werpehowski and Ford.[52] Hauerwas adopts Bernard Williams' notion of a 'real option'.[53] The notion of a real option excludes from the debate about truth those examples which, usually for historical reasons, are not ways of life that could possibly be adopted today. The 'real option' approach does not underestimate the depth of division between those who hold different commitments, or try to formulate a theory capable of defeating relativism. Instead, it deals with confrontations one at a time. Again Hauerwas argues that what we need are not *proofs* to destroy relativism but *skills* to live in a divided world.

The notion of the 'real option' enables Hauerwas to reconceive the command to witness in a plural world.[54] Again Hauerwas resists all attempts to substitute theory and argument for personal encounter and practice. It is not that Christians possess 'a universal truth which others must also implicitly possess or have sinfully rejected'; nor that they can make *a priori* judgements about other faiths. For *all* are sinners and fall short: and all can find redemption through participation in the life made possible by Christ's passion and resurrection. So the Christian community's task is 'to be the sort of community that can become a real option and provide a real confrontation for others', showing the unity in diversity that judges 'the diversity of the world where most of our confrontations are either notional or violent'.[55]

Once again, we see how a thoroughgoing commitment to the social embodiment of truth enables Hauerwas to form a faithful ethic despite the

---

[50] Hauerwas, *Truthfulness and Tragedy* p. 35.

[51] Hauerwas, *A Community of Character* pp. 9–12. See pp. 51–52 above.

[52] In addition to the works cited above, see William Werpehowski, '*Ad Hoc* Apologetics' *The Journal of Religion* 66 (1986) pp. 282–301; David F. Ford, 'The Best Apologetics is Good Systematics: A Proposal about the Place of Narrative in Christian Systematic Theology' *Anglican Theological Review* 67/3 (July 1985) pp. 232–254.

[53] Hauerwas, *A Community of Character* pp. 103–104.

[54] Ibid. pp. 105–106.

[55] Ibid. p. 105.

charges of fideism and relativism. His position is highly consistent, and few have faulted its internal logic. The questions remain on whether a Church of this kind is sustainable or desirable.

Elitism

If truth is to be assessed largely on whether it produces lives and communities of character, does an impossibly heavy burden rest on the shoulders of the faithful? To what extent does human sinfulness reduce the effectiveness of Christian behaviour in demonstrating the truth of Christian convictions? If sinfulness affects the ability of Christians to *act* truthfully, surely it also affects their ability to *speak* and think truthfully as well. In Gary Comstock's assessment, Hauerwas 'seems to have a problem with weakness of will. Can't Christians truly believe the story, want to live by it, and yet fail to do so? But if we can only say that the story is accepted as "true" by those who actually *practise* pacifism, then we could not have Christian pacifists who, through some flaw of character, fail to act on their convictions. Yet there are such people.'[56]

Just as Hauerwas appears anthropocentric on the issue of revelation, since he concentrates on the practices and language of the Church to the near exclusion of God's prevenience, so here he seems anthropocentric for much the same reasons. He appears to be making truth a prisoner of the practice of the Christian community. This certainly takes narrative, incarnation, particularity and embeddedness seriously, but it does seem to underplay the otherness and the sovereign prevenience of God. It seems that the truth of God's presence and action in the Christian community is subject to the community, rather than vice versa. Hauerwas is concerned that Christian belief in grace and the action of the Holy Spirit would be called into question if Christians were never changed by the practice of their faith and the community failed to produce saints. Once again the *communio sanctorum* emerges as the key doctrine. Hauerwas takes seriously Nietzsche's protest – that Christians 'don't look redeemed' – as an appeal to falsification.

Hauerwas perhaps slightly overstates his case here. Nietzsche's objection does not restrict the sovereignty of God. There is a level of theological realism which is not entirely subordinate to the social domain of reality. The Christian who lives unfaithfully yet says 'Jesus is the Son of God' does not thereby invalidate the doctrinal claim. The character of the Trinity is not subject to the performance of the community.[57]

---

[56] Comstock, 'Two Types of Narrative Theology' p. 708 n. 19. It is interesting to note Hauerwas' own comments in his introduction to the second edition of *Character and the Christian Life* (p. xxxii): 'I think this book was enough on the right track that its mistakes have proved fruitful. For finally I think this is the best most of us can do: make interesting mistakes.'

[57] Wallace, *The Second Naïveté* p. 106 calls the Lindbeck/Hauerwas position here 'Donatistlike'. Iain Torrance in 'They Speak to Us across the Centuries: 2. Cyprian' *The Expository Times* 108/12 (September 1997) pp. 356–359 also makes a comparison with Donatism, and commends Augustine's orientation toward Christ as a focus of unity.

In response to this, Hauerwas points out that the inquiry into truth-claims tends to single out individual propositions or historical events as if they could be abstracted from the whole picture. Theology cannot be separated from ethics and narrative in this way. Again Hauerwas insists that one cannot bypass the social and linguistic reality and simply settle on individual external realities. The context of the Christian community is indispensable if the question is to be rightly asked:

> Questions like does God really exist or did Jesus rise from the grave are sometimes taken as the central questions that determine the truth or falsity of religious convictions. God's existence and Jesus' resurrection are not unimportant convictions for Christians, but it is inappropriate to single them out as *the* issues of religious truth. For the prior question is how the affirmations of God's existence and Jesus' resurrection fit into the story of the kind of God we have come to know in the story of Israel and Jesus. The emphasis on story as the grammatical setting for religious convictions is the attempt to remind us that Christian convictions are not isolatable 'facts', but those 'facts' are part of a story that helps locate what kind of 'fact' you have at all.[58]

Here Hauerwas makes an important point that events have meaning only in relation to the story of which they are a part. This corresponds to a similar point about the meaning of human actions, as we have already discussed. It also underlines the conviction that the social reality is the indispensable context for truth. However, the emphasis that this places on the contemporary community to embody the truth of the story is immense – since there is no other available mode of verification. And this brings the argument back to plurality, for when has the Church embodied the truth in the way Hauerwas describes? One can see why Hauerwas increasingly takes to relating stories of faithfulness, and why such stories are integral to his whole project.

The doctrine of the communion of saints emerges as central to Hauerwas' ethics once again. In Chapter 2 I suggested that there were philosophical reasons for suggesting that the community should be seen as the unit of Christian ethics; here it has become apparent that there are good hermeneutical and epistemological reasons for the same conclusion. In this notion of participation in the communion of saints there is, I suggest, a theological impetus for seeing the community as the embodiment of the ethic of Jesus.

An abiding anxiety remains. Is Jesus' ethic just too strenuous? This seems to be the implication of Matthew 5:48, 'Be perfect, as your heavenly Father is perfect'. Is the communion of saints a company of heroes? Hauerwas is determined to deny this charge of ethical élitism. But he is committed to seeing ethics in terms of people rather than principles. Thus he directs his criticism against deontological approaches to perfection which result in moral callousness and self-righteousness. If perfection resides more in the principle than in the person, the result can be legalism. The meaning of

---

[58] Hauerwas, *Truthfulness and Tragedy* p. 73. It is not clear whether or not Jesus' resurrection should be so singled out. Barth tends to treat it in this manner.

absolute commands or ideals is seldom unequivocal; and principles can conflict with each other. Deontological principles tend to be negatively formulated: they can easily slip into a search for moral purity rather than an expression of agape. Nonviolence is not simply a question of not taking life; it requires positive action that respects life. Christian faith is not simply an ethical stance to be kept consistent, or a set of rules not to be broken. This is not perfection.

Hauerwas' positive proposal is based on narrative. Christians seek perfection by imitating God's way of dealing with the world, as set forth in the biblical narrative. Like Yoder, Hauerwas is uninterested in any static, abstract notion of perfection. If God's perfection is displayed in human form and in Israel and the Church, why should human perfection be any different? Hauerwas has a highly pragmatic approach to doctrine: doctrines are tested by the forms of community they produce. He therefore has little interest in a definition of perfection that distracts from the indispensable commitment of the practising community. Human perfection is thus a dynamic, embodied story: participation in the communion of saints.

Part of the problem is that sanctification seems to imply a normative description of the virtues of the Christian life. But a glance at the diversity of virtues recommended by different societies and thinkers reveals a disarming lack of consensus, even upon a principle for determining the key virtues. This leaves the notion of sanctification vulnerable to historical disputes and enquiry: hence the temptation toward abstraction. Hauerwas is anxious to maintain the historical character of virtue, and therefore begins to steer away from the term 'sanctification' toward language that speaks more concretely about participation in the Church. Nonetheless sanctification as a theme remains significant to Hauerwas because it concerns performance and is thus crucial to assessing the truth of Christian convictions.

Perhaps Hauerwas' most successful demonstration that the communion of saints is not a matter of élitism is in his discussion of the role in the Church of people with disabilities. This counters any suggestion of a narrow notion of perfectionism. It emphasizes that the communion of saints refers to the way Christians participate in Christ by entering his community, rather than any idea that sanctification is a reward for ethical heroes. By stressing the vital role in the Christian community played by those whose difference from the majority is most obvious, Hauerwas subverts conventional notions of ethical excellence. His stress on disabilities enhances the embodied, rather than cognitive, dimension of ethics: for those whose rational powers are not their greatest gifts, and for those for whom independence is not conceivable, the priority of community and the social dimension of truth is undisputed.

Performance

The believing community is thus the place where truth is embodied and can be assessed. Hauerwas sees the Christian community as performing the Scripture, and thereby providing the only means of testing its validity. The danger, in his view, in seeing ethics as the performance of theology comes where it is assumed that one 'must begin with beliefs about God, Jesus, sin and the like, and the moral implications of those beliefs'.[59] This makes such beliefs look like a primitive metaphysics which the observer could analyse as a system of belief detached from the Church. Hauerwas insists: 'Christian beliefs about God, Jesus, sin, the nature of human existence, and salvation are intelligible only if they are seen against the background of the church – that is, a body of people who stand apart from the "world" because of the peculiar task of worshipping a God whom the world knows not.'[60] The model for performance comes from the first Christians, whose peculiarity came in 'their social inventiveness in creating a community whose like had not been seen before': 'They thought that their belief in God as they had encountered him in Jesus required the formation of a community distinct from the world exactly because of the kind of God he was.'[61]

Hauerwas addresses the justification of Christianity in pragmatic terms – since a theoretical justification would almost inevitably be foundationalist. In order to avert the charge of relativism or of fideism, he needs to show how Christian claims can be assessed as true or false. Given Hauerwas' reluctance to disembody truth and authority, he seeks an actualized form of truth. Thus he speaks not so much of the truth of Christian doctrines but more of the truthfulness of Christians' lives. Truth is not a virtue or attribute on its own: it cannot be separated 'from other measures of value – from consistency, righteousness, justice, happiness, satisfaction'.[62] One must ask, What forms of life issue from Christian convictions? Do the beliefs form communities, confer courage, patience and hope, develop wisdom, discernment and honesty within the body, offer a spirituality of tragedy that sustains nonviolence, free people from self-deception, sustain worship, produce saints, and help people understand why they do what they do? For Hauerwas, following Wittgenstein, the truth of a story is not just that it provides an accurate description of the past, but that it helps one go on into the unknown – without a false story.[63] Pragmatic tests of Christianity focus on Christian tradition and the 'richness of moral character' it produces in much the same way that science judges its theories by the fruitfulness of the activities they generate, and significant works of art become so in the light of the interpretation and criticism that surround them.

There is a delicate line to tread here. Hauerwas constantly has to steer a path between on the one hand the objectivity that supposes a community can find a place to 'stick our heads above history' and judge all truth-claims

---

[59] Hauerwas, *Against the Nations* p. 42.

[60] Ibid.

[61] Ibid. See pp. 90–93 below for further development of these themes.

[62] Hauerwas, *Truthfulness and Tragedy* p. 80, quoting James McClendon and James Smith, *Understanding Religious Convictions* (Notre Dame: University of Notre Dame Press 1975) p. 15.

[63] Hauerwas, *Truthfulness and Tragedy* p. 80.

from neutral territory, and on the other hand a relativism which suggests that any assessment of truth-claims is circular at best and impossible at worst, because there is no neutral ground from which to begin. His path is to see the *assessment* of truth-claims as itself a skill. One learns how to judge between stories by oneself living truthfully within a story. Who is the person who says Christian claims are false? What story has taught such a person what is good and right and true? Is this person criticizing Christianity for being something it never set out to be – perspicuous, context-independent, objectively justifiable? Hauerwas summarizes his position in concluding his essay 'Story and Theology':

> The true stories that we learn of God are those that help us best to know what story we are and should be, that is, which gives us the courage to go on. Namely, the story that is necessary to know God is the story that is also necessary to know the self, but such knowing is not passive accommodation to an external object. Rather such knowing is more like a skill that gives us the ability to know the world as it is and should be – it is a knowing that changes the self.[64]

It is thus the story of God which forms communities of character whose practice of virtue develops people of the skill required to assess the truthfulness of the story.

One of the key questions that Hauerwas has to face is that of how one knows a narrative is false. Many grotesque evils have been done in the name of Christianity throughout the history of the Church. What criteria may the Christian community use to criticize its own practice? The mass suicide of nine hundred members of the People's Temple at Jonestown, Guyana is an extreme case of the practice of a false story. Hauerwas' response to Jonestown illustrates his assessment of truth as performance.[65]

Hauerwas begins by insisting that Jim Jones was not wrong to make great demands on his followers. What happened at Jonestown was an act of revolutionary suicide – and one that should be respected. The participants felt that to lose Jones amounted to the dissolution of the community; losing the community was tantamount to losing their life: 'so, like the martyrs, they chose spiritual life rather than spiritual death'.[66] And in several respects, Jones' community exhibited the features of spiritual life: blacks and whites found they could be brothers and sisters, the dispossessed found they could be responsible for one another, people experienced the joy of being loved and of loving in return. This gave the people a vision and a sense of mission – a mission to offer this equality and love to wider society: a mission worthy of making sacrifices.

It is important to note the features that Jones shared with Christianity. Like the early Church, the People's Temple thought in terms of a cosmic struggle

---

[64] Ibid. p. 81.
[65] Hauerwas, 'On Taking Religion Seriously: The Challenge of Jonestown' *Against the Nations* pp. 91–106.
[66] Ibid. p. 100.

between good and evil, a struggle that required of the disciple a complete sacrifice both privately and publicly – wealth, status, money, health, family, even life itself. The Christian community took precedence over one's own family. Thus it is not for the Church to follow secular critics and attack the People's Temple for interfering with individual autonomy: the Church should have no stake in underwriting the notion that religion belongs only to the private realm.

The tragedy of Jonestown is twofold. In the first place, the tragedy is that Jones' beliefs were false. The participants died because they believed that Jones told the truth: but they were wrong. They were not wrong to give their lives for their beliefs: they were wrong because the cause of the sacrifice was not worthy. The clue to the falsity of Jones' claims was in the command to suicide itself. This command exposed the emptiness of the whole of Jones' project – a project based on himself, not on the character of God:

> The willingness to take their lives, and the lives of others, manifests the assumption that they must insure their own existence. The Jewish and Christian prohibition against suicide is not based on the inherent sacredness of life but rather on God's sovereignty over all life. Our life is not for us to do with as we please, but rather we must learn to look on our life as a gift that is not ours to dispose of.... Those ... who would contemplate and indeed even practice suicide as did those at Jonestown must be judged worshippers of a false god.[67]

For Hauerwas, the fact that the community had already resorted to violence in killing a congressman and some reporters ought already to have demonstrated the falsity of its performance. For any community that feels the need to use violence of this kind is unlikely to be a community grounded in the truth. This is the centre of his understanding of truth as performance. 'Anytime a religion must resort to violence to secure its beliefs that is a sure sign that something has gone wrong with its claim to worship the God of truth and peace. Unfortunately Christianity provided Jones with many past precedents for the violence he used to protect his community. The use of violence is a sure sign that the community trusts not God, but themselves.'[68] In this summary passage Hauerwas unites the themes of narrative, truth, performance and nonviolence. A point he does not develop is that suicide denies the Christian story by prematurely foreclosing it. A correct perception of the narrative involves an awareness of its ending – that is, it demands eschatology. Violence in general and suicide in particular exhibit a rejection of the ending of the Christian story as portrayed by Jesus. Just as it is the ending of the Jonestown story that exposes its falsity, so it is by confidence in the ending of their narrative that Christians display their faithfulness.

Another dimension of the tragedy of Jonestown is that the Church's contemporary practice is so unused to matters of truth and falsity that no one was able to recognize heresy when they saw it. Fearing themselves to

---

[67] Ibid. pp. 101–102.
[68] Ibid. p. 106 n. 13.

violate people's autonomy, the watchword of tolerance is so honoured by the contemporary Churches that they are reluctant to criticize any but those who interfere with the same autonomy. The only sin seems to be to take religion seriously. The moral, for Hauerwas, is a familiar one: the powers that reigned at Jonestown can only be countered by the kind of convictions that only a community of character can foster. In the absence of such a community, Christians find themselves assenting to secular dismay at how anyone could be so foolish as to be a martyr.

Summary

In this chapter I have considered how Stanley Hauerwas' understanding of the Christian narrative is one which depends heavily on Christian communities for its intelligibility and its relation to truth. Several criticisms of this community narrative can be made, relating to Hauerwas' assumption that the narrative he describes is indeed the gospel as it has been proclaimed by all Christians in all ages. His thoroughgoing antifoundationalism also leaves him open to criticism. Though troublesome, these criticisms may not prove insurmountable, and I shall return to them in Chapter 7.

Sometimes it appears that Hauerwas spends so much time demolishing the presuppositions of Christians who may be tempted to seek common cause with liberal democracies, that there is little time left for constructive proposals. It is clear that a community of the kind he requires needs extensive training in the ways of counter-cultural discipleship. In my next chapter I consider what makes the Church a unique community. The discussion of what exposes a story as false has shown how Hauerwas begins to place nonviolence as the key to the way the Christian imitates the character of God. Community begins as a vehicle for the transmission of tradition and the teaching of virtue: but, when it becomes the Church, it becomes the indispensable location for the embodiment of truth.

5

From Community to the Church

In the previous chapter I demonstrated how Hauerwas' notion of performing the Christian story requires a community. I went on to outline how the community is indispensable for assessing the truth claims of narrative from above. In this chapter I examine how Hauerwas expands the notion of Christian community to describe the central theme of his theological ethics: the Church. How does the Church perform Jesus' story?

Hauerwas' writing has a very combative style: many of his essays bear controversial and confrontational titles. He is not a mild man. For him, conflict is at the heart of life. This is true as much within the Church as elsewhere. Thus the way the Church deals with conflict is central to its mission. In Hauerwas' view, Jesus faced conflict throughout his ministry: and the way Jesus dealt with conflict discloses to the Church what it means to be faithful to the gospel.

Hauerwas roots the Church's character fundamentally in the character of God. His emphasis is constantly on the faithfulness of the Church – its faithfulness to the character of God. If one might adapt the terminology of the Nicene Creed, Hauerwas might be said to stress the Church's holiness and its apostolicity (in this sense its attempt to stand in the tradition of Jesus and the early Church). Hauerwas is deeply suspicious of the assertion of what might be called a false unity or catholicity. It is for this reason that he is often taken to be a sectarian – one who advocates the withdrawal of the Church from mainstream society.

While the last chapter considered the accusation of fideism, this chapter addresses perhaps the most common charge made against Hauerwas: that he is a sectarian. In order to understand this charge, and Hauerwas' response to it, it is helpful to appreciate the extent to which Hauerwas has learned his ecclesiology from the Mennonite theologian John Howard Yoder. This is true most of all in the perception of Jesus as the norm for Christian ethics. In this area, Yoder and Hauerwas are so close that I shall follow their arguments interchangeably. For them both, ethics means imitating the character of God: and the character of God is revealed in Jesus.

The character of God

The sovereignty of God

When Christians follow the ethic of Jesus, they display their faith that the God who is fully revealed in Jesus is sovereign over all things. In the ministry of Jesus, Christians see the subjugation of all powers opposed to God's will, and the establishment of a new kingdom. This new peaceable kingdom is the yardstick for judging all others. Peace becomes the defining characteristic of an ethic and creed based on the character of God:

> Christians believe that the world is deeply bent by sin, most poignantly manifest in the distrust that characterizes all relations between people. Violence and coercion are not accidental to such a world but are integral to its nature. For example, . . . people are not racist because they are ignorant, but racism is a manifestation of fear, fuelled by the corrupt and prideful assumption that the only way to get out of this life alive is by taking control of our existence. . . . The Christian and the Jew believe that they have been given a special mission in such a world. Namely, they have been called to form communities that manifest the trust and love possible between people when they recognize the sovereignty of God over all life. To be sure, they are often unfaithful to the task, but even their unfaithfulness points to the kind of life that should be possible between people.[1]

As soon as Jesus becomes the norm for Christian ethics, the issue of violence emerges as central. Immediately Hauerwas has ruled out a simple evaluation of consequences. Faithfulness to the sovereignty of God is not likely to bring with it much in the way of effectiveness; there is no strategic calculation of appropriate methods for getting one's way. Nonviolence is not right because it 'works'. Hauerwas is well aware that the nonviolence of Christians may make the world a more violent place. His concern is not with effective action but with faithful recognition of the approach to evil that Jesus has made possible.

The path to nonviolence begins with Yoder's insistence that Jesus is no far-away figure. For the situation into which Jesus came, and the forces with which he came into contact, were ones of abiding historical and political relevance: then, as now, the kingdom of God confronted racism, militarism, nationalism, the corruption of justice, mob spirit and action, religious bigotry and the pressures of government. Do these forces constitute the true nature of history? Or did Jesus expose, address and redeem them, and thus define history differently? Yoder and Hauerwas insist that the latter is the case.

The issue is one of sovereignty. If Jesus is Lord, then it is his activity, not that of these competing powers, that determines the meaning of history. Jesus' lordship relativizes the sovereignty of all other powers. All the 'givens' of history have their authority undermined if Jesus is Lord. For Yoder and Hauerwas, Jesus' lordship is revealed definitively in the cross. It is the cross that discloses the meaning of history. Christians are those who have come to see the cross as victory. The revelation of the victory of the cross disarms all the powers the Christian might be tempted to use. Those powers do not have the force they once had. Thus 'when the Christian whom God has disarmed lays aside carnal weapons, it is not, in the last analysis, because they are too dangerous, but because

---

[1] Hauerwas, *Suffering Presence* p. 147.

they are too weak'.[2] This claim is a soteriological one. It is the belief that, through the cross, God decisively dealt with evil: not by responding in kind, but through self-giving, nonresistant love. It is also an eschatological claim – that the lamb that was slain is the lamb that will finally sit on the throne.

Peace is central to the character of the God whom Christians are called to imitate. Learning to be followers of Jesus means being called to imitate God. Hauerwas concentrates on Matthew 5:48: 'you must be *teleioi*, as your heavenly Father is *teleios*'.[3] This is a point that is picked up by Yoder:

> Christians love their enemies not because they think the enemies are wonderful people, nor because they believe that love is sure to conquer these enemies . . . [nor] because they fail to respect their native land or its rulers; nor because they are unconcerned for the safety of their neighbours . . . The Christian loves his or her enemies because God does, and God commands his followers to do so: that is the only reason, and that is enough.[4]

Thus when Christians renounce violence they are recognizing first of all the sovereignty of God, and secondly their vocation to imitate God's character. The sovereignty of God is revealed in the full divinity and the full humanity of Jesus.

Both Hauerwas and Yoder base Christian ethics on the full humanity and full divinity of Christ. Their response to alternative views is thus that such views do not do full justice to this orthodox doctrine. Because Jesus is fully God, his call to love the enemy and not to resist evil is binding. And because Jesus is fully human, his journey to the cross is not simply an impossible ethical ideal. Mistakes made in Christian ethics tend to correspond with the denial either of Christ's full divinity or of his full humanity.

Yoder regards methods which do not treat Jesus as the norm as a denial of Jesus' full divinity.[5] If Jesus is not the norm, other principles come to shape Christian ethics, and Jesus can become almost irrelevant. Yoder lists several grounds on which Jesus' irrelevance is asserted. It is said that Jesus anticipated an imminent *eschaton*; that he thought in terms of simple rural face-to-face relations; that the contemporary Christian faces problems Jesus did not face, particularly problems of the use of authority unthinkable before Christianity became the official religion of the Empire; that Jesus' concern was spiritual not social; that only his death has abiding significance.[6] In addition, there is historical-critical scepticism about whether the text is clear enough to guide us, or about whether it is consistent in its guidance from redactor to redactor; and there is the characteristically Lutheran view that Jesus' ethic is designed

---

[2] J.H. Yoder, 'Living the Disarmed Life' *A Matter of Faith: A Study Guide for Churches on the Nuclear Arms Race* (Washington DC: Sojourners 1981) p. 43.

[3] Hauerwas translates this 'perfect', though it could also be translated 'oriented toward the end', which has implications on the eschatological approach to ethics I outline in Chapter 7.

[4] Yoder, 'Living the Disarmed Life' p. 42.

[5] Yoder has in mind recent situation ethics and Roman Catholic natural law ethics.

[6] Yoder, *The Politics of Jesus* second edition pp. 4–8.

not to tell us what we can do but to bring us to our knees because we cannot do it.[7]

This style of ethics often begins with the rhythms of the world in the realities around us. It tends to be grounded on one or more of 'nature', 'reason', 'creation' and 'reality'. Rather than choose not to follow Jesus, or read the story and find in it a different message, this approach maintains that the particular claims of the Jesus' ethic upon the life of the disciple can be set aside on systematic, logical grounds. Yoder regards this approach as a denial of the absolute relevance, sovereignty and divinity of Jesus.

The opposite mistake Yoder describes as docetism. Docetism involves the perennial subjugation of the historical Jesus to the givens of contemporary theological presuppositions, and thus the undermining of the full humanity of Christ. The most common form of docetism is to make Christology the servant of soteriology. It is not, of course, possible to distinguish clinically the person of Christ from his work; the two cannot be separated. However when today's society, and the social situation of the Church within it, are taken as a given, Christology tends to become distorted. When soteriological issues take a primary place, the character of Jesus becomes a function of the saving acts required of him. His mission defines his person, rather than vice versa. Projected onto Jesus are human desires to be saved, to become like God, to overcome guilt, to make satisfaction for sin, to be perfect in action, purity and trust. The historical Jesus can get left behind.

The narrative character of the gospels discourages such a propositional rendering of soteriology.[8] The gospels do not separate the person of Christ from his work, the incarnation from the atonement. There is no moral, metaphysical, or anthropological point or message that is separable from the story of Jesus as the gospels render it. The character of Jesus is unsubstitutable – he is not a myth but a particular person with particular followers whom he called to do particular things. His identity is not gathered by researching his titles or by assessing the effects of his ministry, but by learning to follow him. He is the only given.

God's sovereignty is for Hauerwas practically identical with the kingdom. The activities of the kingdom of God are the activities which recognize and affirm God's sovereignty. God's sovereignty was perfectly realized in the person of Christ – the embodiment of the kingdom on earth. Thus to imitate Christ is to embody God's sovereignty.

Imitating Christ

There are two dimensions that make the imitation of Christ central to Hauerwas' ethics. First, imitating Christ expresses the continuity of Christian

---

[7] These latter arguments are among those additions noted by Yoder in his second edition, ibid. pp. 15–19.

[8] See Hauerwas, 'Jesus, the Story of the Kingdom', *A Community of Character* pp. 36–52.

ethics with the ethics of the Old Testament. Second, along with Yoder, Hauerwas maintains that Christ's life is still paradigmatic for Christian ethics, in contrast to those who seek foundations elsewhere. I shall consider these two dimensions in turn.

Hauerwas' understanding of imitation begins with the biblical narrative. The early Christians saw in Jesus a continuation of God's dealings with Israel. These dealings included in particular the crossing of the Red Sea, the giving of the law at Sinai, the crossing of the Jordan and the construction of the Temple at Zion. By obeying the commands, by fearing and loving the Lord, Israel believed it was imitating God. '. . . To love God meant to learn to love as God loved and loves'.[9] What made Israel Israel was to remember (in an active, Hebrew sense) the definitive acts of God – the Exodus, the law–giving at Sinai, the crossing of the Jordan, the temple at Zion – and to meditate on the way of the Lord, with the help of the prophet, the priest and the king, living in obedience, fear, love and perfection. Israel's vocation was a call to imitate God, to reflect the character expressed in his deliverance of his people.[10] The prophet, priest and king were to be the models for the people to imitate. In the Servant of Second Isaiah these three functions coalesce. The servant enacts the three offices, of prophet, priest and king, displaying the purpose and task of Israel and revealing the life of God. By imitating God, Israel depicted God's kingdom – his sovereignty – in the world. The early Church saw in Jesus a recapitulation of the life of Israel, and a similar presentation of the life of God before the world. Imitating Jesus was therefore continuing Israel's vocation by imitating God.

The climax of Hauerwas' argument is his use of the temptation narrative.[11] By following Luke's account of Jesus' temptation in the wilderness, Hauerwas brings together his discussion of imitation with his view of the Church's social ethic. The first temptation is to be a grand prophet: it recalls Israel's desire for a certain future of her own choosing. 'Surely it would be a good thing to . . . feed the hungry and poor. But Jesus rejects that means of proving how God reigns with his people knowing that the life offered Israel is more than bread can supply.' The second temptation is to kingship: a dominion that will bring peace to nations. But God's rule is through weakness, his power is love, his peace is not coercion. 'Jesus . . . rejects Israel's temptation to an idolatry that necessarily results in violence between people and nations. For our violence is correlative to the falseness of the objects we worship, and the more false they are, the greater our stake in maintaining loyalty to them and protecting them through coercion.' The third temptation is to be the high priest, forcing God's hand, dictating the manner and timing of God's intervention in history. Jesus' refusal shows his commitment that God's will be done in his life and death.

God does not impose his will upon Israel. Though he constantly calls her back to faithfulness, she retains the possibility of disobedience. This pattern

---

[9] Hauerwas, *The Peaceable Kingdom* p. 78.

[10] Ibid. pp. 76–78.

[11] Ibid. pp. 78–79.

is continued in the gospels. God does not accept violent means, but creates a people who refuse to meet the world on its own terms. Being like Jesus means using the same methods as Jesus did when he was confronted with powerful enemies. Jesus faced the same calls to 'responsible' action in society that the Church faces today. He too was concerned for the downtrodden and oppressed; he too longed for justice on earth; he too saw the potential of political power. Yet he took the path not of power and justice, but of humility and love. Because Jesus chose servanthood and forgiveness rather than force and hostility, he went to the cross. Christians imitate him when they make a similar choice.

The confidence in Jesus as the paradigm for the Church is the second dimension of the theme of imitation, and it is an emphasis Hauerwas owes to John Howard Yoder. Yoder's concern is to establish the life of Jesus as normative for Christian ethics. In order to do this Yoder steers a course between two extremes: those who abstract certain elements from the life of Christ, and those who advocate a step-by-step imitation of Jesus' lifestyle. In common with the first group, Yoder asserts that one point in Jesus' life is indeed more important than the others; in common with the second group Yoder insists that this point is not an abstraction.

Yoder first criticizes those who abstract from the gospel narrative some value such as absolute love or humility or faith. Yet, as we have seen, Yoder also criticizes the 'mendicant' tradition which develops a general concept of living like Jesus. The former approach is insufficiently concrete; the latter is 'a red herring', since it does not offer a political alternative to the 'ethos of Caesar'.[12] Yoder is careful to highlight that there is no general notion of living like Jesus in the New Testament. Neither Paul nor any other writer looks to barefoot mendicancy, the forsaking of home or property, the formation of a close-knit group of disciples, the use of parables, singleness, time on mountains or in the wilderness, or the artisan background for a model for the imitation of Christ.[13] Hauerwas insists that one can only learn to be like Jesus if one joins a community that practises his virtues – not by simply copying his external circumstances. The Christian is called to be *like* Jesus, not to *be* Jesus. This rules out a simple copying of his external circumstances.

Despite his concern for the whole of Christ's life, Yoder does single out one particular element – the voluntary suffering of the cross – as the normative revelation within the normative revelation. There is no exaltation of suffering-in-general. The concept of imitation concentrates on one realm above all others: the 'concrete social meaning of the cross in relation to enmity and power'.[14] Jesus' cross was not a painful sickness or a sudden catastrophe, inexplicable and unpredictable. It was not a simple illustration of all and every kind of suffering. It was the end of a path freely-chosen, a path which refused the use of violence but remained committed to love

---

[12] Yoder, *The Politics of Jesus* second edition pp. 132–133.
[13] See especially Ibid. pp. 130–133.
[14] Ibid. p. 131.

the enemy; a path which demonstrated the reality of the life to come to a world unwilling to see it; a path which confronted the powers of darkness, confident in the faithfulness of the Father. This path led to the cross. And, according to Yoder, it still does.

Yoder describes how Jesus renounces three widely-respected paths. One is the path of quietism – the Church's tendency to withdraw from mainstream society when conflicts arise. Jesus could have avoided Jerusalem and died in ripe old age, still uttering wise words in the purity of a separated community. It was a temptation he faced, but one he resisted. A second path is that of the Jewish religious leaders: the path of conservative social responsibility. They realize the frustrations of being ruled over by the Romans, but are terrified of making matters worse by stepping out of line. It was they who demanded that Jesus be killed. A third approach is that of Barabbas. Barabbas is the man who faces the injustice and oppression of Roman government and responds with violent revolution. Over and over again this option presented itself to Jesus, and over and over again he rejected it. The Church constantly faces a similar choice. Surely there seem to be so many situations where injustice can only be overcome through force of arms, arms that could be used for the protection of the innocent. Jesus too could have thrown in his lot with Barabbas, and attempted to restore Jewish self-rule by helping to throw out the Romans. For him, as for Christians today, the crusade is a constant and attractive path; but Jesus rejected it, and in doing so, took up his cross and walked to Golgotha instead.

Thus in the imitation of Christ we can see several of Hauerwas' themes coming together. The narrative of Jesus is embodied by the practices of the community producing lives of virtue which are committed to nonviolence. Hauerwas makes the journey from community to the Church: the Church is the community that seeks to imitate the character of God. In doing so, it shares God's life, since 'truth, for Christianity, is not correspondence, but rather the *participation* of the beautiful in the beauty of God'.[15] Sharing God's way with his world is a participation in the life of God. It is not just a question of imitating Christ: the readiness to renounce legitimate ends whenever they cannot be attained by legitimate means is a *participation* in the triumphant suffering of the lamb.[16]

Christian nonviolence in this light is a recognition of the incarnation: it is the belief that God participated in human nature so that humanity might participate in God's nature. Jesus Christ

> was not simply a divine figure masquerading as a man whose apparent obedience was therefore irrelevant to the rest of us; he was the true human being. Faith in Jesus Christ is not an arbitrary or magical inscription on heavenly ledgers; faith is rather participation in the being of God, incorporation into the body of Christ. The possibility of obedience is therefore a statement not about our own human

---

[15] Milbank, *Theology and Social Theory* p. 427.
[16] Hauerwas, 'Messianic Pacifism' *Worldview* 16/6 (June 1973) p. 31.

capabilities, but about the fullness of the humanity of Jesus and the believers' identity with him through the Spirit in the Church.[17]

This is the kind of statement with which Yoder and Hauerwas tie together ontology, Christology and ecclesiology. In this context a phrase like 'being (or doing) the truth' makes sense. The Christian should conform him or herself to the perfect obedience of Christ. This is done by participation in the nonviolent community. Participation in this community, the body of Christ, the communion of saints, is in fact participation in the being of Christ – indeed, in the life of God. The life of God is itself nonviolent, as we can see from the manner of both creation and redemption, and God will triumph, as truth must, in the only nonviolent, self-giving way that truth knows. This picture is thus 'the way things really (ontologically) are'. Not to participate in the nonviolent community is therefore to part company with the truth.

The Holy Spirit

It is time to review what Hauerwas has to say about the significance for Christian ethics of Jesus and the Church.[18] Most of the criticisms of Hauerwas have clustered around the issues of sectarianism and fideism. Perhaps because of this, he has not been pushed to clarify some of the more doctrinal features of his position. I believe he could and should do this by developing his description of the role of the Holy Spirit.

It is not clear from Hauerwas' writing whether Jesus was the last of the prophets – the one who finally and definitively broke the barrier between God and his creation, changing the course of history and creating a new reality – or whether he was the first of the saints – inaugurating a new community which would continue his incarnation and work into every age. The latter model is one concerned primarily with revelation – Jesus is seen as revealing how his followers are to live. The former model is more concerned with redemption as a once-for-all event. Has redemption definitively taken place in the resurrection and ascension, or is it still taking place in the Church? One can perceive Hauerwas' eclectic background here. On the one hand is Yoder's strong insistence that history has changed since Christ – a claim Hauerwas uses against Reinhold Niebuhr, who implies that human nature is much as it ever was. On the other hand is the Methodist tradition of the continuing work of the Holy Spirit in sanctification, and the Roman Catholic tradition of the presence and efficacy of Christ in the eucharist.

---

[17] Yoder, ' "Christ and Culture", A Critique of H. Richard Niebuhr' p. 16, quoted in Hauerwas, *Vision and Virtue* p. 201.

[18] The most constructive response to Hauerwas' more dogmatic themes has come from David Fergusson, 'Another Way of Reading Stanley Hauerwas?' *Scottish Journal of Theology* 50/2 (1997) pp. 242–249. Fergusson helpfully points out some of the difficulties that arise from the way Hauerwas integrates his understanding of the ethical centrality of Christ with his emphasis on the Church.

Put in a different way, is redemption a *story* which the community *remembers,* or a *drama* which it *performs*? It is clear now that one is looking straight down the barrel of Reformation debates about the eucharist. Hauerwas has a stake in each of the principal strands of the Reformation – Catholic, Magisterial and Radical. One would therefore imagine that Hauerwas would want to say 'both' – both story and drama. But can one have both? Or, at least, what would Hauerwas have to do to make it clear that the Church can have both?

I believe the way for Hauerwas to have both is similar to the path that Calvin took out of the impasse over the eucharist. It is to develop the doctrine of the Holy Spirit. This is not a device for playing down the significance of Jesus: the Holy Spirit always points to Jesus. But one needs the Holy Spirit if one is to hold together the twin notions that on the one hand redemption has been achieved (as Calvin would say, Christ sits at the right hand of the Father), while on the other hand the Church imitates and continues the work of Christ, hoping thereby to be transformed into his likeness. It is the Holy Spirit that enlivens this part of the story, that unites this story to the story of redemption, that welcomes the drama of the Church into the mystery of the Trinity. The Holy Spirit makes Christ present in the Church's performance, and makes the Church present in the story of Christ. The story of Pentecost unites these two themes.

A fuller doctrine of the Holy Spirit would also help in understanding how God works outside the Church. The Church is a constant reminder to the rest of creation that it is not the Church – that it is taking the freedom not yet to believe. But Hauerwas has no stake in maintaining that God thereby leaves the rest of creation alone. God reigns over the whole of creation; he has particularly ordained that the Church be the visible community that manifests his grace to his creation. But he also sends his Holy Spirit, less visibly, to renew the face of the earth. As well as the performance of the story of Jesus, the Church must surely concentrate on the discernment of the activity of the Spirit. The Holy Spirit is not, I repeat, a second authority, to which resort can be made when following Jesus does not appeal. But it does offer a way in which the Christian community can perceive how God's purpose is being and has been revealed and brought about through practices and people that do not call themselves Church. This perception is desperately needed in Hauerwas' writing, lest Christians be paralysed in their membership of other communities besides the Christian one. If the Church genuinely intends to remain committed to communities other than itself, it must be because it believes that there too God lives and reigns, and it wants to be where God is, with the people he has made for his service. In this complex ministry the Church is sustained by the story made present by the Holy Spirit.

The politics of the Church

The Church realizes the kingdom by recognizing the sovereignty of God which was fully present in the person of Jesus Christ. Thus the vocation of the Church is to imitate Christ. Christ embodied the sovereignty of God particularly in the way he went to the cross and renounced the rival paths of Essene, Sadducee and Zealot. The Church therefore reflects the character of God when it establishes practices and patterns that face conflict without violence. How is this to be done?

The first step towards this, for Hauerwas, is for the Church to rediscover its integrity and identity. This is the force underlying his stress on narrative, virtue and community. The first form of politics is the politics that takes place within the Church itself, between Christians committed to imitating Christ as a community. It is because Hauerwas so explicitly emphasizes the priority of Christian identity that he attracts charges of being a sectarian. He sees this charge as surprising, since he regards the Church as the most political of institutions. The second form of politics is that which takes place as the Church interacts with the world in which it lives. Hauerwas can seem sectarian here also, since he insists that the Church should always be present *as the Church*, and should be cautious about translating its distinctive narrative into supposedly common ethical foundations. The following words are among his most characteristic: 'The first social ethical task of the church is to be the church – the servant community. Such a claim may sound self-serving until we remember that what makes the church the church is its faithful manifestation of the peaceable kingdom in the world. As such the church does not have a social ethic: the church is a social ethic.'[19] If there could be a summary of Stanley Hauerwas' ethical foundation, this is it.[20] The third form of politics, how different parties in the world outside the Church relate to one another, does not particularly interest Hauerwas. When he does address such issues – for instance in some of his essays on medical ethics – he often does so in order to show the poverty of the 'politics of the world', particularly when it is based on liberal-democratic principles. Again, this appears to some like a sectarian concentration on the Christian community and downgrading of the world in general.

Thus while the key area for Hauerwas ought logically to be the way Christians relate to each other, the controversial area has become the way Christians as individuals or as the Church relate to the world in general. Hauerwas has always resisted concentrating on the latter question, a decision which has at times caused considerable exasperation from both sides of the argument. To follow his approach I shall begin with politics within the Church, before proceeding to the relation of Church and world.

Politics within the Church

Being rather than having a social ethic entails offering a model of how to be peaceful. The unity-in-diversity of the Church offers an alternative to

---

[19] Hauerwas, *The Peaceable Kingdom* p. 99.
[20] 'This is not only Hauerwas' departure point. It is also his conclusion.' Wilson Miscamble, 'Sectarian Passivism?' *Theology Today* (April 1987) p. 72.

the often violent divisions found elsewhere. Hauerwas laments the scandal of the disunity of the Church – a disunity based not only on doctrine, history and practice, but more sinisterly on race, class and nationality. It is this disunity that hinders the Church's task of reminding the world that it is the world.

Yoder's Mennonite background accounts for a good deal of more 'mainstream' discomfort with Hauerwas' ecclesiology. Hauerwas and Yoder talk extensively of the 'politics' of the Church. Both have written significant meditations on Matthew 18:15ff.[21] For Yoder, Christian ethics happens in the Church rather than at the desk. Obedience to Christ's will is promised to the community gathered in his name around Scripture, in the face of a given moral challenge. Yoder relies on Matthew 18:15: 'What you bind on earth shall be considered as bound in heaven'. Yoder renders this in carefully chosen words: 'A transcendent moral ratification is claimed for the decisions made in the conversation of two or three or more, in a context of forgiveness and in the juridical form of listening to several witnesses.'[22] Thus there is conversation – not the deductive application of universally valid rules. The conversation begins with the two parties of the conflict and gradually involves others only in so far as is needed to achieve reconciliation. The decision is ratified in heaven. The intention is to reconcile.

Since this is the mission of the Church, the ministry required is that which can sustain this mission. Yoder identifies four kinds of people in particular who are needed in such a community. The Church needs prophets who have a vision of the place of the community in history. It needs scribes who know what to bring out of the storeroom of community memory – and when to do so. It needs teachers who are aware of the tyranny of language. And it needs agents of due process whose business is to facilitate and sum up.[23]

Stanley Hauerwas' discussion of Matthew 18 greatly illuminates what it means when he says that the Church's first social task is to be itself. For Hauerwas, the peacemaking that is based on Matthew 18:15ff is not the avoidance of conflict but the creation of the right kind of conflict. His essay is a call for the Church to be 'the most political of institutions', given that, unlike politics as it is generally understood, it is interested in truth. Hauerwas sees 'political' peacekeeping as 'the development of the processes and institutions that make possible confrontation and resolution of differences so that violence can be avoided'; as such, peacemaking 'is not simply one activity among others but is the very form of the church'.[24]

---

[21] Yoder, 'The Hermeneutics of Peoplehood' *The Priestly Kingdom: Social Ethics as Gospel* (Notre Dame: University of Notre Dame Press 1984) pp. 15–45, especially pp. 26–28. Hauerwas, 'Peacemaking: The Virtue of the Church' *Christian Existence Today* pp. 89–97.

[22] Yoder, 'The Hermeneutics of Peoplehood' p. 27.

[23] Ibid. pp. 29–34.

[24] Hauerwas, 'Peacemaking' pp. 96, 95.

The passage from Matthew 18 is central because it unites the themes of confrontation and forgiveness. Christians are called to confront their enemies. In the process they may discover they have been mistaken about being wronged, or even that their enemy might repent and they will therefore have to be reconciled. For the Church to be 'a community of truthful peace' it must not fail to challenge sinners, for this would abandon them to their sin. There is no limit to forgiveness (Matthew 18:22); but the wronged person always approaches the confrontation as one who has been forgiven. This is not to be a recipe for self-righteousness (another form of power). Those who are excluded from the process and treated as Gentiles or tax-collectors, are the self-righteous themselves – those who act like they have no need of forgiveness. 'There is no more violent act than the unwillingness to accept reconciliation freely and honestly offered.'[25]

In relation to those outside the Church, the Church must be as truthful with the world as it is with itself. It must call for a peace based on forgiveness rather than forgetfulness. It must challenge 'the false peace of the world which is too often built more on power than on truth'; in doing so it realizes the world may become a more violent place. Yet humanity is 'not naturally violent' but is 'created for peace'. Thus it is the Church's task to 'help the world find the habits of peace' by witnessing in its own life the right kind of conflict. For 'without the example of a peacemaking community, the world has no alternative but to use violence as the means to settle disputes'.[26]

What is missing in Hauerwas is a lengthier discussion of these themes. If the Church's first social-ethical task is to be itself, one needs to know more what 'being itself' involves. Hauerwas sometimes concentrates on what it does *not* involve, much to the consternation of Niebuhrians. It still remains for Hauerwas to write more essays like 'Peacemaking: The Virtue of the Church' to show what practices are required to be the Church. Once the focus has settled on the internal working of the Christian community, more needs to be said on how that community works.

While I have suggested in Chapter 2 that the final cause or purpose of Christian ethics is the Church itself – in other words that the Church is an end in itself – this would only make sense to Hauerwas so long as one understood that serving the world was part of the definition of 'Church'. For being a distinct community that practises the truthful politics of peace is the chief way that the Church serves the world in general.

---

[25] Ibid. p. 94. In *The Politics of Jesus* Yoder provides helpful insights into the nature of the forgiveness that Hauerwas recommends. 'The personhood which [Jesus] proclaims as a healing, forgiving call to all is integrated into the social novelty of the healing community. This ... would be even more clear if we could read the Jesus story with a stronger sense of the Jewishness of his context and with Amos ringing in our ears' (p. 108). 'The forgiveness of sins is not, for Jesus, a mere assuaging of personal guiltiness or interpersonal estrangement; it is a sign of the new age and the presupposition of a new possibility of community' (p. 108 n. 16).

[26] Hauerwas, 'Peacemaking', p. 95.

George Lindbeck picks up a theme dear to the heart of Yoder when he points out that the Church gains little by pursuing relevance for its own sake:

> Religious communities are likely to be practically relevant in the long run to the degree that they do not first ask what is practical or relevant, but instead concentrate on their own intratextual outlooks and forms of life. . . . A religious community's salvation is not by works . . . and yet good works of unforeseeable kinds flow from faithfulness. It was thus, rather than by intentional effort, that biblical religion helped produce democracy and science . . . ; and it is in similarly unimaginable and unplanned ways, if at all, that biblical religion will help save the world . . . from the demonic corruptions of these same values.[27]

Hauerwas has no hesitation in asserting the positive role of Christians within the public realm. This does not compromise the 'Church being itself': for the Church seeks service rather than dominion. Therefore the Church does society an important service by being a community capable of developing people of virtue. One does not have to have an Aristotelian notion of political life to regard it as important that at least some citizens be people of robust moral character. Hauerwas insists that any society will gain by honouring honour.

One of the chief virtues of the community is to preserve a language of discourse that enables imaginative approaches to ethical enquiry to be sustained. 'Christians should . . . provide imaginative alternatives for social policy as they are released from the "necessities" of those who would control the world in the name of security'.[28] I shall develop this theme of imagination in Chapter 6. Here it will be enough to say that the false unity of the nation-state may tend to impose a false 'realism' which suggests that there is no alternative to the necessary course of events. It is the peaceable practice of the kingdom that pictures a world that does not have to be this way, and makes possible a resistance to this naturalistic fallacy.

Michael Quirk points out that Hauerwas is related to the tradition of civic republicanism revived by Alasdair MacIntyre, Michael Sandel, Michael Walzer and Charles Taylor. As Quirk notes, Hauerwas parts company with this movement in so far as its roots are humanist rather than Christian.[29] The litmus test tends to be that of violence. To the extent that the state demands that Christians commit violent acts to further its policy, the Church will be deeply suspicious of the state. Up to that point, Hauerwas and the civic republicans have much in common.

If one were to summarize Hauerwas' discontent with charges of advocating withdrawal from political life, one would hear him asking the question, 'If one has renounced violence, how is one to resolve disputes without

---

[27] Lindbeck, *The Nature of Doctrine* p. 128. In its theme and its place in the book, this paragraph appears to be a gesture toward the last paragraph of Alasdair MacIntyre's *After Virtue*.

[28] Hauerwas, *A Community of Character* p. 11.

[29] Michael J. Quirk, 'Beyond Sectarianism?' *Theology Today* (April 1987) pp. 78–79.

politics?' Politics is not excluded by Hauerwas' ethics; it is positively *demanded* by his requirement that Christians ask, 'How can I be a reconciling presence in the life of my neighbour?'

Hauerwas is adamant that what society needs is not theories of justice or theories of the state. What is required is people prepared to be formed with the virtue of justice by being shaped by the practices of a characterful community – not a disembodied theory which can be applied in all situations and attempts to bypass the need for community. Here, if anywhere, is Hauerwas' common ground with the civic republicans. If, as society fragments, politics is not preserved in the Church, where else are civic republicans to look in search of an embodiment of the justice they seek? It is perhaps Hauerwas' chief frustration with the United States of America that many of its constitutionalists have assumed that the place to begin social formation is with an understanding of rationality and a blank sheet of paper. The Church and the Jews have millennia of reconciling experience upon which to draw: and if civic republicans learn from their practices they may avoid repeating some of their failures.

Hauerwas is not interested in the Church providing a blueprint for secular society. He welcomes the way Millbank demonstrates that particularity is central to Christian witness. Milbank shows how positivist and dialectical social sciences tried to replace Christianity's inherent dependence upon particular revelation by establishing universals. But these universals were inevitably founded on their own metaphysic. Milbank relates how in the postmodern era an apparently infinite number of discourses claim to represent humanity: universality can do no more than take its place among them.[30] Christian moral judgements are related to regeneration, to forgiveness, to the Church, to Christian hope: they cannot simply be moralized into a blueprint for a non-Christian society.

Because the Church claims no special insight into the general form of the good society, its witness will always be expressed in specific criticisms and suggestions, addressing particular injustices at a given time and place. There is no level to which the state could rise beyond which the Christian critique would have nothing more to ask. The Church should not attempt to speak on every matter that arises: only when it is engaging with the problem itself, and when it has something to say.

Church and world

A great deal of subtlety is necessary for Hauerwas to affirm the particularity of the Church without suggesting a dualism between Church and world. The Church, 'the people capable of remembering and telling the story of God we find in Jesus', exists for the world. The world is God's good creation; God has redeemed it, even though it refuses to acknowledge the fact. Thus the Church attempts to show the world what it is meant to be. Church and world

---

[30] Milbank, *Theology and Social Theory* p. 260.

cannot survive without each other; and each sins in frequently forgetting this. The Church is constantly tempted to a dualism that suggests God's redemption extends only to itself, or to a triumphalism that confuses servanthood with domination as its mode of relation to the world. The Church has no right to determine the boundaries of God's kingdom, for such is to limit the sphere of God's sovereignty.

It is important to stress that although 'wider society [is] the institutionalization of unbelief and sin,'[31] Church and world are not concepts which are intelligible without the other. The 'world' is not an ontological designation;[32] it is not inherently sinful. As often, Hauerwas invokes Yoder when in need of subtle distinctions: 'The distinction between church and the world is not something that God has imposed on the world by a prior metaphysical definition, nor is it only something which timid and pharisaical Christians have built up around themselves. It is all of that in creation that has taken the freedom not yet to believe.'[33] In Hauerwas' language:

> the world consists of those, including ourselves, who have chosen not to make the story of God their story. The world in us refuses to affirm that this is God's world and that, as loving Lord, God's care for creation is greater than our illusion of control. The world is those aspects of our individual and social lives where we live untruthfully by continuing to rely on violence to bring order.[34]

There is no room for Christians to be self-righteous, since the distinction between Church and world runs through every agent. Christians will no doubt find non-Christians who manifest God's peace better than they themselves do; co-operation with such people is based not on a generally shared natural morality but on the boundless width of God's kingdom, which the Church has no right to circumscribe.

Through having an identity distinct from the world, the Church offers the correct perspective from which to describe and understand the world. The story that stands at the centre of the Church is one which, Christians believe, correctly describes the world. An insight that Hauerwas originally gained from Iris Murdoch is that people act in the world that they see. What they are to do will be determined by what they perceive to be 'going on'. How Christians see is learned through being a people who are formed by the preaching and practice of their narrative. Hauerwas calls for the Church to be 'a community which tries to develop the resources to stand within the world witnessing to the peaceable kingdom and thus rightly understanding the world'.[35]

---

[31] Hauerwas, 'The Nonresistant Church: The Theological Ethics of John Howard Yoder' *Vision and Virtue* p. 206.

[32] Hauerwas, *The Peaceable Kingdom* p. 100.

[33] Yoder, *The Original Revolution* (Scottdale, Pennsylvania: Herald Press 1971) p. 116.

[34] Hauerwas, *The Peaceable Kingdom* p. 101.

[35] Ibid. p. 102.

In Yoder's words:

> The search for a public moral language is motivated ... by embarrassment about particularity, which is not willing to break through the embarrassment to confession by taking the risk of a specific encounter, preferring to posit something argued to be more solid and less threatening than an open market place, even if that 'something' be nonexistent or vacuous ... The way to affirm our respect for others is to respect their particularity and learn their languages, not to project in their absence a claim that we see the truth of things with an authority unvitiated by our particularity.[36]

There is no question that some in the world are bound to hate this people for describing the world in these terms. For this reason the price of being unafraid to speak the truth may be geographical mobility. Just as their saviour was often on the move, Christians may find they have no earthly home but the Church itself. It is in no one's interest for the Church to abandon particularity in order to seek some less particular moral consensus; for Christians believe that the way they see reality is the way reality really is.

The Church begins its social ethic by seeking to understand the world rather than rush into acting in it. For John Milbank, theology is a social science which claims to read and criticize what is going on in other societies. Meanwhile Christ and the Church are a new social practice, critiquing all others.[37] On the basis of its counter-ontology – the priority of nonviolent creating – the Church sets about 'out-narrating' a politics based on coercion and falsehood.

This is the only context in which terms such as the 'ghetto' make any sense. If the Church insists on calling attention to what the world is, if it has no reason to fear the truth, if it is able to exist in the world without resorting to violence to maintain its presence, it is not likely to be popular. When 'ghetto' is used as a slogan, it tends to be forgotten that historically a ghetto was not an enclave chosen by a self-righteous group but a refuge into which society drove those whose loyalty to the God of the Hebrew Scriptures made them cosmopolitans and therefore misfits in medieval Europe.[38] This is highly significant: if the Church does come to be isolated, it will not be from withdrawal or from deliberately provoking the world's violence. It may, however, mean that the only available path of resistance is to leave one place for another. Christians are at home in no nation: their only home is the Church itself.

If the Church is not the world, then neither is the world the Church – or the kingdom. In several essays, Hauerwas argues that Christians have only a

---

[36] Yoder, *The Priestly Kingdom* p. 42. There is a clear link here with Hauerwas' rejection of ethics from the neutral observer's perspective. See pp. 13–20 above.

[37] Milbank, *Theology and Social Theory* p. 388.

[38] Yoder, *The Christian Witness to the State* (Newton: Faith and Life Press 1964) p. 88 n. 10. Hauerwas is aware that although initially most Anabaptists did not withdraw but were forced to the periphery, 'this forced withdrawal later became a self-fulfilling prophecy as Anabaptists misdescribed their own theological and social commitments by making a virtue of necessity.' Hauerwas, 'Will the Real Sectarian Stand Up?' *Theology Today* 44/1 (April 1987) p. 91.

qualified loyalty to the nation-state.[39] Hauerwas is anxious to resist the presumption of the state; he also wishes to resist the supposition that the world's way of ruling is the only way to rule. In resisting the presumption of the state, Hauerwas is most at odds with those such as Richard Neuhaus who suppose that the Church should choose sides between totalitarian and democratic states. A demand of this kind makes democracy an end in itself. It expects Christians to kill in order to preserve the democratic state against her enemies; and yet that Church persists in supposing that it is free to recognize idolatry. In Hauerwas' view, the Church in the United States is the captive of the state. The overriding conflict of the twentieth century has not been that between freedom and oppression, or democracy and totalitarianism. It has been, as ever, the conflict between

> those that would remain loyal to God's kingdom and those that would side with the world. And the world is exactly those people and institutions claiming that Christians too must be willing to choose sides and kill in order to preserve the social orders in which they find themselves. As Christians when we accept that alternative it means we are no longer the church that witnesses to God's sovereignty over all nations, but instead we have become part of the world.[40]

With great clarity, Hauerwas charts how Christians have assumed that it was their task to make the 'liberal' world work. In this 'liberal' world, Christian belief and practice was restricted to the private realm; the result was a peaceful society. Hauerwas characterizes the ethics of Reinhold Niebuhr as one which focuses on love and justice, requiring a balance of freedom and equality; Hauerwas, perhaps exaggerating somewhat, describes this as 'functionally atheistic'. 'In the name of Christian responsibility to the "world", theologians became "ethicists" so they could be of service to liberal political regimens'. In a sardonic tone, Hauerwas recalls Jeffrey Stout's observation that liberalism arose out of the chaos of the Thirty Years' War:

> The whole point . . . of the philosophical and political developments since the Enlightenment is to create people incapable of killing other people in the name of God. Ironically, since the Enlightenment's triumph, people no longer kill one another in the name of God but in the names of nation-states. . . . The ultimate pathos of our times is that we live in societies and polities formed by the assumption that there is literally nothing for which it is worth dying. The irony is that such societies cannot live without war as they seek to hide in war the essential emptiness of their commitments.[41]

---

[39] See especially 'The Reality of the Church: Even a Democratic State is Not the Kingdom' *Against the Nations* pp. 122–131, 'A Christian Critique of Christian America' *Christian Existence Today* pp. 171–190 and 'The Politics of Salvation: Why there is no Salvation Outside the Church' *After Christendom* pp. 23–44.

[40] Hauerwas, 'The Reality of the Church' p. 129.

[41] Hauerwas, 'The Politics of Salvation' pp. 31, 33, 44. See also Reinhold Niebuhr, *The Nature and Destiny of Man* (volume 2 New York: Scribners 1949) pp. 244–286 and Jeffrey Stout, *Ethics after Babel: The Languages of Morals and their Discontents* (Boston: Beacon 1988).

What Hauerwas has done here is to show that war exposes the limitations of liberal democracies just as much as medicine does. Christians do no favours to such societies by simply adapting their narrative to suit the prevailing culture. It is chiefly in the distinct witness of the Church to a particular kind of politics that it both reflects the character of God and best serves its society.

Hauerwas' response to claims that his ecclesiology looks sectarian is to say that the alternative to the Church is the nation-state and if ever there were a sect, the nation-state is it. 'The closest approximation we have to a universal society is in fact the church through its unwillingness to be captured by narrow national loyalties'.[42] This is a bold claim for catholicity based on the rejection of 'Constantinianism'. Hauerwas calls the kingdom 'God's international'.[43] Those who give their primary loyalty to the nation-state (for instance because it preserves democracy against totalitarianism) have the more reason to be called sectarian

> since they are usually the ones that develop justifications for Christians in one country killing Christians in another country on grounds of some value entailed by national loyalties. Surely if any position deserves the name 'sectarian' it is this, since it qualifies the unity of the church in the name of a loyalty other than that to the kingdom of God.... What kind of unity is it that would have us eat at the same table to which we have been invited by a crucified saviour only to be told at the end of the meal that the peace of that table does not mean we cannot kill one another for the goods of the nations in which we find ourselves living?[44]

Hauerwas thus faces the charge of disunity head on, by confronting the idolatry of the nation-state. What claims to be the voice of general well-being may be no more than the voice of a particularly influential economic or political interest. It requires an alternative conversation to give a different reading of what may otherwise be taken for granted. The Church provides such an alternative conversation.

It is important for Hauerwas that the conversation should not take place in a language defined only by the nation-state. It is a common assumption that once Hauerwas has adopted Christian pacifism he must correspondingly envisage the withdrawal of the Christian community from political life. Hauerwas strenuously denies this assumption. He exposes the assumption that to be involved in politics requires that one is prepared to kill on behalf of the state. There is plenty of politics that does not require killing. A further underlying assumption is that all politics is in the end a cover for violence. For Hauerwas, by contrast, it is the disavowal of violence that is the beginning of politics. Hauerwas advocates not withdrawal but 'selective service': there are times when participation in some aspects of education, law or government

---

[42] Hauerwas, 'Will the Real Sectarian Stand Up?' p. 88.

[43] Hauerwas, *The Peaceable Kingdom* p. 151.

[44] Hauerwas, *Against the Nations* pp. 7, 128. See also 'A Modest Proposal for Peace: Let the Christians of the World Agree that they will not Kill One Another' *Unleashing the Scripture* pp. 63–72.

will not be appropriate; but these times will be determined by the political commitments of the community of character.

Power

The change in Christian social practice and ecclesiology symbolized by the conversion of Constantine is so significant to the thinking of John Howard Yoder and those inspired by him that it is worth considering in detail. Yoder gives his most thorough exposition of this profound shift in his essay 'The Constantinian Sources of Western Social Ethics'.[45] Yoder's concern is not with the year 311 or with Constantine the man: it is with how, for example, Christians went from rejecting the violence of army and empire in the third century to considering it their vocation and duty to fight in the fourth and fifth.

What had happened? First of all, the forbidden had become the obligatory. From persecuting Christians the empire before long began to persecute heretics. It became increasingly difficult to identify the minority of 'true' Christians. In various interpretations the 'invisible Church' were seen as the Elect (chosen by God), the sincerely faithful (practised by humans), the 'religious' (who retained some social nonconformity) or – most visibly – the hierarchy.

Second, eschatology and ecclesiology swapped places. The confession that 'Jesus Christ is Lord' meant, for the early Christians, that in a largely hidden way Christ subdued even the rebellion of the principalities and powers under his lordship and used it for his ultimate purpose. With the conversion of Constantine, Christ's lordship was hidden no longer. Providence was now an object no longer of faith but of empirical observation. A Christian (and therefore Christians) ruled the world. The millennium was not a far-off dream but a present reality:

> Before Constantine, one knew as a fact of everyday experience that there was a believing Christian community but one had to 'take it on faith' that God was governing history. After Constantine, one had to believe without seeing that there was a community of believers, within the larger nominally Christian mass, but one knew for a fact that God was in control of history.[46]

Before the shift, the beleaguered Church represented God's providential working in the world. Afterwards, the empire supported the Church, and the success of the two went hand in hand. It was now the empire as a whole, rather than simply the Church, which made God's providence visible. There was no reason for the Church to confront society: its new duty was to support society. When faced with non-Christians outside the empire, the cause of throne and altar was identical; the outsider was the 'infidel'; the result was the crusade.

---

[45] Yoder, *The Priestly Kingdom* pp. 135–147.
[46] Ibid. p. 137.

Third, the ruler or emperor replaced Jesus as the norm for Christian social ethics. Ethics concerned what was possible for rulers to do in positions of power. Only a minimum standard of behaviour applied to all Christians; the state maintains justice and need not seek sanctity. The strenuous commands of Jesus were left to the 'religious'. What, after all, if everyone were to give all their money away or love their enemies? The trend is highly utilitarian, favouring what Yoder calls the 'engineering approach to ethics': 'Once the evident course of history is held to be empirically discernible, and prosperity of the regime is the measure of good, all morality boils down to efficacy. Right action is what works; what does not promise results can hardly be right.'[47]

Fourth, the prevailing metaphysic was dualist. The tension of the visible and the invisible, the personal and the structural, the natural and the revealed, the needs of justice and the counsels of the gospel: all these justified the new social arrangements. Interiorization and individualization were functional explanations and justifications for the displacement of the gospels as the primary authority for the ordering of the external world of the Christian community. The sovereignty of Jesus in Christian social practice became increasingly qualified by other values – power, mammon, fame, efficacy. Such other values, known as responsibility, nature, efficiency or wisdom tended to become part of the meaning of 'Christ', speaking where Jesus was silent or inappropriate.[48]

These four dimensions of 'Constantinianism' are significant because of their influence on the thinking of Hauerwas and of theologians in the Mennonite and believers' Church tradition.[49]

John Howard Yoder's influence on Hauerwas is also significant in the way he characterizes the way Christians have understood their role in society in *The Christian Witness to the State*. Yoder describes four principal approaches. The medieval view understands two kinds of persons each with their respective vocation. The saints, a small minority, act on the level of love. Those responsible for the economic and political function of the world can, indeed should, operate on a level of justice. This level of justice is fixed, attainable and knowable outside the revelation of the incarnate Christ: it is based on natural law. Lutheranism accepts the distinction between love and justice. Instead of dividing people into religious and lay, however, it sees all people in a tension between both levels, being nonresistant with the neighbour while justly following the 'orders of creation' in society. While as sinners Christians

---

[47] Ibid. p. 140.

[48] Ibid. pp. 85–86.

[49] J. Denny Weaver extends Yoder's analysis into the field of soteriology. Weaver argues that the 'classic' or 'victory over the powers' theory of the atonement, so prominent in the early Church, fell out of favour in the post-Constantine era. After the Church moved to a position within the mainstream of society, its theologians gradually acknowledged that the 'victory over the powers' theory had become irrelevant. This was not because of its demon imagery or the objections to tricking the devil, but because social circumstances had changed and confrontation was a distant memory. See J. Denny Weaver, 'Atonement for the NonConstantinian Church' *Modern Theology* 6 (July 1990) pp. 307–323.

can never attain perfect love, justice is possible. The Reformed thinkers dispensed with the distinction between reason (or nature) and revelation. It would be wrong for individuals to try to act in a more loving way than the entire people: to do so would deny their common responsibility for the civil order. If a government is unjust, the responsible Christian must rebel. Reinhold Niebuhr accepts the Greek and Roman insights which supplement Christian revelation to guide responsible witness to the state. He also accepts Luther's distinction between face-to-face relations and those of social responsibility. Justice is no longer a fixed quantity, but a balance between present practice and a line higher – but not so much higher as to make it irrelevant. The duality, such as it is, is between the Christian and sin.

Yoder argues that what these four approaches have in common is that they all formulate the problem in Constantinian terms. The issue is posed as if the only alternatives for the Christian were 'responsibility' or 'withdrawal'. 'Responsibility' is a slogan whose use assumes the loss of the Church's visible distinctiveness in order to leaven the whole of society. Thus the Church tries to formulate an ethic that will work as well for non-Christians as for Christians. The implications are subtle but considerable. 'Responsibility' assumes the Christian has a stake in the survival of the contemporary social order, an interest which surpasses what most of these thinkers acknowledge to be the law of nonresistant love found in the gospel. This law of love is no longer decisive but is substituted by a new autonomous moral absolute called 'responsibility'. In the name of 'responsibility', orders of creation, and natural law, Christians depart from Christian revelation when grounding the authority of their witness. There are held to be insights or ways of working which claim Christ-like authority yet which call people to do things that Christ does not call people to do. Each of these alternatives bases its social ethics and conception of justice on a reality other than the redemption that is in Christ.

The Constantinian formulations of Christian social ethics all assume that it is the Christian's duty to make the world come out right. They tend to posit metaphysical distinctions between the orders of creation and redemption or God-given levels of righteousness. They are also concerned to ensure survival by establishing a general, fundamental ethical norm which can be met by those who do not confess Jesus Christ as Lord as much as by those who can. This is what Hauerwas and Yoder are determined to avoid. Yoder's writing, which has been so deeply influential on Hauerwas, especially in the areas of ecclesiology and pacifism, presupposes a minority community. Yoder is not interested in public ethics – one cannot do 'ethics for anyone': 'The obedience of faith does not make sense apart from the context of faith. . . . Cross-bearing in the hope of resurrection, enemy love as a reflection of God's love, forgiving as one has been forgiven . . . do not make sense in the context of unbelief.'[50]

The duality in Christian social ethics is one not of orders but of agents: some believe and some do not. If the Christian knows and does the good on

---

[50] Yoder, 'Radical Reformation Ethics in Ecumenical Perspective' *The Priestly Kingdom* p. 110.

the strength of the forgiveness and regeneration of the gospel, how can one expect a society which has not encountered the gospel to do likewise? The resources for making such redeemed behaviour possible are lacking:

> The Christian is a person who ... by the power of God working in him or her is a new person. Conflict before was a normal built-in part of one's nature; but now the person has been disarmed ... The believer knows how to deal with [enmity] as with any other temptation – in repentance, confession, and spiritual victory.... We cannot impose [Christian behaviour] on entire nations ... We do not wait for the world to be ready to follow us before we follow Christ.[51]

It does require some subtlety to separate minority ethics from a world-denying tendency. Yoder does this with a thoroughly postmodern twist:

> The dominant moral views of any *known* world are oppressive, provincial or (to say it theologically) 'fallen'. This is true even if the terrain of the provincialism is large or the majority holding the views is great. There is no 'public' that is not just another particular province. We need a communal instrument of moral reasoning in the light of faith precisely to defend the decision-maker against the stream of conformity to his own world's self-evidence.[52]

In his attack upon the 'Constantinian' presuppositions of much Christian social ethics, Yoder points out as a cause for repentance that which is generally taken for granted. His essay 'The Kingdom as Social Ethic' is a discussion of the logic and psychology of weakness and how they differ from the logic and psychology of control. For instance, 'in a situation of majority control, if something happens it is because you let it happen and you are to blame for it, even for results which are partly evil'. Christians in majority or large- minority contexts often assume that 'perhaps the only way to do moral deliberation is to work out a consequentialist calculation of the direction one wants the whole social system to take'.[53] Ethics done by the weak looks very different:

> There are things that we cannot control, which are nonetheless going to happen. ... This means that it will be an expression of wisdom, and not of self-righteousness or unconcern or isolation, if we accept the fact that those deeds are going to be done and that we cannot stop them, and concentrate for ourselves on doing other things which no one will do. This looks to our friends of a majoritarian cast of mind like acquiescence in evil. It is; one of the differences between being powerful and powerless is that one has thought more about the fact that there are evils one cannot prevent.[54]

Yoder sums up his position in two pairs of questions. 'Instead of asking about one's action "if I do this how will it tip the scale ... ?", one rather asks "in a

---

[51] Yoder, 'Living the Disarmed Life' p. 43.

[52] Yoder, 'The Hermeneutics of Peoplehood' p. 40. In *The Politics of Jesus* he writes 'The Church does not attack the powers; this Christ has done. The Church concentrates on not being seduced by them' (p. 150).

[53] Yoder, 'The Kingdom as Social Ethic' *The Priestly Kingdom* pp. 96, 100.

[54] Ibid. p. 101.

situation in which I cannot tip the scales, on what other grounds might I decide what to do?" '[55] 'If everyone gave their wealth away what would we do for capital? If everyone loved their enemies who would ward off the Communists? . . . Such reasoning remains ludicrous wherever committed Christians accept realistically their minority status. Far more fitting than "What if everybody did it?" would be its inverse, "What if nobody else acted like a Christian, but we did?" '[56]

Christian ethics is therefore done by powerless people who recognize that their faithfulness will inevitably result in their being a minority community. It is not so much that they have renounced control as that the forms of life they have adopted mean that control is unlikely to come their way. They do not believe that the forces that determine the march of history are controlled by the leaders of the armies and markets, so it is not inevitable that Christians must become lords of the state and the economy so as to use that power towards the ends they consider desirable. Yoder roots the central theme of powerlessness squarely in the New Testament itself: 'The cross and not the sword, suffering and not brute power determines the meaning of history. The key to the obedience of God's people is not their effectiveness but their patience (Revelation 13:10). . . . The relationship between the obedience of God's people and the triumph of God's cause is not a relationship of cause and effect but one of cross and resurrection.'[57] In the worship life of the late New Testament Church is displayed the most desperate encounter of the Church's weakness – John in exile, Paul in prison – with the power of evil rulers. This, says Yoder, is simply a logical unfolding of the meaning and work of Jesus Christ himself, whose life followed suffering servanthood not violent lordship, who was 'so faithful to the enemy-love of God that it cost him all his effectiveness; he gave up every handle on history'.[58]

It is important to note that while faithfulness is a more important goal than effectiveness, the two are by no means in opposition, and many churches that have not claimed direct social significance or concern for society have often had the most social significance. Indeed to accept an opposition between faithfulness and effectiveness would be to accept a typology imposed by the 'responsibility' school. It is no more true to suppose that the 'responsible' use of power always gets results than to presume that minority faithfulness is by definition ineffective. Yoder details a number of ways in which social results can be a by-product of suffering love. The minority group can maintain awareness of an issue, doing jobs no one else is doing, until social circumstances alter to make the issue one of general concern. The Quaker experience of fair trading in the eighteenth century eventually rewarded faithfulness rather than effectiveness by creating a body of trust. Faithful minorities can move the public conscience, as with Mahatma Gandhi and Martin Luther King. They can represent those who have no one to speak

---

[55] Ibid.
[56] Yoder, *The Priestly Kingdom* p. 139.
[57] Yoder, *The Politics of Jesus* p. 232.
[58] Ibid. p. 233.

for them. They command respect when their social goals are in the interest of others.[59] Yoder's examples of the social significance of minority faith communities make it clear that in following the gospels' social ethic the Church is not withdrawing from public or political life. What the Christian withdraws from is the responsibility to transform society from the top down.[60]

The question of effectiveness is fundamentally an eschatological matter, as I shall explain in Chapter 7. For the story which is told by the consequentialist, and results in the conclusion that the Christian should take 'responsibility' for public life, is a story whose ending is premature. Hauerwas' understanding of ethics is teleological, that is, oriented to the end of the story, where the story is going, rather than in foreclosing the story by determining all consequences and thus being 'effective'.

In his more recent work, Hauerwas has come to an understanding that the contrast between faithfulness and effectiveness is a caricature arising from the shortcomings of the consequentialist perspective. How long a timescale does the consequentialist envisage? How often do things turn out as their perpetrators expect? It is, in the end unnecessary to have to choose between a faithfulness ethic and a principle ethic: since both are different forms of a principle ethic. In the same way, the contrast between pacifism and 'responsibility' is a contrast between two different eschatologies:

> The person who says, 'You must give up some of your scruples in order to be effective', is still saying that because the goal for the sake of which to be effective is *in principle* a good goal. So the argument which takes the clothing of 'principles versus effectiveness' really means this principle versus that principle. It really means that goal, for the sake of which I want you to give up other scruples, is so overridingly important that those other things are less important. That's an ethic of principle.... Likewise, the people who say 'You must simply be true to God' ... and 'let the heavens fall' ... really say that because of a conviction about Providence, trusting that if the heavens fall God has another better set of heavens ready, which is part of the process, so even that is not thumbing your nose at results. It's trusting God who gave the rules to know more about the results than we know. So I am increasingly convinced that the debate between the effectiveness ethic and the principle ethic is a false debate.[61]

---

[59] Yoder, *The Priestly Kingdom* pp. 96–99.

[60] This 'ad hoc politics' may be compared with the '*ad hoc* apologetics' discussed in Chapter 3. Yoder gives a social-ethical embodiment to Hauerwas' postliberal distrust of the 'large battalions' of systematic theology, rooted in the medieval era when Church and state were so close. See pp. 114–116 below for de Certeau's impressive contribution to this argument.

[61] Yoder, *Christian Attitudes to War, Peace and Revolution: A Companion to Bainton* (Elkhart Indiana: Goshen 1983) pp. 436–437, quoted in Hauerwas, 'Epilogue: A Pacifist Response to the Bishops' in Paul Ramsey, *Speak Up for Just War or Pacifism: A Critique of the United Methodist Bishop's Pastoral Letter 'In Defense of Creation'* (University Park: The Pennsylvania State Press 1988) p. 180. See also Hauerwas and William Willimon, *Resident Aliens: Life in the Christian Colony* (Nashville: Abingdon 1989) p. 46.

What this quotation from Yoder shows is that consequentialist criticisms of the ethic developed by Hauerwas are making ethical distinctions that are finally unsustainable. Hauerwas' pacifism is founded on the sovereignty of God and on faithfulness to the definitive practice of Jesus. There is no guarantee that a consequentialist calculation would be more catholic.

The tactic of the Church

Underlying most of the scholarly discussion of the issue of social engagement in the twentieth century has been an assumption that the language of the debate has been set by Ernst Troeltsch and H. Richard Niebuhr.[62] The rejection of their two typologies is the subtext of Hauerwas' polemic. Troeltsch assumes the 'church type' is superior to the 'sect type'; Niebuhr assumes (in practice if not in theory) the superiority of the 'Christ the transformer of culture' model. It is not at all clear that Troeltsch's typology is adequate to cover the nuances of a host of different positions; while Niebuhr's study is uncritical of the term 'culture', which begs the question of what culture is, and whether it is ever in the singular.[63]

By being tied into the 'responsibility' model, what both Troeltsch and Niebuhr miss is the subtle way that unity can be a construction imposed by the powerful. A key dimension of an eschatological understanding of unity is that it sees unity as a gift from God, not a static norm to be imposed. Hauerwas ties this insight into his thought in his introduction to *After Christendom*, where he employs a very helpful distinction made by Michel de Certeau.

De Certeau distinguishes between 'strategies' and 'tactics'. A strategy is any

> calculation (or manipulation) of power relationships that becomes possible as soon as a subject that will empower (a business, an army, a city, a scientific institution)

---

[62] Ernst Troeltsch, *The Social Teachings of the Christian Churches* (New York: Macmillan 1931) and H.R. Niebuhr, *Christ and Culture* (New York: Harper and Row 1951). In *Christian Existence Today* (p. 19 n. 2) Hauerwas quotes Troeltsch's definition of a sect: 'a voluntary society . . . (who) live apart from the world, are limited to small groups, emphasize the law instead of grace, and . . . set up the Christian order, based on love . . . in preparation for the coming Kingdom of God' (*The Social Teachings* II 993). See pp. 3–12 above for the wider context to the conflict with Troeltsch.

[63] See Duane Friesen, 'Normative Factors in Troeltsch's Typology of Religious Association' *Journal of Religious Ethics* 3/2 (Fall 1975) pp. 271–283. If Yoder can come up with seventeen varieties of religious pacifism, one might look for more subtleties in the larger area of relationship of Church and 'society'. See Yoder, *Nevertheless: Varieties of Religious Pacifism* (Scottdale: Herald 1992). In *Resident Aliens* (pp. 39–47) Hauerwas and Willimon refer to Yoder's more helpful threefold typology of the *activist* church (religiously-glorified liberalism), the *conversionist* church (oriented inward and thus religiously-glorified conservatism) and the *confessing* church (determined to worship Christ in all things). See Yoder, 'A People in the World: Theological Interpretation' in James Leo Garrett Jr. (ed.), *The Concept of the Believers' Church* (Scottdale: Herald 1969) pp. 252–283.

can be isolated. It postulates a *place* that can be delimited as its *own* and serve as the base from which relations with an *exteriority* composed of targets or threats (customers or competitors, enemies, the country surrounding the city, objectives and objects of research etc.) can be managed. As in management, every 'strategic' rationalization seeks first of all to distinguish its 'own place', that is, the place of its own power and will, from an 'environment'. A Cartesian attitude, if you wish: it is an effort to delimit one's own place in a world bewitched by the invisible powers of the Other. It is also the typical attitude of modern science, politics, and military strategy.'[64]

Hauerwas follows this quotation with an observation which I shall develop in Chapter 7. 'Strategy provides for a triumph of place over time insofar as it allows one to acquire advantages, to prepare for future expansions, and in general to create an independence against contingency'.[65] The key to Hauerwas' defence against charges of sectarianism lies here. Hauerwas enjoys expressions such as 'outside the church there is no salvation'.[66] To his detractors this sounds like downright sectarianism. But this would only be true if in his understanding the Church had a 'strategy'. Hauerwas maintains that on the contrary it is the *Constantinian* version of the Church that adopts a 'strategy', demarcating a world in which it is safe.

The Church that Hauerwas describes does not have that kind of power. Instead, it adopts a 'tactic'. A tactic, according to de Certeau, is a 'calculated action determined by the absence of a proper locus. No delineation of exteriority, then, provides it with the conditions necessary for autonomy. The space of a tactic is the space of the other, thus it must play on and with the terrain imposed on it and organized by the law of a foreign power.'[67] Hauerwas explains how a tactic does not form a general strategy: it makes *ad hoc* engagements and must take advantage of such opportunities that arise. It has no 'base where it can build up stockpiles for the next battle'. It is always on the hoof – at best a resident alien. The tactic is 'the art of the weak'.

Once the Church's social ethic is seen as tactic rather than strategy, the concept of withdrawal becomes meaningless. Whither is the Church to withdraw? There is no safe place, no citadel, no barricade to patrol. The Church is always occupying 'the space of the other'. In this regard the subtitles of two of Hauerwas' books – '*Church, World and Living in Between*' and '*Life in the Christian Colony*' are unfortunate. Such phrases only suggest that Hauerwas is a sectarian after all, because they imply a separate space. More in keeping is the subtitle of his '*Unleashing the Scripture*' – '*Freeing the Bible from Captivity to America*'.

---

[64] Michel de Certeau, *The Practice of Everyday Life* translated by Stephen Rendall (Berkeley: University of California Press 1988) pp. 35–36, quoted in Hauerwas, *After Christendom* pp. 16–17 (original italics).

[65] Hauerwas, *After Christendom* p. 17.

[66] See, for example, *After Christendom* Chapter 1.

[67] Quoted in ibid. pp. 17–18.

Thus Hauerwas' argument is that it is the Constantinian Church, rather than the community of character, that is sectarian. The Constantinian Church, like an army, marks out a territory that it can defend, considers the exterior in terms of targets and threats, and then makes forays across the boundary. I would add to Hauerwas' discussion that the community of character inhabits not a different space but a different time. This different time arises from the eschatological perspective, which I shall discuss in Chapter 7.

The imagination of the Church

Because Hauerwas' argument is so consistent, criticizing it tends to become a circular business. To criticize usually means to step out of a tradition to a supposedly neutral standpoint – which is the very habit Hauerwas doubts so much. In the rest of this chapter I shall discuss how the Christian narrative and practices form the Church. For if people are to develop character, and act out of habit rather than decision, they must be nurtured and formed. Hauerwas' writings in this area cover the whole of his career, but profit from being drawn together. Only a community can train people to take the right things for granted.

Seeing the world

The essay 'The Significance of Vision: Toward an Aesthetic Ethic' is such a landmark in Hauerwas' early work that it is worth outlining its argument in full.[68] It anticipates a transition that later takes place as Hauerwas' centre of gravity shifts from character to narrative. The transition outlined in this early article is from ethics as right action to ethics as the vision of God. Hauerwas describes how the ethical worlds people inhabit vary enormously. One cannot simply adjudicate correct choices based on an even assessment of the facts – for people act in the world that they see, and they see different worlds. It is not just that people select different facts from a common world: they actually see different worlds. One can only choose from within the world one sees. Ethics considers and recommends these different worlds, rather than different choices.

The important thing about the world one sees is that it should be the world as it really is. Virtue is the pursuit of this real world, divested of selfish consciousness. Ethics is directed toward seeing the Good without illusion or fantasy: only love enables us to see, in the unique particularity of circumstance, the key to ultimate destiny. In a phrase that anticipates Milbank, Murdoch describes love as 'the nonviolent apprehension of differences'.[69] Like great

---

[68] Hauerwas, *Vision and Virtue* pp. 30–47.

[69] Ibid. p. 39. See Iris Murdoch, 'The Sublime and the Good' *Chicago Review* 13 (Autumn 1959) p. 54. Compare John Milbank's phrase 'Christianity ... is the coding of transcendental difference as peace' *Theology and Social Theory* (Oxford: Blackwell 1990) pp. 5–6.

art, therefore, love shows aspects of reality to which fantasy or convention usually keep us blind. Love and art require us to allow the existence of things and persons other than ourselves. It is love that makes freedom possible: we learn to be free as we learn to respect and accept things and persons other than ourselves. Freedom is a matter of degree, not an absolute; it concerns the degree to which we respect difference and the other; in short, the degree to which we have adapted to reality. Murdoch's term for the process by which we learn to love the other as an equal is attention. To form our attention, and thus our vision, is a matter of 'moral imagination and moral effort'.[70]

Hauerwas draws two principal conclusions from his discussion. Each of them is picked up in his subsequent work on narrative. The first conclusion is that once vision becomes integral to ethics, the latter becomes not so much a debate about decisions as an attempt, through loving attention, to become more like the world that one sees. This point is developed in later work as Hauerwas more fully articulates his Christology under the guidance of Yoder. The reality of the world is disclosed by Jesus Christ, and it is the Christian's vocation to imitate God's way of dealing with the world as disclosed in the incarnate Son. The second conclusion is that 'attention' reaffirms the ethical commitment to the everyday and particular, by contrast with the temptation to concentrate on occasional crises.[71] The Christian life is constantly tested by its encounter with reality.

Vision drops out of Hauerwas' subsequent discussion to such an extent that it does not even register in the index of *The Peaceable Kingdom*. Why is this? The answer lies partly in the flaws in Hauerwas' early writing, and partly in the emergence of a new theme that absorbed the chief elements of vision.

Vision came in for criticism from some of Hauerwas' early critics. Gene Outka points out three ways in which an ethics of vision is incompatible with an ethics of character.[72] Thomas Ogletree correctly anticipates that issues of vision will be absorbed into the emerging category of narrative.[73] Wesley Robbins objects to Hauerwas' assertion that a total vision of life is a necessary

---

[70] Hauerwas, 'The Significance of Vision' p. 42.

[71] For illustrations of this from another perspective, see Janet Martin Soskice, 'Love and Attention' in Michael McGee (ed.) *Philosophy, Religion and Spiritual Life* (Cambridge: Cambridge University Press 1991) p. 61.

[72] Outka's concerns are (a) that Hauerwas has talked of the self as agent whereas Murdoch criticizes this; (b) that Murdoch's notion of submission to a vision of reality sits uneasily with human freedom (one can see the influence of Simone Weil here); (c) that Murdoch sees the ego as the enemy of the moral life whereas Hauerwas' early work inclines more toward seeing the enemy as human passivity. Murdoch's understanding of human freedom is largely derived from Simone Weil. For further discussion of freedom, see pp. 23–28 above. For Outka's criticisms, see Gene Outka, 'Character, Vision, and Narrative' *Religious Studies Review* 6/2 (April 1980) pp. 110–118. Hauerwas moves in Murdoch's direction and away from his emphases in *Character and the Christian Life* on all of these issues.

[73] Thomas Ogletree, 'Character and Narrative: Stanley Hauerwas' Studies of the Christian Life' *Religious Studies Review* 6/1 (January 1980) pp. 24–30.

precondition of having any specific morality at all.[74] Most of the criticisms hint at the interminable underlying tension between the (broadly Platonic) vision of the good and the (broadly Aristotelian) commitment to the pragmatic outworking of theory in the everyday. Hauerwas' increasing sympathy with theologians such as Lindbeck who concentrate on the detail of cultural practice and with philosophers such as Midgely who affirm the complexity of human life inclines him in an Aristotelian direction. Murdoch's own response to this tension is found largely in the detail of her novels.

I suggest that more important than these criticisms is a general broadening of Hauerwas' understanding of the ethical background – what might be called the prolegomena of morality. In his later work he is less anxious to distance himself from decisionists, and more aware of the communal dimension of moral discernment. What he once focused on as moral vision, he comes to see as part of the whole area of the moral imagination. Imagination encompasses both vision and projected action, both formation and instinct. In the following quotation one can see that his earlier interest in Murdoch's notion of attention is alive and well, but now thoroughly assimilated into his category of narrative:

> There is perhaps no more serious Christian offence than to fail in imagination, that is, to abandon or forget the resources God has given us as the means of calling us to his kingdom.
>
> The Christian community lives through a hope fastened on the imaginative world created by God. . . . His reality as the Christ is the resource empowering Christians with the courage to create the necessity of being a peaceable people in a violent world. . . . Christians live on hope and learn to trust in an imagination disciplined by God's peaceable kingdom into accepting the cross as the alternative to violence. Our imagination is the very means by which we live morally, and our moral life is in truth the source of our imagination.[75]

In this and several other places Hauerwas suggests that imagination may rightly take the place in Christian ethics that he had once earmarked for vision. Imagination is the active, inward assimilation of the insights of vision.

---

[74] Robbins claims (a) that Hauerwas' understanding of morality as a 'total vision of life' is as restrictive as those theories Hauerwas opposes – do we, for example, exclude those whose lives are disorganized? (Hauerwas replies that a vision of life is not a *sine qua non* for having morality, but simply a way of affirming the cohesiveness of the Christian story); (b) that theists and polytheists may often act in similar ways (Hauerwas responds that this statement does not therefore mean they have the same morality: to suggest so would artificially separate what people do from why they do it); (c) that Hauerwas' understanding leads to moral relativism (Hauerwas does not provide a theory against moral relativism: he simply challenges people to live out the implications of their position). See J. Wesley Robbins, 'On the Role of Vision in Morality' and Hauerwas, 'Learning to See Red Wheelbarrows: On Vision and Relativism' *Journal of the American Academy of Religion* 45 (1977) pp. 623–641 and 643–655. See also Paul Nelson, *Narrative and Morality: A Theological Enquiry* (University Park and London: The Pennsylvania State University Press 1987) Chapter 7.

[75] Hauerwas, *Against the Nations* p. 59.

It would help Hauerwas' argument a great deal if he were to distinguish between what might be called the everyday imagination, which enables one to see and interpret the world, and the more creative imagination, which enables one to perceive what the world *might* be. When this distinction has been made it becomes easier to see the tension in the Hauerwas' ethics. On the one hand lies that which is in the nature of human society – doing most things by habit, sharing assumptions between members of a community, not being aware of most of the decisions one has made – in short, what I have earlier described as 'narrative from below'. On the other hand lie the themes of Hauerwas' later period – the particularities and distinctive claims of the Christian story, the challenge nonviolence makes to the imagination, the significance of martyrdom: these correspond rather more with the Barthian character of the postliberal 'narrative from above'. The first category moves away from an ethics of decision toward an ethics of habit; the second category suggests that these habits, though perhaps undemonstrative, may well be very distinctive, and very hard to develop. Hauerwas moves from commending an ethic of character to recommending what specific character that ethic should have. It is important to recognize that both of these steps involve the moral imagination.

Are the two sets of arguments reconcilable? I suggest they are, and that the point at issue is that identified in Hauerwas' early essay on Murdoch, 'The Significance of Vision'. The key to the tension lies in what one perceives to be the first task of ethics. For Murdoch, ethical debate is less about choices than about different worlds. Moral theologians and philosophers seek to commend the world that they see as the true one. In Hauerwas' later work, he is more influenced by the postliberal claim that the scriptural world is the real world, and thus he elaborates how Christians are to live in this world.[76] The important point is that for Hauerwas the moral effort takes place in terms of Christian *formation* – the establishment and maintenance of communities of character; Christian *practice*, by contrast, which others see as an agony of moral choice, is for Hauerwas more a matter of habit and instinct – of not realizing, for example, that some time ago one did without thinking what others might regard as an act of great courage.[77] The creative side of the imagination is largely about forming people of character. Moments of moral crisis, by contrast, are emphatically *not* moments of creativity: they are times for doing the obvious – or what has come to seem obvious within the creative formation by the Christian narrative. For example, the practices of nonviolence can only be maintained by people who have become used to establishing other means of resolving

---

[76] 'Intratextual theology redescribes reality within the scriptural framework rather than translating Scripture into extrascriptural categories. It is the text, so to speak, that absorbs the world, rather than the world the text' (Lindbeck, *The Nature of Doctrine* p. 118).

[77] I am grateful to Ben Quash for helping me to clarify the relation between moral imagination and moral effort in Hauerwas' work.

conflict: nonviolence is not a spontaneous one-off tactic to disarm an attacker.

In *The Peaceable Kingdom* Hauerwas, in contrast to the general Roman Catholic tradition, recasts the practice of casuistry as an imaginative enterprise. The novelty of associating casuistry with the imagination perhaps reflects a number of misconceptions about imagination and morality. As Hauerwas points out in his essay 'On Keeping Theological Ethics Imaginative',[78] the field of imagination is customarily associated with spontaneity, originality, creativity, the artist, the unexpected, the unpredictable – a world not subject to discipline and necessity, a world full of wayward but tolerated individuals, a world which challenges, threatens and disrupts the established conventions of our social morality. By contrast the field of morality is that of fulfilling expectations, furthering the common good of society, keeping obligations and maintaining trust, staying in the real world, not escaping to an imaginary one.

According to Hauerwas, this dichotomy is a false one. It makes several very doubtful assumptions. Imagination is not the unique preserve of a few talented individuals but a necessity for the whole Christian community. It does not depend entirely on the inspiration of the moment but can be developed through training. Christian ethics is not primarily about fulfilling expectations of the common good of society: many of the conventions of our social morality need threatening and disrupting. Maintaining trust is not a virtue in itself: it depends on the parties maintaining the trust and what practices are required to maintain it. Staying in the real world presupposes that ontological reality corresponds with the necessities of the passing moment – even though retrospect, let alone eschatology, suggests otherwise.

Hauerwas maintains that it is not the task of Christian ethics to underpin the social *status quo*. Rather its task is to describe the world in which Christians perceive themselves to live and act, and to help the Christian community form practices consistent with life in such a world. When ethics is understood as the adjudication of tricky cases of conscience by balancing moral principles, the practice is implicitly socially conservative – since it assumes there is nothing fundamentally wrong with the *status quo*, only with its anomalies. In contrast, the Christian community lives within a tradition based on a story which in many respects contradicts the assumptions of the contemporary social *status quo*. How then does the community faithfully live out its story? This is the field of casuistry. Casuistry, for Hauerwas, is

> the process by which a tradition tests whether its practices are consistent (that is, truthful) or inconsistent in the light of its basic habits and convictions or whether these convictions require new habits and behaviour. . . . We . . . only recognize certain dangers and challenges because we have been trained to do so by the narrative that has bound our lives. It is true that in the beginning we perhaps do not recognize such dangers to be part of the narrative but as we 'grow into the

---

[78] Hauerwas, *Against the Nations* pp. 51–60.

story' we see more fully its implications. Casuistry is the reflection by a community on its experience to test imaginatively the often unnoticed and unacknowledged implications of its narrative commitments.[79]

Once a community has made a prior commitment that, for instance, the kingdom of God embodied in Jesus demands a response which must be nonviolent, imagination is essential if Christian practice is to be delivered from a callous self-righteousness which preserves its own integrity at the expense of the welfare of others. Many pacifists assume, like those they oppose, that it is the armies and markets that determine the meaning of history. It is possible for a community to deny that this is the case; but it takes imagination for such a community to live as if it believes that it is the cross, rather than the armies or markets, that determines history's meaning. Such a commitment assumes the formation of people used to the practices of nonviolence. Ethics in a given situation then becomes less a matter of making a decision than of using the imagination (informed by a truthful narrative) to describe the situation in a perspective that enables the community to act in a manner consistent with its moral commitments and habits. This perspective may well reveal that less in the situation is 'given' than at first appeared.

It is in the area of how to form this imagination in a community that gaps in Hauerwas' work are most noticeable. His essays on the various ways it is done are spread across the twenty-five years of his career, but have never found the focus they require. If truth is to be assessed by performance, more needs to be demonstrated of the way the Christian narrative brings about Christian communities whose character is formed such that their habits are more significant than their decisions. Nonetheless, Hauerwas has made forays into this territory, and it is time to discuss these.

Worship

How does Hauerwas believe the Church should go about forming the character of Christians? The most instructive place to begin is to recall that Hauerwas is himself an educator, charged with forming the character of those called to be Methodist ministers. How does he teach Christian ethics to them?

In a fascinating essay, worthy of expansion into something much longer, Hauerwas outlines how he structures his course at Duke University. He recognizes the degree of confusion about what power ordination confers; but perceives that the one thing all ministers do is lead their congregations in worship. If all the aspects of the Christian life are of value to the extent that they build up the Church, then the Church is definitively embodied when it gathers for worship. Holiness is the way Christians seek to imitate the character of God, and holiness is what Christians seek in worship. Ethics arises

---

[79] Hauerwas, *The Peaceable Kingdom* p. 120.

at the intersection between knowledge of God and knowledge of one's human self. The interdependence of the two is a feature of worship. In worship the Church is 'made part of God's praise and joy'. It is this joy that principally distinguishes the Church from the world. The task of ethics is 'to assemble reminders from the training we receive in worship that enable us to rightly see the world and to perceive how we continue to be possessed by the world'.[80]

Hauerwas organizes the course around the movement of the eucharistic liturgy. The congregation gathers and greets, then confesses the sins that inhibit community and fail to reflect God's character. The Scripture is proclaimed, and the hearers respond through baptism. They make an offering, then share the eucharistic sacrifice. Finally, they are sent forth.

Gathering focuses on ecclesiology. Gathering is eschatological, since it foreshadows the unity of the saints. It points to the scandal of those who are not present, particularly those who have been excluded ('Eleven o'clock remains the most segregated hour in North Carolina'). Greeting focuses on the name of God – Father, Son and Holy Spirit – and the recognition that theology is primarily about the character of God, rather than our own characters. Confession is the place where the role of the virtues emerges. It is placed in the context of the penitential tradition derived from Matthew 18:15ff. The practice of proclamation discloses the importance of authority and the character and virtues required for such a ministry. This leads to further discussion on the place of the virtues. Baptism is the response to proclamation: baptism addresses the Christological character of ethics, and the way the sacraments maintain the unity between Christ and the Church. Suicide, abortion, marriage and sex are discussed here. Then to the eucharist, which sums up all that has gone before: the sharing of Christ's body is the place to consider issues of economic justice and the ethics of war. Finally the sending forth commissions the congregation to serve the world: this can never be as a sect, but neither does it mean unqualified loyalty to a state. What is required is the skill that has been developed in worship – and in this course.

This course outline shows much more thoroughly than any of Hauerwas' other essays the overall coherence of his project. The great themes of his work are set in an appropriate context. This is not a method abstracted from both the details of life and the revealed character of Scripture and tradition: instead this is a demonstration of how a community shapes its whole life around the God it believes in. Largely missing from the outline is the lengthy engagement with other ethicists, and particularly the onslaught against liberalism, which tend to make the constructive proposals difficult to see. These are no doubt heavily present in the course itself, but a Hauerwas essay shorn of them is a rare treasure. The emphasis on worship brings together themes and hints across the whole body of Hauerwas' work: habits, community, practices, memory and eschatology; the balance between witness and service, between distinctiveness and universal claims; and the presence of the stranger.

---

[80] Hauerwas, *In Good Company: The Church as Polis* (Notre Dame and London: University of Notre Dame Press 1995) p. 156.

The stranger becomes a key figure in Hauerwas' assessment of his colleague Will Willimon's sermons in Duke Chapel. Hauerwas considers the Greek tradition of hospitality. Strangers might not share the stories that shaped civic occasions, but could nonetheless join in the festivals and perhaps contribute additional stories. Barbarians were those who could not hear the Greeks' stories, and thus had to be killed. For Christians, says Hauerwas, 'there are many strangers but no barbarians'. Because Christianity is widely presumed to concern people's private lives, and politics is largely concerned with achieving co-operation between strangers, 'most preaching is done before strangers'.[81]

This fact makes preaching highly problematic – for the temptation will always be to translate the Christian story into the established habits of the hearers, and cease to seek transformation of preacher and hearer. Yet Hauerwas has published an increasing number of his own sermons, despite his awareness of the drawbacks of extracting the sermon from its proper setting in worship. It is arguable that the essay, as a genre, is open to some of the uncomfortable assumptions that Alasdair MacIntyre identifies with the lecture.[82] In this sense the sermon offers Hauerwas the freedom to be more confessional in style. He talks of the need to display his convictions in an appropriate manner: yet surely it would be more consistent to concentrate on a more explicitly communal exercise than proclamation by a preacher. He does this most successfully in his essay 'The Ministry of a Congregation', where he considers a board meeting at a local United Methodist Church.[83]

What is so far lacking in Hauerwas' writing is a substantial treatment of how the moral imagination is formed over time. The broad outlines are in place: the emphasis on the centrality of forgiveness, offering and receiving, is widespread in his work; the way a commitment to nonviolence shapes the life of a community is frequently illustrated; the way discipleship is best compared to apprenticeship and the role of saints as great artisans; and the way worship determines the shape of practice has been detailed in the essay already quoted.[84] Yet Hauerwas has not yet shown how these ingredients can be integrated in a larger educational programme. Most of his comments about education concern how difficult it is and how little Christians share with some of the academic principles of liberal democracies, and how easy it can be to lose sight of the truth.[85] His writing is at its most attractive when he

[81] Hauerwas, *Preaching to Strangers* pp. 5–6.

[82] Alasdair MacIntyre, *Three Rival Versions of Moral Enquiry* (London: Duckworth 1990) pp. 216–236.

[83] Hauerwas, *Christian Existence Today* pp. 111–132.

[84] On forgiveness, see Hauerwas, *The Peaceable Kingdom* pp. 87–91, *Unleashing the Scripture* pp. 140–148, *Dispatches from the Front* Chapter 2. On nonviolence, see *Against the Nations* pp. 107–121. *Christian Existence Today* pp. 67–99, 253–266. On discipleship, see *After Christendom* pp. 93–112.

[85] See Hauerwas, *Christian Existence Today* pp. 221–236, Stanley Hauerwas and John Westerhoff (eds.), *Schooling Christians: 'Holy Experiments' in American Education* (Grand Rapids: Eerdmans 1992) pp. 214–234.

makes constructive proposals for how to train disciples and when he describes circumstances in which disciples are tested and grow.

Summary

The single characteristic that summarizes the journey from community to the Church is nonviolence. This is the last of Hauerwas' key themes to emerge – after virtue, character, narrative, truthfulness and community – but it becomes the theme that underpins all the others. Hence Hauerwas begins to look like a sectarian when he advocates the distinct character of the Christian story; but in time it becomes clear that what is at stake is the way the 'responsible' Church accommodates violence in a way that Hauerwas' 'faithful' Church could never do. There are six principal claims involved in his ecclesiology.

First, the practices of peace are the way the Church imitates Christ and thus opens itself to the kingdom by acknowledging the sovereignty of God. The more false one's god is, the more one needs violence to protect it. Hauerwas has no doubt that in advocating nonviolence he is being faithful to the gospels, and he rejects the criticism that this has not always been the interpretation of the church as a whole: 'Show me where I am wrong about God, Jesus, the limits of liberalism, the nature of the virtues, or the doctrine of the Church – but do not shortcut that task by calling me a sectarian.'[86]

Second, a commitment to peace creates a disciplined community which has to use all its imagination formed by Christian Scripture and tradition to form a politics by which it can live. Pacifism creates politics, because it requires the establishment of practices for resolving disputes short of violence. It rejects the assumption that all politics is ultimately a cover for violence.

Third, the Church best serves the world by remaining a distinct community with a strong sense of its own identity. If it believes its story to be true, ontologically as well as historically, then the painfully time-consuming practices of peace are of greater worth than the apparently responsible haste into government. The first task of the Church is to develop these practices which accord with its gospel.

Fourth, the danger of a social ethic which seeks to control the world from the top down is that it is always in danger of replacing God's sovereignty with the sovereignty of something or somebody else. Yoder's characterization of Constantinianism is controversial, but in its details it is not essential to Hauerwas' argument. Power is not an evil unless it is assumed that power is required for the imitation of God. Hauerwas' treatment of the temptation narratives is seminal.

Fifth, it is not the Church that is sectarian, for the Church has no walls and crosses every frontier. Instead, it is the nation-states that are sectarian in their demand that one Christian should kill another in the name of abstract

---

[86] Hauerwas, *Christian Existence Today* p. 8.

ideas such as the right to self-determination. This is a strong but flawed argument, since a great many people have died in history for belonging to the wrong Church.

Sixth, there is an embryonic argument, which I shall develop in Chapter 7. A commitment to nonviolence is ultimately an eschatological belief that the God who does not always at present intervene to right wrongs and heal wounds will ultimately do so. It is this faith in the ultimate justice of the world that abolishes the distinction between faithfulness and effectiveness and enables the Church to care for the world even when unable to cure it.

Four abiding areas remain for Hauerwas to expand upon. A fuller display of the Holy Spirit would clarify the relationship between the definitive work of Jesus and the ongoing role of the Church. Given the emphasis on the internal politics of the Church, more stories and description of this politics would be helpful. Meanwhile, since there has been a thorough discussion of the distinction between Church and world, some more particular examples of how the Church can engage faithfully would finally lay to rest the charges of sectarianism. Lastly, it would be helpful to have more illustration of how the moral imagination of the Church is formed over time.

6

Performing the Church's Story

The faithful Church

Chapters 2, 3, 4 and 5 of this book form a story: a story that starts with the dilemmas of the individual and ends with the practices and faith of the Church. I have chosen to tell a story, not because it describes an exact chronological progression in Hauerwas' thought, but because a narrative best expresses the way Hauerwas' mature position grows out of his early commitments. In this chapter I shall summarize what has gone before in a more systematic way.

One of the most regular features of Hauerwas' writing is his constant frustration with the shortcomings and pretensions of liberal–democratic ways of thinking – the 'story that we have no story'.[1] In this book as a whole, and in this chapter in particular, I hope to draw out Hauerwas' more constructive position, and thus understand the nature of his criticisms and why he makes them. In the process it will become easier to understand the origin of the most common criticisms of his position and how he sets about addressing them.

In keeping with the style of this book and the body of Hauerwas' work, I shall illustrate the conclusions of this chapter and explore Hauerwas' proposals as a whole by considering a 'test case': do Hauerwas' descriptions of and prescriptions for the Church match the story of a particular community of character? The story of a particular village in Vichy France will help to answer this question.

Summary of Hauerwas' constructive proposals

We can summarize the positive proposals of Hauerwas' theological ethics in five theses.

1. Stanley Hauerwas believes in the *holy God* who has revealed himself through the patriarchs, through Moses and the Exodus, through the joys and struggles of Israel, through Jesus and the coming of the Spirit, and through the Church. He believes in the sovereignty of this God, in the way God rules

---

[1] Hauerwas, *A Community of Character* p. 12.

through creation, providence and coming *eschaton*, in the definitive way God shows the character of his kingdom in the crucifixion and resurrection of Jesus Christ. Hauerwas also recognizes that the creation is not all that it was intended to be, that sin has infected the world to such a degree that, even after the coming of the Son of God, human projects are invariably subject to pride, jealousy and fear.[2]

2. Hauerwas maintains that the holy character of the God of Jews and Christians is not self-evident from the workings of nature or the moral law in the human heart or the collective yearnings of humankind. Instead, it is revealed in a *holy story*, the story of Israel, Jesus and the Church, begun in the Scriptures and developed through the history of the Church. From this story Christians learn that God is revealed through human contingency. This means that human contingency is the location for understanding both the character of God and the nature of human response. The way Jesus went to the cross, despite the pressing demands that the world be saved some other way, is the definitive part of the holy story.[3]

3. Though these two convictions underlie his constructive position, Hauerwas does not elaborate on them in great detail. Instead he concentrates on the human response to revelation. Christians are called to be a *holy people*, the communion of saints, imitating the character of the one, sovereign, holy God. Like Israel and Jesus before them, the Church's vocation is to imitate God[4] – to be perfect even as the heavenly Father is perfect.[5] Christian ethics is about forming the human response to God's revelation. And the human response is the Church – a holy people, a historical community.

It is this conviction that lies behind Hauerwas' assault upon the conventional approach to ethics. Ethics is too often a matter of forming principles or guidelines that work regardless of what kind of person is putting them into practice. Yet the kind of person involved is, for Hauerwas, precisely what matters.[6] Actions are good if they lead to the formation of good people;[7] good people are those who imitate the reconciling, serving character of God;[8] to sustain such people, and to teach them the holy story that reveals God's character, requires a community;[9] and that community must begin by being nonviolent, because Christ was, and because refusing to use force demonstrates faith that God, rather than the means of force, is sovereign.

---

[2] For a view of sin, see Hauerwas, *Suffering Presence* pp. 147–148.

[3] See particularly Hauerwas, *The Peaceable Kingdom* pp. 78–79.

[4] Ibid. pp. 76–86.

[5] See also Yoder, *The Politics of Jesus* pp. 116–117 and 225.

[6] See, for example, Hauerwas, *A Community of Character* pp. 114–115, *Truthfulness and Tragedy* pp. 15–39.

[7] Hauerwas, *Character and the Christian Life* pp. xxiii.

[8] Hauerwas, *The Peaceable Kingdom* p. 81.

[9] Hauerwas, *A Community of Character* pp. 9–35.

The key to faithful performance by the community is that its witness is peaceful.[10] The uniqueness of Jesus lies fundamentally in his acceptance of the cross as the way of disarming the powers that oppress us, and in the vindication of his nonviolent witness in the resurrection. Christ is at the centre of Hauerwas' theology, in so far as Christ inaugurates and makes possible the peaceable kingdom – the nonviolent witness of the Christian community.[11] It is a mistake to speak of Christ in a way that might suggest the New Testament reveals a redeemer independent of the Church. The fact that the New Testament communicates the Christ that was known to the early Church is, to Hauerwas, its virtue rather than its flaw. For in ecclesiology lies Hauerwas' epistemology and his Christology.

The Church is called to be holy in the way that Jesus is holy: it should be wary of the temptation to control the wider society, since this invariably results in setting up some norm other than Jesus as the path for all to follow.[12] The resort to violence indicates a lack of trust in God, a lack of faith in his definitive revelation in Jesus. In order to avoid resorting to violence, the Church must set up a form of politics which creates the right kind of conflict – thus showing the rest of creation that politics is not simply a cover for violence. The politics of the Church is based on the practices of forgiveness.[13]

Hauerwas resists all efforts to bypass the historical Christian community as the focus of God's purpose in the world. Hence the Bible is not self-explanatory, but is holy in the sense that it conveys the holy story to the holy people.[14] Hence also the social purpose of the Church does not lie in creating 'a more just America', or any such thing, but in witnessing to a truthful way of living by embodying the holy story.[15] The relation of the Church to the state is significant, and it has a bearing on the kind of ethic the Church espouses.[16] Meanwhile if the Christian community, reflecting the character of God, is the centre of ethical reflection, then the Enlightenment emphasis on moral rationality becomes secondary. Things are no longer expected to be true or right for 'any thinking person' (the conventional 'neutral observer'):[17] and this opens the door to many people excluded by the rationality of the Enlightenment but included by the Church, such as the mentally handicapped, infants and the mentally ill.[18]

4. The questions in ethics should focus on what kind of person one wants (or is called) to be. One will want to develop practices that help to make one such a person, and learn to see the world as such a person would. This process

---

[10] Hauerwas, *Against the Nations* pp. 101.
[11] Hauerwas, *The Peaceable Kingdom* pp. 81–91, *A Community of Character* pp. 36–52.
[12] See especially Yoder, *The Politics of Jesus* pp. 1–20.
[13] Hauerwas, *Christian Existence Today* pp. 89–99.
[14] Hauerwas, *Unleashing the Scripture* pp. 15–38.
[15] Hauerwas, *After Christendom* pp. 45–68, *Against the Nations* pp. 122–131.
[16] Hauerwas, *Against the Nations* pp. 122–131, *Christian Existence Today* pp. 171–190.
[17] Hauerwas, *Truthfulness and Tragedy* pp. 15–39.
[18] Hauerwas, *Vision and Virtue* pp. 187–194, *Truthfulness and Tragedy* pp. 147–168.

is the formation of Christian *character*. Character is where Hauerwas begins his work, with his doctoral thesis;[19] and he returns to this theme again and again. Character is most fully displayed in the way a person or a community responds to adversity. For example a person of character may show great courage by acting in a way that, for another person, might simply be recklessness.[20] In the face of death, a community of character does not assume that life is the only criterion of value;[21] in the face of martyrdom, the person of character recognizes that some things are indeed worth dying for.[22] In the face of the stranger – the undesired pregnancy, the retarded baby – the community of character recognizes the contingency and gift of all forms of life, and affirms that the Church is a form of community prior to the family.[23] Self-deception is a lurking trap, and only the truthful story of God can enable Christians to be truthful about their own stories.[24] Novels and many other sources provide stirring accounts of character and the ways it is formed.[25]

5. The Church seeks to reflect the character of the God revealed in the Christian story. In order to do so, it develops particular *habits* and *practices* modelled on its understanding of *virtue*. Just as one needs to study and train if one is to be a medical doctor,[26] or to do an apprenticeship if one is to be a good bricklayer,[27] or to learn skills of community-forming if one is to be a scholar in a healthy university,[28] so one needs to practise with experts if one is to become a Christian disciple.[29] Hauerwas' early work on Aristotle, Aquinas and Barth frequently reappears as he develops the relationship of virtue to the practices of the peaceable kingdom. Cautious about the way love can become an abstraction,[30] and starting from a position of faith, Hauerwas concentrates on hope. The key hopeful virtue is that of patience.[31] From watching others raise lemurs or play baseball,[32] one can learn the

---

[19] Hauerwas, *Character and the Christian Life* pp. 83–128. Though Hauerwas begins with character, he does so because of the connection he sees between Aquinas' recovery of Aristotle and Barth's theological agenda.

[20] Hauerwas and Pinches, *Christians Among the Virtues* pp. 149–165, *A Community of Character* p. 114.

[21] Hauerwas, *Truthfulness and Tragedy* pp. 101–115.

[22] Hauerwas, *Christian Existence Today* pp. 199–220.

[23] Hauerwas, *A Community of Character* pp. 167–174.

[24] Hauerwas, *Truthfulness and Tragedy* pp. 82–98, *A Community of Character* pp. 129–152.

[25] Hauerwas *Dispatches from the Front* pp. 31–88.

[26] Hauerwas, *Truthfulness and Tragedy* pp. 184–202.

[27] Hauerwas, *After Christendom* pp. 93–112.

[28] Hauerwas, *Christian Existence Today* pp. 237–252.

[29] Hauerwas, *Resident Aliens* p. 126.

[30] Hauerwas, *Vision and Virtue* pp. 11–29, 111–126.

[31] Hauerwas, The Peaceable Kingdom pp. 135–142, Hauerwas and Pinches, *Christians Among the Virtues* pp. 113–128, 166–178.

[32] Hauerwas, *Christian Existence Today* pp. 253–266.

time-consuming nature of that which is done well: thus worship[33] and having children,[34] two time-consuming activities, gain great significance in a patient community. Every society will gain from having communities that honour honour: the Church helps wider society not by leaving the practice of virtue in order to enter the world of hasty achievement, but by improving its own practice of virtue.

Summary of the principal criticisms of Hauerwas' work

Having drawn out in five movements the principal lines of Hauerwas' theological ethics, I shall now summarize the principal criticisms of his work under the same five themes.

1. In his orthodox Christian realism, Hauerwas comes under familiar criticism from those who consider Christian truth-claims to be inadequate. This is especially focused by the way Hauerwas has been associated with the postliberal theologians George Lindbeck and Hans Frei. Postliberals have many critics: there are of course those who refuse to acknowledge any of the serious hermeneutical issues raised in the last three centuries; more significantly there are those who allege that postliberalism rests on claims it cannot justify. In the latter group, the claim is that unless one makes a detailed explanation of what one means by revelation, one should not hide behind its apparent certainties. A further claim is that unless one details the ontology behind one's theological statements, one looks like a *fideist* – one who believes without rational grounds.[35] Hauerwas does not speak much about revelation or ontology, and thus he has been called a fideist. A more constructive criticism, that does justice to his whole theology, concerns whether he adequately details the relationship between the centrality of the Church and the finality of Christ, and whether he could elaborate upon his theology of the Holy Spirit.[36]

2. In his commitment to antifoundationalist narrative theology, Hauerwas comes in for further criticism. Is there such a thing as 'the Christian story'? Even with regard to the Bible, different denominations recognize different collections as the definitive canon. And is it one story? Do the different books witness to a variety of stories, some more complementary than others, and do the different styles of books witness to a variety of understandings of the genre of revelation? Who decides, and is the story in any case controlled by those who have generally told it – generally white educated males? Should one not abandon the notion of a single all-encompassing narrative, when

---

[33] Hauerwas, *In Good Company* pp. 153–168.
[34] Hauerwas, *Truthfulness and Tragedy* pp. 147–156, *A Community of Character* pp. 155–174, see Chapter 8 below.
[35] See pp. 77–89 above.
[36] See pp. 97–98 above.

such a story has led in the past to such violence? How wide can the variety of understandings be before the notion of 'story' becomes incoherent? What justification is there for regarding some texts as more significant than others – why for example does Hauerwas concentrate on the synoptic gospels and particularly on the passion? Meanwhile since the Scriptures were written, the Church has provided a huge diversity of ways of interpreting them. Does this not undermine the truth-claims of the 'story'? Because Hauerwas is quiet on ontology, he is accused of being a *relativist* who can give no reason why Christianity should be more worthy of adherence than any other virtuous form of life. If there is no universal court of appeal, how can stories (and their communities) communicate? Where is the proof that Christianity is true, story or not? Why should one read this story, rather than another?[37]

3. Perhaps the loudest criticisms have come in the third area. Hauerwas, it is said, leaves the world to itself as if it were unclean and advocates a *sectarian* concentration on the enclosed Christian community. In the process, he develops a world-denying theology which lacks a doctrine of creation, and seriously undervalues the priceless qualities of the liberal democracy so many strove so long to establish. He gives no indication of how Christians are to emerge from their self-imposed ghetto, and his views, if widely implemented, would probably return liberal nations to inter-religious conflict. He gives no indication of how his ethic can be translated into legislation, and he implies that Christians who have worked hard to attain positions of influence in society should not be there. His view that nonviolence is required by the passion of Jesus has not been borne out by the majority of the Church's practice over the centuries; nonviolence would make the Church a parasite on the rest of society when a serious threat such as Hitler came along. He too readily adopts from Yoder the caricature of 'Constantinianism', which does little justice to the complexities of social ethics; and he and Yoder misconstrue the work of Reinhold Niebuhr and others in making Christianity relevant to contemporary America. He offers no suggestion of how America should use her influential place in the world for positive ends. His understanding of Christian community is idealized, and bears little relation to contemporary, rootless society.[38]

4. The criticisms of the stress on character come largely from those who feel that ethics is still primarily about decisions and choices, and the *principles* and

---

[37] See above, Chapter 4. See also Julian Hartt, 'Theological Investments in Story: Some Comments on Recent Developments and Some Proposals' and 'Reply to Crites and Hauerwas' *Journal of the American Academy of Religion* 52 (1984) pp. 117–130 and 149–156. From a feminist perspective, see Gloria Albrecht, *The Character of our Communities*, which I have discussed in pp. 68–73 above.

[38] See especially Wilson Miscamble, 'Sectarian Passivism?'; Michael Quirk, 'Beyond Sectarianism?' *Theology Today* 44 (April 1987) pp. 69–77 and 78–86; James Gustafson, 'The Sectarian Temptation: Reflections on Theology, Church and the University' *Proceedings of the Catholic Theological Society* 40 (1985) pp. 83–94.

duties that undergird them. Surely some things are just right and others just wrong, so clearly wrong that one cannot afford to dilute the force of condemnation by introducing the language of character. Some criticisms point out the differences between Hauerwas and Iris Murdoch on these issues.[39] Others dispute Hauerwas' portrayal of the current ethical scene.[40] Others see Hauerwas as almost Pelagian in appearing to set aside the role of grace and focusing instead on sanctification.[41] Many of the criticisms that follow from here are similar to those referred to in the previous paragraph – particularly since character is so difficult to build through legislation, whereas some bad choices can be punished. Meanwhile if Hauerwas genuinely wants to stress the importance of character, he needs to say a great deal more about how disciples of character can be nurtured and educated.

5. The criticisms concerning virtue tend to be much more technical, and have become quieter as virtue ethics has re-established itself. Some of these criticisms overlap with those in (2) above, since they point out that many non-Christians also live virtuous lives, and that Hauerwas offers no argument against moral relativism.[42] Other criticisms point out the potential tension between the notions of vision and virtue in Hauerwas' early work.[43] A more valuable criticism is one that questions whether the antique notion of virtue presumes violence, and consequent control, and thus whether Aristotelian virtue will always be in tension with peace.[44] This is a part of a wider debate about the place of Aristotle in relation to the Christian story. Albrecht questions whether the practices Hauerwas commends, such as reading novels and raising children, are really so virtuous after all, when set in the context of the violence such practices implicitly countenance in other spheres.

Hauerwas' responses to his critics

1. On the issue of the justification of his theological convictions, Hauerwas sometimes takes the path of modesty and says that his principal interest is in ethics, and he cannot write in detail about everything. Yet when goaded he goes on the offensive, pointing out that the transformation of the self (and the community), that lies at the heart of his work, lies at the heart of Christian claims to truth also. Christians have to learn that they are sinners – and to have learned this is to have begun the path of sanctification. The proposals

---

[39] Gene Outka, 'Character, Vision and Narrative' *Religious Studies Review* 6/2 (1980) pp. 110–118.

[40] J. Wesley Robbins, 'On the Role of Vision in Morality' *Journal of the American Academy of Religion* 45 (1977) pp. 623–641.

[41] Thomas Ogletree, 'Character and Narrative: Stanley Hauerwas' Studies of the Christian Life' *Religious Studies Review* 6/1 (January 1980) pp. 24–30.

[42] Ibid.

[43] Outka, 'Character, Vision and Narrative'.

[44] This is the criticism made by John Milbank. See pp. 31–35 above. See also Hauerwas and Pinches, *Christians Among the Virtues* pp. 61–69.

that challenge the Christian understanding of truth presuppose an ethic of their own.[45] Christian truth-claims refer not to propositions but to lives: this makes Hauerwas an unusually pragmatic realist. Again, the centrality of the communion of saints is clear.

2. Hauerwas' understanding of narrative has developed in the course of his work. He lets go of the more formal claims made for narrative in his earlier writing, and concentrates on the scriptural narrative – while continuing to illustrate his claims with other narratives, particularly fiction. Narrative gradually ceases to be a theme on its own, but becomes the servant of the Church. This focuses the scandal of the disunity of the Church, which is a serious problem to Hauerwas because of his stress on faithful performance. While distancing himself from the wilder extremes of ethical practice,[46] he sees no objective way of disputing between Jew, Christian and Muslim.[47] Because of his stress that the Christian story does not end with the Scriptures, his ethics would still benefit from an extensive engagement with Church history, the location of much of the story.

3. In response to charges of world-denying sectarianism, Hauerwas' response is again a mixture of modesty and, when goaded, the defence that his opponents are sectarians themselves. His frustration with H. Richard Niebuhr is that 'culture' seems to receive unqualified loyalty, while 'Christ' is a secondary description.[48] The best form of society is not a static truth, but will always grow and change. He sees no reason why Christians should not be involved in law, government, or general public life, so long as their participation is selective. It is not a matter of total involvement or total withdrawal. The key is the issue of violence: on this issue rests the selection. Hauerwas is most anxious to insist that nonviolence makes Christians more political, rather than less. The doctrine of creation is a teleological doctrine – creation was set up for a purpose, and that purpose is fully known in Christ and the Spirit: the kingdom of God is wider than the Church, and Hauerwas makes no claims that God only cares about or works through the Church.[49] At times it seems that his continued admiration for the Jews might lead Hauerwas to regard them as a model of the selective involvement he commends.

When frustrated by repeated charges of sectarianism, Hauerwas pursues a further line – that it is the nation-state, rather than the Church, that is a sect,

---

[45] Hauerwas, *Christian Existence Today* pp. 1–21.

[46] Hauerwas, *Against the Nations* pp. 91–106.

[47] Hauerwas, *Christian Existence Today* pp. 10–11.

[48] Hauerwas, *A Community of Character* pp. 72–86. See also Arne Rasmusson, *The Church as Polis: From Political Theology to Theological Politics as Exemplified by Jurgen Moltmann and Stanley Hauerwas* (Notre Dame: University of Notre Dame Press 1994) pp. 231–245.

[49] Hauerwas, *Christian Existence Today* pp. 1–21.

calling as it sometimes does for withdrawal from other forms of life, and demanding that Christians fight each other in the name of some higher claim than their faith.[50]

4. and 5. Hauerwas' responses to the criticisms of his work on character have led him to develop his understanding of narrative and of the Church, and eventually to single out the organizing principle of peace. He responds to criticisms of his use of vision by distancing himself from Iris Murdoch.[51] He does not define 'the standard account of moral rationality' succinctly, but he does address its representatives individually,[52] and the ire of some of them suggests that at least some of his criticisms are pertinent. His most successful responses lie in the stories of character he tells.[53]

A test case: Le Chambon-sur-Lignon

In his book *Lest Innocent Blood Be Shed* Philip Hallie tells the story of how the people of the village of Le Chambon-sur-Lignon in the south of France resisted the Nazis during the years 1940–44.[54] The story is more thoroughly documented in a large collection of papers edited locally by Pierre Bolle.[55]

Le Chambon-sur-Lignon is one of two closely related villages in a particular part of the Massif-Central. Both villages have a fiercely-protected identity of Protestantism stretching back to the sixteenth century. After the collapse of France to the Germans in 1940, the area was controlled first by the Vichy government and gradually more directly by the Nazis. Yet the leaders of the village community set about doing all they could to provide a safe haven for Jews and other refugees fleeing from central Europe. Gradually during 1941 and 1942 it became known that this village called Le Chambon was a community where Jews would be protected, often being put up in boarding houses and private homes and farms away up in the hills and mountains above the village. From time to time groups were spirited away across the 200 miles to safety in Switzerland. The Nazi army and the French police knew what the villagers were up to, and often raided houses in the

---

[50] Hauerwas, 'Will the Real Sectarian Stand Up?' *Theology Today* 44:1 pp. 87–94.

[51] Hauerwas, 'Murdochian Muddles: Can We Get Through Them If God Does Not Exist?' *Wilderness Wanderings: Probing Twentieth-Century Theology and Philosophy* (Westview: Boulder, Colorado and Oxford 1997) pp. 155–170.

[52] Hauerwas, *The Peaceable Kingdom* Chapter 2. The lurking rival is generally Reinhold Niebuhr.

[53] For example, Hauerwas, *Christian Existence Today* pp. 67–88.

[54] Philip Hallie, *Lest Innocent Blood Be Shed: The Story of the Village of Le Chambon-sur-Lignon and How Goodness Happened There* (London: Michael Joseph 1979). Hauerwas refers to this work in *Against the Nations* pp. 87–88 n. 37.

[55] Pierre Bolle (ed.), *Le Plateau Vivarais-Lignon: Accueil et Résistance 1939–1944* (Le Chambon-sur-Lignon: Société d'Histoire de la Montagne 1992). I am grateful to Imogen Draperi for her help in translating this work.

village, but only very seldom found any refugees stored away. Somehow the bush telegraph almost always beat them to it, and the refugees hid in the mountains for a few days until the coast was clear. Hallie describes the story of Le Chambon in these years as 'a kitchen struggle, a battle between a community of intimates and a vast, surrounding world of violence, betrayal and indifference'.[56]

An examination of some of the features of this story illuminates the themes of Hauerwas' work summarized in the foregoing discussion. Hallie is not a Christian, and Hauerwas' mention of the book is concerned largely with pointing out how little Hallie understands the theological grounds of the nonviolence of the leaders in Le Chambon.[57] But this drawback is simply an invitation to concentrate on the undisputed facts of the story. In what follows I take several themes of Hauerwas' ethics and look at the Le Chambon story in their light.

Community

The first of Hauerwas' claims to be considered is that the practices of a community are formed by a narrative. Integral to the self-understanding of the village of Le Chambon was the fact that more than two-thirds of its three thousand residents were Protestants in a country where Protestants formed perhaps one per cent of the population. Their ancestors had survived through three centuries of persecution, often losing their property, their liberty or their lives; worship had to be conducted in darkened homes or secluded fields or woods. Pastors and people had been burned in Le Chambon since the sixteenth century. The population had remained remarkably stable: the thousand refugees who arrived after the Edict of Nantes was revoked in 1685 had long been assimilated. History was very much alive in the mind.

Centuries of persecution left among Protestants a tradition of resistance to the law of the land and devotion to their pastors who maintained their solidarity. Le Chambon's response to the revocation of the Edict of Nantes came not in battle but in 'the devices peculiar to mountain people: silence, cunning and secrecy ... they resisted by quietly refusing to abjure their faith, and by quietly conducting their services in meadows within the pine forests ... This was ... the resistance of exile'.[58]

This tradition was written on the hearts of even those on the fringes of the congregational life of Le Chambon. Hallie records a conversation with a daughter of a woman who had run a boarding house which hid Jewish girls. Resistance came by habit: 'One of the Marion daughters said "What they were asking us to do was very much like what the Protestants have done in France ever since the Reformation. Pastors were hidden here in Le

---

[56] Hallie, *Lest Innocent Blood Be Shed* p. 57.
[57] Hauerwas, *Against the Nations* pp. 87–88 n. 37.
[58] Hallie, *Lest Innocent Blood Be Shed* p. 167.

Chambon from the sixteenth century through the period of the 'desert' in the eighteenth century." "[59] This quotation vividly expresses what Hauerwas means by a community being formed by a narrative.

In his sermons the pastor, André Trocmé, emphasized that the community was a continuing part, not only of the Protestant narrative, but of the narrative of the Jews in exile. As early as March 1939 he took as his text for a sermon Deuteronomy 10:19 – 'And you are to love those who are aliens (*étrangers*), for you yourselves were aliens in Egypt'. At Christmas 1942 he recalls a town in Samaria where an old lady gave everything she had to a Jewish couple hunted by Herod (whom he equates with Pétain) and Archelaus (whom he equates with Laval, the head of the police). Her generosity inspired others, and the town became known as the most hospitable in Samaria.[60]

Narrative

A second claim is that the narrative of Jesus reveals God's way with the world. Faithfulness to the narrative of Jesus is what Hauerwas regards as the heart of Christian ethics. In Hallie's account, the faithfulness of the community as a whole is not described at length. Hallie concentrates on the thinking of the pastor, André Trocmé, whose nonviolence Hallie associates primarily with a personal journey in which he recognized the precious character of human life. Hauerwas points out the humanism of Hallie's account, and quotes from Trocmé's own *Jesus and the Nonviolent Revolution* to broaden the picture of Trocmé's theological position. Trocmé understands nonviolence as related to the delay of the coming kingdom granted to humanity because of Jesus' sacrifice.[61]

Notwithstanding Hauerwas' criticisms, Hallie outlines the key dimensions of Trocmé's 'apostolic' nonviolence. In a passage very similar to Yoder's arguments, Hallie quotes Trocmé's words to a men's circle meeting: 'If Jesus really walked upon this earth, why do we keep treating him as if he were a disembodied, impossibly idealistic ethical theory? . . . If he existed, God has shown us in flesh-and-blood what goodness is for flesh-and-blood people.'[62]

Hallie describes Trocmé's desire to be with and imitate and obey Jesus, like the obedience of a lover to his beloved. 'Jesus was for Trocmé the embodied forgiveness of sins, and staying close to Jesus meant always being ready to forgive your enemies instead of torturing and killing them.' Hallie mentions

---

[59] Ibid. p. 179.

[60] Francois Boulet, 'L'Attitude Spirituelle des Protestants devant les Juifs Réfugiés' in Bolle (ed.), *Le Plateau Vivarais-Lignon* pp. 402–404.

[61] André Trocmé, *Jesus and the Nonviolent Revolution* (Scottdale: Herald 1973). Trocmé's view that Jesus had inaugurated a social revolution based on the jubilee year was influential on Yoder's *The Politics of Jesus*.

[62] Hallie, *Lest Innocent Blood Be Shed* p. 68.

later that nonviolence gives the enemy an opportunity to repent, whereas killing the enemy leaves no time to do so.[63]

Virtue and habit

A third claim is that virtue arises more through habit than through decision. Hallie begins his narrative with the arrest of the leaders of Le Chambon in February 1943. During the arrest comes an incident which demonstrates the way the practices of a community make nonviolence a matter of habit and instinct rather than decision. It exemplifies Hauerwas' insistence that the ethics of a community are more about what all its members take for granted than about what an individual may decide to do by consulting a moral law or assessing likely consequences. When the police arrived to arrest André Trocmé, and sat in the dining room awaiting his return with a suitcase, Magda Trocmé invited the two policemen to dine with them. This was despite the presence in the house of refugee Jews, concealed upstairs. When asked by Hallie how she could be so magnanimous to men who were there to take her husband away, perhaps to his death, she replied, 'It was dinner time . . . the food was ready. What do you mean by such foolish words as "forgiving" and "decent"?' Hallie sums up the general attitude of the Chambonnais to what they did in these years: 'How can you call us "good"? We were doing what had to be done. Who else could help them? And what has all this to do with goodness? Things had to be done, that's all, and we happened to be there to do them. You must understand that it was the most natural thing in the world to help these people.'[64]

The villagers of Le Chambon did not decide that the village was to become a haven for refugees. They did not cast themselves in the role of rescuers. They simply found themselves incapable of turning refugees away. It was in the process of caring for the refugees that they realized how dangerous was their guests' position. If the Gestapo could kill an unarmed person for protecting a refugee, what would they do to the refugees themselves? Gradually the villagers took on increasing danger and increasing hunger in addition to the hardships of the Occupation. Eventually André Trocmé established a more formal scheme in some of the houses funded by the Quakers from Marseilles – but this was not a 'decision', so much as an extension of what was already taken for granted.

The stranger

A fourth claim is that the nonviolent community is open to luck, surprise and the stranger. One of Yoder's emphases in discussing issues of nonviolence

---

[63] Ibid. pp. 161, 34, 220. Consider Yoder's discussion of the ethics of killing someone who was attacking a third party: 'To keep out of heaven temporarily someone who wants to go there ultimately anyway, I would consign to hell immediately someone whom I am in the world to save.' J.H. Yoder, *What Would You Do?* (Scottdale: Herald 1992) p. 40.

[64] Hallie, *Lest Innocent Blood Be Shed* pp. 196–197.

is the importance of considering luck, surprise and accident. Things seldom turn out as predicted, especially when the prediction entails the wholesome fruit to be borne by violence: 'By assuming that it is my business to prevent or bring judgement upon evil, I authorize myself to close the door upon the possibilities of reconciling and healing. When I take it into my own hands to guarantee that events will not turn out in a way that is painful or disadvantageous to me, I close off the live possibilities of reconciliation which might have been let loose in the world.'[65]

Hallie's account contains a remarkable incident which bears this out. After the three leaders were arrested, they were taken to the internment camp of Saint-Paul d'Eyjeaux near Limoges. After a month, they were offered release on condition that they sign a promise to obey without question the orders of Marshal Pétain's government. Trocmé and Edouard Theis refused to sign, to the consternation of fellow inmates who recommended they be 'a skunk with the skunks'. The following morning, to everyone's amazement, they were released on the orders of the prime minister of France – no one has discovered why. Days later the other prisoners were deported to labour and concentration camps in Poland and Silesia, where few survived.

Another characteristic story concerns the churchwarden Amélie who refused to ring the church bells to mark the anniversary of the Légion Francaise des Combattants, later to become the Milice. Challenged by two women who tried to do it themselves, she bravely defended the church and was rescued by a downpour which drove the women away.[66]

The unexpected was common and essential to the life of the village. It came most frequently in the form of the stranger. Several times in Hallie's account the stranger disturbs and reveals the truth to the community. It is a German soldier during the First War who convinces the young Frenchman Trocmé that it was possible and necessary not to carry weapons. It is the strange policemen who receive the presbytery's hospitality. It is a young Jewish girl knocking on the door of the pastor's house who elicits the response from Magda Trocmé, 'Naturally, come in, and come in'. It is this response which Hallie takes to sum up the whole character of the village; and in the conclusion of his book, it appears that Hallie himself has become this stranger. The fact that the stranger may be the bringer of the gospel is underlined by the strangeness of Trocmé himself: from a bourgeois family, educated in Paris, married to an Italian, yet acting as the yeast to a farming community.[67]

---

[65] Yoder, *What Would You Do?* pp. 31–32. The consequentialist negotiation tends to leave no room for providence by assuming that history is our slave. Providence, for Yoder, 'designates the conviction that the events of history are under control in ways that are beyond both our discerning and our manipulating, although their pattern may occasionally be perceived by the prophet, and will later be celebrated by the community' (ibid. p. 35).

[66] Georges Menut, 'André Trocmé, un Violent Vaincu par Dieu' in Bolle (ed.), *Le Plateau Vivarais-Lignon* p. 398.

[67] Ibid. p. 399.

Imagination and politics

A fifth claim is that Christian nonviolence provokes the imagination and demands engagement in politics. Throughout the period described by Hallie, the initiative lay with the occupying power. The villagers were not in control of the situation; they could only survive by day-to-day responses to moves from the powerful. They were therefore not in a position to calculate likely outcomes in a consequentialist way. André Trocmé described predictions in such circumstances as 'a refuge for cowards'.[68] The position corresponds to de Certeau's distinction between strategies and tactics. The villagers were in no position to contemplate a strategy; they had no safe space from which to make forays into 'enemy' territory. They had to manage a tactic, constantly adapting to initiatives coming from others. Likewise politics was an inevitable form of life: right relationships with the village as a whole, with the resistance, and with the occupying power were a day-to-day issue.

Hallie records how Trocmé had learned from his time as a soldier with the French army in Morocco in 1921.[69] This taught him that it was no use professing a commitment to nonviolence half-way through a campaign. The conviction had to be embodied from the word go. This required a whole change of heart, rather than a temporary change in strategy. It stimulated the imagination to find ways of living peaceably. Trocmé met weekly with the key members of the village. In these meetings they evolved 'practical plans for overcoming evil with good': 'nonviolence was not a theory superimposed upon reality; it was an *itinerary* that we explored day after day in communal prayer and in obedience to the commands of the Spirit'.[70] 'Nonviolence goes beyond violence, and allows us to create new situations. It brings hope by inventing ways of breaking through the deadlock the world finds itself in. It creates unshakeable hope. It will no doubt be a long road which will demand patience as new ways are gradually invented day by day.'[71]

Summary

The story of Le Chambon-sur-Lignon demonstrates the claims and the issues at stake in Hauerwas' approach. There is no question of withdrawal: the community of character is surrounded. A history of dealing with minority status illustrates the significance of narrative in forming the virtues of a people. It is crucial that this community regarded Jesus as God's definitive ethical embodiment, not as merely an abstract ideal or pious principle. Once the commitment to nonviolence had been made, moments of decision did not

---

[68] Hallie, *Lest Innocent Blood Be Shed* p. 285.
[69] Ibid. p. 92.
[70] Ibid. p. 173. My italics.
[71] Jacques Martin, 'La Nonviolence, une Question à Notre Temps' in Bolle (ed.), *Le Plateau Vivarais-Lignon* p. 377.

disappear but were subservient – they explored the itinerary of nonviolence and demanded imaginative responses from those involved in protecting Jews. There was no rejection of politics: rather, constant wheeling and dealing was the rule in order to keep the community alive.

The drawbacks are equally clear. Although there is no question of withdrawal, Le Chambon is a geographically isolated community made up largely of one oppressed denomination. Once again, it proves very difficult to avoid spatial conceptions in describing the community of character. And on the question of catholicity, there remains the abiding question of why the wider Church did not act in the way the Le Chambonnais pioneered. Hauerwas' answer to this would no doubt be that this is a question for the wider Church, not for the heroic people of Le Chambon. To echo Yoder's words, the question is not, 'What if everyone were to act in this way?', but, 'What if no one acted in this way, but we did?'

Hauerwas' strongest argument against those who assume his advocacy of nonviolence is sectarian is that the Church requires and embodies a different form of politics. The reason why his response to the charge of sectarianism has not been completely convincing is that he has not yet fully displayed what he expects the politics of the Church to be. Much of his work amply demonstrates that the Church *needs* a politics, but with some exceptions this has not been mapped out in detail. He has shown convincingly that 'withdrawal' is a meaningless term to describe his approach. I suggest the underdeveloped regions lie less in how Christians relate to the world than in how they relate to each other. The question is less about the sanctity of the communion of saints, but more about in what resides their communion. Perhaps the weakness of Methodism's sacramental tradition lets Hauerwas down here.

Hauerwas' reluctance to be specific about the politics of the Church is understandable, given his misgivings about providing an ethical blueprint. Nothing can substitute for the actual practices of a community. What Hauerwas does do is to move towards telling the stories of those who have been part of communities of character. The community of Le Chambon-sur-Lignon is one such community (although Hauerwas mentions it only in a footnote). By telling the story of Le Chambon, I hope to have shown the strengths and weaknesses of Hauerwas' politics. The Le Chambon story in some ways confirms the more friendly criticisms of Hauerwas' approach: for it is realized in the story of an isolated village in a minority denomination in a time of crisis. Nonetheless, this heroic story shows that what Hauerwas commends can be done, has been done, and does produce people of virtue.

7

From Space to Time

The three most common criticisms of Stanley Hauerwas' work are that he is a sectarian, that he is a fideist, and that he lacks a doctrine of creation. My intention in this chapter is to show how greater attention to the eschatological implications of his theological ethics would enable Hauerwas successfully to respond to his critics.

Eschatology and time

Hauerwas offers a number of responses to the charge of being a sectarian. One of the problems he makes for himself is the use of spatial metaphors concerning the 'territory' occupied by Church and World. Consider the titles and subtitles of some of his books: *Essays on Church, World and Living in Between* (1988); *Life in the Christian Colony* (1989); *Dispatches from the Front* (1994); *The Church as Polis* (1995). All of these encourage an assumption he then has to deny – that he is describing the life of a separated community that has set up boundaries with the rest of the world. Each of these titles comes from his later period, well after the criticisms have become commonplace.

Hauerwas' most helpful discussion of this issue is in his employment of Michel de Certeau's distinction between a strategy and a tactic.[1] A strategy is the art of the strong: it concentrates its power in one place and makes systematic forays into enemy territory. A tactic is the art of the weak: it has no front line since it is perpetually surrounded. It thus entertains *ad hoc* encounters with powerful forces.[2] De Certeau's distinction suggests that it is not the Christian community that is sectarian: on the contrary it is the dominant secular forces that adopt strategies and thus power bases. However it seems Hauerwas will go on being accused of sectarianism (and go on being exasperated by the accusation) until he ceases to use confusing spatial metaphors.

---

[1] See 114–116 above.
[2] Thus, for example, Hauerwas' observation that Christianity 'must always be a Diaspora religion' *Against the Nations* p. 77.

It is my argument that it makes much more sense of Hauerwas' approach to understand the Church as existing in a new *time*.[3] It is this observation that enables us to see how Hauerwas' perspective on Christian ethics is profoundly eschatological. The distinction between Church and world is not about living in different spaces, but about having a different perception of time. The Church is a community of the new time. This has a considerable bearing on ethical reasoning. Rival ethical systems each have an implicit understanding of time. Deontological reasoning underestimates the significance of time. Consequential reasoning tends to foreshorten its story by concentrating on the destiny one can oneself determine. Eschatological reasoning, by contrast, has a longer view of time, and commends action in accordance with the End of the story. The centre of that story is not the acting subject but the sovereign God. God has and is the last word. The problem with consequential reasoning is not that it considers consequences, but that it is insufficiently eschatological: in other words, it seldom projects far enough into the future to make its calculation of benefits adequate, and by assuming the responsibility of the agent it inadequately acknowledges the sovereignty of God.

The theme of time emerges as a unifying theme of Hauerwas' work. Each of his major claims is a claim about the significance of time for Christian ethics. In Philip Kenneson's words, 'all of the categories that have become the hallmark of Hauerwas' work – character, narrative, memory, virtue – all are attempts to make connections between the self's communal nature and the community's irreducibly temporal character.'

In exploring eschatology therefore, I am examining the direction implicit throughout Hauerwas' work. If one takes the great themes of Hauerwas' work – the sovereignty of God, the Christian narrative, the new community, and Christian character – one can see how time is implicit in each of them.

A commitment to the sovereignty of God, particularly in the doctrine of the last things, carries several implications concerning time. The sovereign God shapes history to his good will and purpose; his kingdom will be fully established in his good time. The relationship of time to eternity is at the heart of the tension between immanent and transcendent notions of God.

God's sovereignty is expressed in traditional eschatological portrayals by the second coming of Christ and the last judgement. Christ's sudden, personal, bodily return has significant ethical implications. These implications lie particularly in the area decisive for Hauerwas – the attitude of the Church to the existing order. By contrast, belief in a catastrophic, personal, bodily return encourages Christians to be faithful and ready, rather than successful. It challenges the existing order, but avoids a triumphalist approach which might suggest Christians should seize power. Because it is sudden, it undermines gradualism; because it is personal, it keeps continuity with the ministry

---

[3] I derive this idea from Philip Kenneson, 'Taking Time for the Trivial: Reflections on Yet Another Book from Hauerwas' *Asbury Theological Journal* 45 (Spring 1990) pp. 65–74.

and passion of Jesus; and because it is bodily, it avoids versions which seek to make Christian transformation an interior event.

The last judgement picks up another issue closely related to time and authority – the Christian approach to evil. The righteous suffer – the apparently wicked prosper. Is God good and is his reign universal? Belief in the last judgement is belief that there will come a day when evil is abolished and righteousness reigns, when the significance of history is revealed, the secrets of all hearts made plain, the plot unravelled; when the agony of poverty, violence, starvation, loneliness and despair is lifted. Things will not always be this way. The horror of the last judgement has already been revealed in the agony of the cross; the glory of the last judgement has been seen in the resurrection on the third day. The crucifixion was not a ghastly mistake. History has already come out right in Christ. In Christ God has revealed the way he deals with the world and the way he would have his world governed. Because forgiveness and love have been vindicated in the resurrection, there can be confidence that he will end the story justly, in a manner not unlike the manner in which he has already decisively acted.

Nevertheless, evil is still present, and Christians constantly pursue a nonviolent commitment to turn against it. To do so they need courage. Courage is an eschatological virtue because it consists in recognizing that the End does not lie in the death of the self but in the final *eschaton*. The paradigm of Christian courage is martyrdom. Martyrdom requires an extraordinary courage, made possible by the belief in a last judgement that vindicates the righteous.

> Through Christ [Christians] have been given power over death and all forms of victimization that trade on the power of death. . . . Though our enemies may kill us they cannot determine the meaning of our death. . . . We refuse to let our oppressors define us as victims. We endure because no matter what may be done to us we know that those who would determine the meaning of our life by threatening our death have already decisively lost.[4]

It may appear that Hauerwas' emphasis on martyrdom is due to his overemphasis on the cross. However this discussion has shown such a criticism to be misplaced. For the courage that makes martyrdom possible is an eschatological virtue, drawing its strength from belief in the last judgement.

A constant theme of Hauerwas' writing is the need for patience among members of the Christian community. It is one of the most important of all the virtues – perhaps the definitive virtue, next to charity. A key fault of consequentialist reasoning is that by assuming it can predict outcomes it foreshortens the story. Belief in the second coming and last judgement remind the Christian that the end of the story comes much later – or very much sooner – than may be supposed. Tragedy can only be sustained by a belief in

---

[4] Hauerwas, 'On Developing Hopeful Virtues' *Christian Scholars Review* 18/2 (1988) p. 113.

the ultimate wiping away of every tear from every eye: too much social ethics tends toward violence precisely because it seeks to wipe away the tear all too hastily.

Hauerwas would profit considerably from drawing out the eschatological features of belief in God's sovereignty in these ways. His theological ethics are deeply eschatological, and the notion of being a community of a new time is one which conveys his insistence on Christian identity without appearing sectarian.

Moving on to the second theme of Hauerwas' work, narrative is the way Christians understand the revelation of God over time. The faithfulness and providence of God would be meaningless if there was not a continuity to the story stretching from Israel through Jesus to the Church. Just as when Christians guide their ethical behaviour by asking 'of what story am I a part?', so they seek the character of God by considering his revelation over time. Part of this revelation lies in the history of the Church. The communion of saints is the way doctrine speaks of the Church over time.

If narrative expresses continuity over time, it might appear that an interruption to that continuity, in the *eschaton*, would undermine narrative. But the *eschaton* is part of the story, and in one particular respect it restores continuity. What traditional eschatology has to offer to the continuity of the story is the role of the millennium. The millennium ties eschatology to concrete history. Most importantly, for Hauerwas' concerns, the millennium reintegrates the Jewish people into the Christian story. It is only in eschatological terms that the role of the Jewish people, before Christ and since, begins to make sense. If God has 'rejected his people whom he foreknew', then it puts into question all his promises and his faithfulness – the foundation of the gospel.

Hauerwas' commitment to narrative inclines him to seek continuities in the Old and New Testament story. Thus when speaking of the kingdom, he stresses how Israel is the context for Jesus' life and still a part of the story: 'The kingdom does not start with nature, with the notion that the perfection implicit in creation be reformed by divine assistance; rather, the kingdom starts as the hope of a people formed by God, which for Christians is defined by the life and death of the crucified Christ. . . . What we can know of this God and his kingdom is always given through the history of Israel filtered through the light of Jesus' cross.'[5]

Hauerwas' interest in the Jews is wholly consistent with his stress on narrative, and with his emphasis on the call to be a holy people. It is here in particular that one can discern why the communion of saints becomes even more significant to him than the centrality of Christ. For the communion of saints is also an eschatological doctrine, and accommodates the history of Israel without great difficulty. Thus the communion of saints unites Hauerwas' great themes of holiness, narrative, apprenticeship and community, with the pressing need to understand God's purpose for the Jews. It is not possible to

---

[5] Hauerwas, *Against the Nations* p. 115.

perceive this connection without the eschatological dimension offered by the millennium.

The third theme of Hauerwas' work is that the new community is founded on the eschatological event of resurrection. The resurrection is, for Hauerwas, the foundation of Christian forgiveness, which is the key practice of the community of character. Forgiveness is both a personal and a political necessity: and in both cases it requires letting go. To forgive, one must let go of the ways one gives significance to one's life, of the impulse to control the world to make it right, of the power gained by forgiving without receiving forgiveness. Hauerwas draws attention to the violence that lies behind the refusal to receive forgiveness freely offered. Accepting forgiveness makes one powerless; a forgiven people are a people deeply aware of grace and the contingency of their lives, of the way they depend on one another and on God.

Forgiveness relates to the new time particularly in the way it concerns the past. It implies being at peace with one's history. This is not an ethic which tries to abstract the individual or the community from its history. The community and its members are able to claim their past, inexorably sinful, as their own, with no need to tell themselves false stories, because they can accept forgiveness for what they have done and not done. Only then can they live in peace with themselves and one another.[6]

The resurrection makes possible the love of the enemy. Eventually the love of the enemy comes to symbolize the eschatological ethic. For on the cross, Christ became the enemy – the victim. The kingdom was given over into the hands of God's people. The kingdom to which they belonged became the kingdom that belonged to them, to do with as they wished. Yet the story is not limited by the limitations of God's people. In the resurrection, victim is transformed into hope.[7] This takes away from God's people their control over the consequences of their own sin, and leaves them deeply dispossessed. They are empty handed, just as they will be on the day of their own resurrection. And just as on that day, it is a time for offering forgiveness where it has not been deserved – to the enemy and the stranger.

The resurrection of Christ inaugurates the end-time and creates a people of the new time. Both these eschatological themes are implied in Hauerwas' work. For example, he sees the resurrection as bridging the gap between Jesus and the *eschaton*: 'The resurrection, therefore, is not an extra-ordinary event added to this man's life, but a confirmation by God that the character of Jesus' life prior to the resurrection is perfectly faithful to his claim to proclaim and make present God's kingdom. Without the resurrection our concentration on Jesus would be idolatry, but without Jesus' life we would not know what kind of God it is who has raised him from the dead.'[8] In the same way, through

---

[6] See especially Hauerwas, 'Resurrection, the Holocaust, and the Obligation to Forgive' in *Unleashing the Scripture* pp. 140–148.
[7] Hauerwas, *The Peaceable Kingdom* p. 90.
[8] Ibid. p. 79.

the resurrection the Church sees that the imitation of Christ accords with the life of the new time: 'The kingdom is *present* in so far as [Jesus'] life reveals the effective power of God to create a transformed people capable of living peaceably in a violent world.... His life is the life of the end – this is the way the world is meant to be – and thus those who follow him become a people of the last times, the people of the new age'.[9]

The new time that is made possible by the resurrection is a restored time – the restored sabbath. Hauerwas describes the resurrection of Jesus as 'the embodiment of God's sabbath as a reality for all people'.[10] Since life is in God's hands, since the end of the world has been revealed, it is possible to rest: the sabbath becomes a form of life, a new time, a peace between people and between people and the world. Life is valued not as an end in itself, not as the foundation of all value, but as valuable because God has valued and created it.

Hauerwas' fourth theme is Christian character. Time arises in the study of character at the point where character requires narrative. Hauerwas expresses this in his essay 'Character, Narrative and Growth in the Christian Life'. 'The growth of character, and our corresponding ability to claim our actions as our own, is a correlative of our being initiated into a determinative story. For it is only through a narrative which we learn to "live into" that we acquire a character sufficient to make our history our own.'[11] A key difference between a 'determinative story' and a story of one's own choosing is that a determinative story is a communal thing. In practice the term 'character', for Hauerwas, means a person's ability to identify the place or part they fulfil in a narrative. Thus a phrase such as 'my story' is almost meaningless: the story is always communal, and communal identity is prior to personal identity. Character and community emerge as the way Hauerwas ensures the identity of the self over time.

Character and community can be seen as eschatological themes if one places them in the perspective of heaven. The kingdom of heaven is the final eschatological category that has an implicit bearing on Hauerwas' ethics. Heaven speaks not of a territory over which God rules but of God's reign as dynamic and transforming, and met with obedience, service and joy. The coming of heaven to earth means a radical transformation of the way we do and are done by. 'The ultimate eschatological hope, then, is not that individuals will go to heaven but that heaven will fully and finally pervade earth. It is that "the earth will be filled with the knowledge of the glory of God as the waters cover the sea".'[12]

Thus the eschatological hope is embodied by people who see heaven not so much as a 'space' but as a way of acting in time – as a verb, rather than as a noun. The ethical implications of this last dimension of eschatology

---

[9] Ibid. pp. 83, 85, italics original.
[10] Ibid. p. 87.
[11] Hauerwas, *A Community of Character* p. 151.
[12] Ibid. p. 158.

make time more important, rather than less. Thus the hope of heaven avoids
the chief danger associated with eschatology – the danger of transforming
a living hope into a secret knowledge that disengages the gnostic community from its surroundings. Kenneson points out how tempting it is to talk
of salvation in ahistorical terms – particularly when the Church seems such
a poor witness to the kingdom. The temptation to be ahistorical is especially
common when discussing the doctrine of the atonement. Very often talk
of salvation bypasses the human community that salvation creates. This is a
gnostic tendency since it implies that salvation is simply a matter of God's
achievement and human knowledge of it. However humanity is not just
saved *from* something, it is saved *to* something. That latter something is the
new people, the eschatological community, that lives as if God, not
humanity, rules. The life of this community cannot be bypassed when
describing salvation: its very life is a crucial, albeit insufficient, manifestation
of God's rule. Indeed it may not be possible to know what salvation means
apart from such a community. Salvation saves humans *within* time, not *from*
time. In Hauerwas' words, 'That God "saves" is not a pietistic claim about
my status individually. . . . Rather, the God of Israel and Jesus offers us
salvation insofar as we are invited to become citizens of the kingdom and
thus to become participants in the history which God is creating'.[13]

Once one is committed to an ahistorical salvation, an ahistorical eschatology comes close behind. The heresy involved in both is docetism. God is so
other that he could not stoop to be involved in time. The moral consequence
is that Christ has no decisive relevance for ethics. In these circumstances the
temptation towards either human control or despair is almost irresistible. A
historical salvation is a salvation that establishes a new time. Salvation creates
a new people, the eschatological people: and a characteristic of this new
people is that they live in a new time – an eschatological time. In this new
time the priorities of existence are transformed: activities are significant to
the extent that they proclaim and accord with the new time.

Hauerwas draws these themes together (without drawing out the implicit
eschatology) in his essay 'Taking Time for Peace: The Ethical Significance of
the Trivial'.[14] His argument is that Christians witness by distinguishing
survival from life; and the way Christians affirm that God has done what is
necessary to ensure life is by taking time to do apparently trivial things. The
unity of the themes comes through in the following passage:

> The virtues . . . are timeful activities. This is not just because the virtues can only
> be developed through habitual formation, but because the virtues bind our past
> with our future by providing us with continuity of self. Because we are virtuous
> people, as we are peaceful people, we do not confront just any future but a future
> of a very definite kind. Just as fears of a courageous person are not the fears of a

---

[13] Hauerwas, *The Peaceable Kingdom* p. 63. In *Against the Nations* p. 115, he adds 'The
kingdom of God is a category which presumes and creates a people.'
[14] Hauerwas, *Christian Existence Today* pp. 253–266.

coward, so the future of the virtuous person is not the future of those who lack character.[15]

Thus far, I have shown that eschatological time is a dimension that underlies all of Hauerwas' writing, and yet is never made explicit. In what ways can this notion of time be developed?

One of the simplest ways to tell whether someone is powerful or powerless in contemporary culture is to examine their attitude to time. One might think of time as being something that all people experience equally – after all when it is ten o'clock in one's own home, it is ten o'clock in every other home for hundreds of miles, whether that home is a palace or a cardboard box. But one can find out how people relate to time by listening to the language they use.

For many people, time is a commodity.[16] It is treated like one of the most valuable things money can buy. People who are busy and important use commodity-language to describe time. They 'buy' time, or 'spend' time; they talk of 'using' time, or even of 'investing a great deal of time', or sometimes of 'putting time aside'; they 'save' time or 'waste' time, 'lose' time or 'find' time. Not any old time: they are only interested in 'quality' time. All of these words treat time as a product, like something one could buy in the supermarket. Occasionally it is pointed out that 'time is money'. It is considered a very good thing in these circles to save time – though it is not always clear how one is to spend the time one has saved.

Another group of people would love to be busy and important, but for a variety of reasons they feel that they are not. Yet because commodity-language is the way so many people speak of time, this second group are made to feel that because they are not in a hurry, they are 'wasting' time, or 'losing precious time' in life's race. For these people, time quickly becomes an enemy. Because the commodity-language does not fit, they often use battle-language. Time is 'against' them, or 'presses in on' them; it 'weighs heavy' on their lives. They seem to be failing the 'test' of time. The saddest language is that which speaks of 'killing' time, since those who set out to kill time almost always lose the battle.

In the Church's calendar, Advent is set aside for considering the dimensions of time. Advent is a reminder that just as the history of the world has a beginning and a middle, it also has an end. Several times in the gospels Jesus predicts that there will be a dramatic climax to the story of the world. At the end of the world, God finally intervenes and brings justice and peace to his whole creation. Talk of the end of the world may sound like a frightening thing. Of course, for those who treat time as a commodity, the end of the world is indeed a frightening thing: what will happen to all that precious time they have 'saved'? But for everybody else, the end of the world is tremendously good news, because it is a reminder that God is in control of

---

[15] Ibid. p. 265.

[16] Many of the ideas in these paragraphs are inspired by Kenneson, op. cit.

history – and that even if his people keep on getting it wrong, he will finally make all things right.

What Jesus does by showing his people the end of the world is to take time out of human hands. He says, 'If you're going to treat time as an enemy or as a commodity I'm going to take time away from you. I shall give you back a new time, but you must treat this time differently: you must now treat time as a gift and as a friend.' So time is a gift, because it is God's time, not one's own; and time is a friend, because there is nothing to fear from what God has in store. Time is 'on our side'. One cannot buy time with God. One must learn to enjoy God's time.

If time is a friend, the Christian community can enjoy time with those who do not promise to make the world a better place. It can give a special place to spending time with prisoners, the severely retarded, the very elderly – for that is where the Church believes God spends his time. If time is a gift, it is a gift that can be enjoyed with all sorts of people who do not contribute to conventional ideas of status – with the very sick, with the homeless, with the mentally ill. When the Church is full of people like this, it is evidence that the Church is living in a new time. This is what is meant by the 'kingdom breaking in'. The kingdom of God breaks into the Christian community when people recognize the sovereignty of God, and start living as if God is king. The community will be marked out by its attitude to time, for the way it sees time is a measure of its faith. Every bit of time Christians spend with a powerless person is part of the Church's proclamation of Advent hope.

It is easy to slip into old ways, and treat time and people as commodities for one's own advancement. But gathering together in worship, Sunday by Sunday and many times besides, is a constant reminder to the Church that it is living in God's time, not its own. The church gathers because worship is the most profound recognition of God's sovereignty over time: hence there is nothing better in life than to worship God with others who love him. And if it takes all the time in the world it does not matter – because it is God's time.

The Christian community is therefore exactly where Jesus is, at the place where the new time breaks into the old, at the edge of possibility. Anthony Harvey puts it like this:

> Jesus' ethical teaching [lies] . . . at the very edge of what we usually believe to be possible. Jesus' message has power not in spite of, but because of, its promise of a future which is not ideal or utopian, nor a mere variation on what we know already, but is both radically new and able to be envisioned on a human time-scale, 'in our generation'. Faithful and eager attention to such a future introduces a new dimension to the present; for the present becomes, not a mere working out of the consequences of the past, but a transition to an altogether different future. The present is transformed by the discovery of possibilities which were not apparent until it was seen in the light of the future.[17]

---

[17] Anthony Harvey, *Jesus and the Constraints of History* (London: Duckworth 1982) p. 97

What is vital is that the community is able to see that it is at the edge of possibility, and thus learn to act in witness to the kingdom breaking in. Like realists, Christians want to earth ethics in the real world. But the community of the new time sees the world at the edge of possibility; and the way the Church acts depends on the way it sees the world in which it acts. The ethic of the kingdom and the Sermon on the Mount trains Christians in how to see the world. The Beatitudes extend the practice of Jesus into the promise of an in-breaking kingdom. This is ethics on the very edge of possibility, an ethic which is breaking into a new time, where the demands of reality are very different. This is the eschatological ethic, implicit in Hauerwas' work, and occasionally explicit, as in this passage in *Resident Aliens*:

> If the world is a society in which only the strong, the independent, the detached, the liberated, and the successful are blessed, then we act accordingly. However, if the world is really a place where God blesses the poor, the hungry, and the persecuted for righteousness' sake, then we must act in accordance with reality or else appear bafflingly out of step with the way things are.... So discipleship, seen through this eschatology, becomes extended training in letting go of the ways we try to preserve and give significance to the world, ways brought to an end in Jesus, and in relying on God's definition of the direction and meaning of the world – that is, the kingdom of God.[18]

Eschatology and Hermeneutics

If Hauerwas aligned himself more explicitly with eschatological ethics of the kind I have described, it would not only free him from charges of being a sectarian, but also make clear that he is not a fideist. An eschatological approach can resolve many of the problems associated with postliberal hermeneutics.

Eschatology can play a similar role in Hauerwas' narrative ethic to the role played by *telos* for Alasdair MacIntyre. MacIntyre affirms the indispensability of teleology when he says there 'is no present which is not informed by some image of some future and an image of the future which always presents itself in the form of a *telos* – or a variety of ends or goals – towards which we are either moving or failing to move in the present'.[19] MacIntyre sees human life as a narrative quest – a journey directed toward a determinate goal. As one journeys, one learns about the goal one seeks and also about oneself. For the Church, the *telos* is formed by Christians' perception of the *eschaton*. It is the sense of an end to the story that makes it possible to speak of a story at all. The Church learns about its hope by

---

[18] Hauerwas and Willimon, *Resident Aliens* pp. 88–89.
[19] MacIntyre, *After Virtue* p. 216.

seeking it. It seeks, or quests, by embodying its belief in God's sovereignty in the way it structures its own life and acts in the world. Hauerwas appears to endorse such a view when he commends virtues according to their eschatological significance – faithfulness, courage, hope, patience – and insists on keeping love tied to hope and patience, in order to maintain its eschatological character. The difference between *eschaton* and *telos* is that *telos* is an incomplete goal which the agent is obliged to bring about, whereas *eschaton* is something that has already happened in Christ, and its ethic rests on the faithfulness of the Church as the *eschaton's* proleptic presence.

Eschatology not only has much to offer in the discussion about sectarianism, but it can also help Hauerwas in his problems over truth. Postliberals such as Hans Frei and George Lindbeck insist that the scriptural world is the real world – indeed Lindbeck says that the Scripture absorbs the world rather than vice versa. The text makes such a demand on the reader that one cannot properly read it unless one is performing it. One cannot step outside the world one inhabits in order to justify that world.

Critics of this position question whether Scripture creates one coherent world or several; whether there is any reason to opt for this world in the first place; and in what sense this world can be said to be 'revealed'. The question becomes one of whether there can be any access to ontological truth except by stepping through the contextual hoops of social practice, culture and language. Those who say there can are accused of being foundationalists, since they suppose one can bypass human community in search of truth; those who, like Lindbeck, are more sanguine, are challenged to come up with some justification for entering the 'world' they propose.

Stanley Hauerwas develops the notion of narrative so that it incorporates the history and tradition of the Church. This potentially eases some of the problems associated with the somewhat static view of the text held by Frei and Lindbeck, and introduces the idea of a continuing conversation. The emphasis moves from Holy Scripture to holy people, the communion of saints. Hauerwas opposes any efforts to set up a theory of revelation or knowledge or religion that attempts to bypass the community of faith. The ontological level is definitely there – there is no doubt that he is a theological realist – but the narrative of the community is the only way to get to it. He advocates performance as the only way to assess the truth of Christian convictions. This is not because performance provides unequivocal proof – he is well aware of the host of hermeneutical problems such as who should assess and how they should go about it – but because of the impossibility of assessing any other way.

How can the numerous areas of continuing criticism be resolved? I suggest that the feature of story that has yet to be fully discussed is the fact that a story has an ending. When a story has been told, whether non-fiction or fiction, one can look back over the story and see which actions and people in the story were oriented towards the story's ending, and which actions and people hinted at a possible alternative ending. One can trace what one might call a 'critical path' through the story, of actions and people which, though not necessarily bringing the ending *about*, had the same *character* as the ending.

I suggest that it is the role of the Church, placed as it is in the 'middle' of the narrative, to strive to live on that critical path. This is what it means to live teleologically – according to the end. For Christians the end, or closure, of the world is identical with its *telos*, or purpose. Thus a teleological Christian ethic involves developing and sustaining the practices that conform to the *end* of the world – in both senses. Actions can be said to be truthful to the extent that they follow that critical path. Doctrines and ontological claims can be described as true to the extent that they describe that ultimate state of affairs.

Questions of hermeneutics are part of the continuing conversation of the Church with its defining moments. But I argue that an eschatological approach resolves some criticisms from the hermeneutics of suspicion since its 'critical path' of 'actions and lives oriented to the end' provides a way of rehabilitating many neglected parts of the tradition. What a critic such as Gloria Albrecht might regard as groups excluded by gender, class, or nationality, may be seen eschatologically as seriously neglected parts of the tradition. The extent that the Church has neglected and still neglects those parts is the extent to which it will face eschatological judgement. Some parts may be unheard today, since they perhaps played a small or forgotten part in getting the Church to its present circumstances; but they will finally be judged by the extent to which they were oriented to the final reality, the End.[20]

I also believe that an eschatological approach is more faithful to intratextualism than some other approaches. For if the text is a *narrative*, then one must follow the direction in which it points. And while most of the narrative is contextual, concerning Israel's responses to Yahweh's covenant and the early disciples' responses to Jesus, there can be little doubt that the end that the narrative points to is the fulfilment of ultimate closure.

An eschatological approach can help with the stalemate that sometimes appears in intratextualist attempts to make sense of Christian witness. A serious danger for some intratextualists is that they seem to assume that describing Christian practice and what Christians mean by what they say is as far as they can go, without assuming any common ground with the stranger. But the New Testament, part of the text in question, assumes witness and conversion. What therefore is a postliberal Christian witness? Lindbeck offers a dismal picture of the contemporary 'unchurched masses . . . immunized against catechesis' – but he offers no alternative.[21] He is limited by his purely retrospective understanding of narrative. Of course it

---

[20] One example is Hauerwas' concern for the place in the narrative of the Jews.
[21] Lindbeck, *The Nature of Doctrine* pp. 132–133.

is difficult to re-educate adults with an alien theological language. The teleological approach which I am suggesting does not begin by asking people the somewhat unappealing question 'Would you like to come from where we are coming from?', but instead focuses on the more accessible, but no less intratextual and antifoundationalist question, 'Would you like to be going where we are going?'

I further believe that the approach I suggest is more contextual than that of some cultural-linguistic approaches. Lindbeck speaks of the 'world' of the text as the 'real' world. But if we are to sustain his commitment to context, then surely this must include space and time. Is it not escapist to see the only real world as that of Sinai, Zion, Babylon and Galilee – at a time separated from ours by millennia? Is not the ultimately real world, to which Lindbeck refers, the one which ultimately will be the only world, that of the reign of God – that could at any time be suddenly upon us, ending the story? The biblical stories, which hardly constitute one single coherent world, inaugurate this ultimate world, instantiate it, anticipate it and most importantly direct our attention towards it – but they surely do not *constitute* that world. If scripture is itself the world in which Christians act, the result for ethics can only be confusion over the difference between their world and the scriptural world, or escapism into a disembodied scriptural world.

Attention to the ending of the story makes more sense of the plurality of Christian practice. For if one's narrative only enables one to look *back*, then any deviation from the practice of Israel, Jesus and the early Church is bound to look like unfaithfulness. But if one's narrative is concerned with where one is going, one's method of getting there is bound to be affected by where one is starting from. A contextual approach recognizes that Christians are currently in different places, but emphasizes that they are all going to the same place.

The tragic story of Jonestown shows that performance can be used as a valid criterion for assessing truth.[22] Jonestown is an example of the way a premature closure of the story is a form of unfaithfulness: advocates of such foreclosure could be described as heretics. Once again, one is not simply looking back to the story of Jesus to assess faithfulness: one is asking 'In the light of the story of Jesus, what ending of this story is appropriate?' Suicide was clearly not an appropriate ending – not because the participants were too faithful to Jim Jones, but because they were not sufficiently faithful to God.

To be sure Hauerwas is right when he directs attention to the memory of the community of faith, for it is only in this narrative that the community finds itself directed towards the 'life of the end'. The problem with decisionist ethics is that it is unhistorical – dealing simply in the present, without reference to memory, character, context, or the practices of the end of the

---

[22] See pp. 85–89 above.

story. A further problem of consequentialist ethics is that it has a highly premature conception of the end of its particular story. The eschatological approach broadens the picture to reconceive the terms of the story the consequentialist tells.[23]

Finally, revelation is not an abstract doctrine of the manner of the knowledge of God, but an anticipation of the revealing of the full picture in the future. More important than revelation is how one comes to trust in the God described in scripture. The resurrection of Jesus is a key event in scripture, since it is this event that leads Christians to trust in the God to whom the life and death of Jesus point, and helps them to see Jesus as the instantiation of the end – the full appearance of the reign of God. Thus the resurrection of Jesus unites the emphases of Hauerwas' early work – the ethics of Christ's life and passion – with the emphasis I am commending – the eschatological perspective.

Eschatology and creation

Only when one can see how, in Hauerwas' scheme, eschatology can relate to creation and salvation, can an overall assessment be made of whether eschatology fits into a coherent theology for the community of character.

There is an abiding danger among those who write about Christian ethics that a split will emerge between those who incline to 'creation ethics' and those who demand 'kingdom ethics'. The tendency of the former is to concentrate on the created order, often in terms of natural law, to the neglect of salvation and eschatology. Stanley Hauerwas is in no danger of falling into this former camp. He has, however, been accused of belonging to the 'kingdom' camp – having a world-denying tenor, hand-in-hand with suggestions of sectarianism, deriving from his refusal to do 'ethics for everybody'. This is how he explains his position, in an unusually explicit eschatological passage:

> Those who emphasize apocalyptic often are accused, of course, of failing to do justice to God as creator. Despite the apparent centrality of creation to Christian faith, as actually employed, creation talk often serves as a means for the domestication of the Gospel. Appeals to creation are meant to suggest that all people, Christian or not, share fundamental moral commitments that can provide a basis for common action. These appeals to creation too often amount to legitimating strategies for the principalities and powers that determine our lives. This type of creation talk is fundamentally false to the biblical profession of faith in the Lord of creation because it implicitly underwrites the lordship of the principalities and powers.[24]

---

[23] Hauerwas does this on the nuclear annihilation issue. See *Against the Nations* Chapters 8 and 9.

[24] Hauerwas, *Dispatches from the Front* p. 111.

In this style of scepticism about using a 'doctrine of creation' for ethics Hauerwas has been much influenced by John Howard Yoder.[25] It has brought Hauerwas into conflict with those, such as Oliver O'Donovan, who have sought to mediate between 'creation ethics' and 'kingdom ethics'. Hauerwas criticizes O'Donovan for using resurrection as a way of bringing creation and natural law in by the back door. 'I fear such appeals to order, and the correlative confessions in God's creation that sustain them, because I do not believe such order is knowable apart from cross and resurrection. O'Donovan seeks an account of natural law that is not governed by the eschatological witness of Christ's resurrection. We cannot write about *Resurrection and Moral Order* because any order we know as Christians is resurrection.'[26]

In reply O'Donovan doubts whether Hauerwas has a view of the resurrection which sufficiently differentiates it from the crucifixion. To some extent O'Donovan misses the point here, because Hauerwas is talking of the resurrection as an *eschatological* witness, rather than more narrowly of an event tied to Jesus' death. Yet O'Donovan is perceptive in pointing out Hauerwas' increasing 'tendency to privilege the crucifixion over other moments of the Christ-event, in keeping with an emphasis on martyrdom and death as the

---

[25] The following passage is a virtuoso display of Yoderian polemic: 'Historical study shows that it has been possible to understand under "order of nature" just about anything a philosopher wanted; stoicism or epicureanism, creative evolution or political restorationism, Puritan democracy or Aryan dictatorship.... "Nature" may be the struggle of the species for survival; it may be the existing social order in its interplay of hierarchies and power claims; or, on the other hand, it may be the essence of a person or thing that he is called to become. The word thus includes two different scales of variability; when nature is understood to mean a quasi-platonic essence, distinct from what things appear to do, we have the whole gamut of ideals which have not yet been actualized in experience: if, on the other hand, by nature we understand "things as they are", we must deal with the entire scale of empirical realities. The conviction, almost universally shared, that nature is a reliable source of knowable and binding ethical norms rests on failure to clarify either the content which it claims to have proved or the truth claims which it presupposes' (Yoder, *The Christian Witness to the State* Newton, Kansas: Faith and Life Press 1964 pp. 33, 82).

This is a devastating critique of natural law foundationalism. Yoder goes on to say that we may be able to establish the structures of 'things as they are' – this is the aim of 'natural' science – but this structure cannot be a critique or a moral imperative. Alternatively we may be able to understand 'the nature of things' as some sort of philosophical essence to be distinguished from things as they are – this could be a moral imperative, but it gives up any claim to be empirically ascertained from nature; moreover for a Christian this essentialist approach must justify itself since it is foreign to the historical thrust of the Biblical revelation.

The 'almost universally shared' conviction that nature is a reliable source of ethical norms is not simply a harmless fallacy, in Yoder's view. There is within the logic of natural law and corresponding natural (or universal) rights a powerful justification for violence.

[26] Hauerwas, *Dispatches from the Front* p. 175.

normative expression of Christian witness'.[27] What O'Donovan does not point out, but is implicit in his criticism, is that by over-emphasizing the cross and underplaying creation, Hauerwas falls short of his own criteria. By this I mean that Hauerwas is failing to do full justice to the *narrative* form of Christian convictions. This narrative has a beginning, a middle and an end. By concentrating too much on one point (the crucifixion), Hauerwas may be led to neglect those other dimensions of the narrative.

Hauerwas develops this point in response to another of his critics, James Gustafson. Hauerwas is unimpressed by Gustafson's suggestion that an independent doctrine of creation is required as a basis for ethics: 'Why doesn't Gustafson simply say that what is needed is a morality in which all people can agree?' Hauerwas is concerned that when abstracted from reference to Israel and Jesus, creation (and redemption) become ciphers. For Hauerwas, common ground lies not in the breadth of shared humanity but in the wideness of God's mercy, stretching beyond the Church. What a commitment to revelation through narrative enables Hauerwas to say is that creation only has theological substance when it is seen as part of the Christian story: 'creation in Christian theology is an eschatological act that binds nature and history together by placing them in a teleological order.' Christ's resurrection unites nature and history so that they can no longer be talked of as separate orders.[28]

It would not be fair, however, to ignore steps Hauerwas has made towards a more positive view of creation. For these steps we need to look to two essays published in his recent book *Wilderness Wanderings*, one distancing himself from Iris Murdoch, another aligning himself with John Milbank.

In 'Murdochian Muddles: Can We Get Through Them If God Does Not Exist?', Hauerwas recognizes that Iris Murdoch's philosophy is finally incompatible with Christian ethics for a number of reasons, of which two are pertinent here. The first concerns Murdoch's confidence in the myth of the demiurge, the 'paradigmatic artist making beauty out of necessity'.[29] As convinced as Murdoch is by this model, the ontological argument demonstrates to her the fact that no such God can exist. In response, Hauerwas asserts that the doctrine of creation *ex nihilo* affirms the free decision of God, a decision exercised spontaneously and graciously. The transition from Murdoch to Hauerwas is expressed in the transition from talking of the 'contingent' to talking of the 'created'. Each created thing is a gift whose purpose is to praise the creator. Hence a definition of sin arises from the doctrine of creation:

---

[27] Oliver O'Donovan, *Resurrection and Moral Order: An Outline for Evangelical Ethics* (Grand Rapids: Eerdmans 1994²) p. xv. The emphasis on the crucifixion is a theme Hauerwas shares with Yoder.

[28] See Gustafson, 'The Sectarian Temptation: Reflections on Theology, the Church, and the University' *Proceedings of the Catholic Theological Society* 40 (1985) pp. 83–94; Hauerwas, *Christian Existence Today* pp. 1–19.

[29] Hauerwas, 'Murdochian Muddles: Can We Get Through them if God Does Not Exist?', *Wilderness Wanderings* pp. 155–170.

For the Christian 'sin' names the training we must undergo to discover our lives are possessed by powers, by narratives, whose purpose it is to hide from us the fact that we are creatures of a gracious God. Such 'knowledge' does not come 'naturally', but rather from being made part of a community with practices that offer the transformation and reordering of our lives and relationships. . . . Only through [forgiveness and] reconciliation do we believe we can fully acknowledge our contingency and particularity.[30]

Murdoch's second unacceptable belief is in the absolute pointlessness of existence. Hauerwas responds to this claim by demonstrating the way the doctrine of creation initiates the Christian story, whose purpose is that all creation should worship God. This narrative needs constant retelling: indeed the whole story must remain open to renarration, due to the constant creating work of providence. In his dialogue with Murdoch, Hauerwas is drawn to emphasize the importance of Christian community in demonstrating that what appears to be contingent is in fact created.

With his second dialogue partner, John Milbank, the concern is more with the character of the God that does the creating. In his essay 'Creation, Contingency, and Truthful Nonviolence', Hauerwas combines a view of creation with an eschatological perspective, while still maintaining his emphasis on witness through martyrdom.[31] In this essay Hauerwas commends Milbank's view of creation as the ongoing nonviolent work of the Trinity. The reason why Milbank is so important to Hauerwas is that Milbank gives Hauerwas a way of talking about creation. Hauerwas has tended to avoid talk of creation because it seemed to underwrite the project of universalist epistemology. Having accepted the critique of 'foundationalist' epistemology of this kind, Hauerwas was left with no way of talking about creation.

What Milbank does is to talk of God's *nonviolent* creation. This gives Hauerwas the opportunity to extend to creation the insights he has derived (originally from Yoder) from God's nonviolent salvation. The crucial link between nonfoundationalism and nonviolence that connects them with creation is the fact that they accept, acknowledge and encourage *difference*. Difference is at the heart of nonfoundationalism, because unlike liberalism it does not assume that all accounts of knowledge and existence are at root the same. Difference is at the heart of nonviolence, because without a commitment to nonviolence, the conflict that inevitably arises from difference would be destructive (especially given the foundationalist presumption that unity is in the nature of things).[32] It is in this context that Milbank's

---

[30] Ibid. p. 165.
[31] Hauerwas, 'Creation, Contingency, and Truthful Nonviolence: A Milbankian Reflection', *Wilderness Wanderings* pp. 188–98.
[32] In *Against the Nations* (p. 84 n. 26), Hauerwas quotes Reinhold Niebuhr's indictment of the violence of universalism: 'The logic of the decay of modern culture from universalistic humanism to nationalistic anarchy may be expressed as follows: Men seek a universal standard of human good. After painful effort they define it. The painfulness of their effort convinces them that they have discovered a genuinely

understanding of creation in terms of harmonious difference is so fruitful. For Milbank, the Trinity itself is a social being embodying harmonious difference. This is his foundation. Creation is thus the bringing-about in existence of the Trinity's own harmonious difference. This is how Milbank summarizes his position:

> Christianity . . . recognizes no original violence. It construes the infinite not as chaos, but as a harmonic peace which is yet beyond the circumscribing power of any totalizing reason. Peace no longer depends on the reduction to the self-identical, but is the *sociality* of harmonious difference. Violence, by contrast, is always a secondary willed intrusion upon this possible infinite order (which is actual for God). . . . It is Christianity which exposes the non-necessity of supposing, like the Nietzscheans, that difference, non-totalization and indeterminacy of meaning *necessarily* imply arbitrariness and violence. . . . Christianity, by contrast, is the coding of transcendental difference as peace.[33]

This summary is tremendously important for integrating the whole of Hauerwas' theology. Creation, prior to this, has undoubtedly been the missing ingredient. It was missing because it seemed to open the door to formal theories of natural law, foundational accounts of knowledge, and in the end to a violence that denied the particularity of story, Christian or otherwise. Milbank offers a way for Hauerwas' perception of the Christian narrative to have a greater emphasis on the *beginning* of the story. Thus Hauerwas can finally bridge the divide between creation ethics and kingdom ethics.

The way he does this is expressed in his only foray into the relationship between humans and animals.[34] He rejects the notion of animal rights, since he sees rights as linked to a Cartesian view of the rational individual – a view that excludes animals. In addition, the language of inalienable rights assumes a conflictual account of the world, which differs from the Milbankian priority of peace. Hauerwas grounds the human relationship with animals in an eschatological view of creation. Humans are distinguished from animals in that they have a particular purpose: they are the image of God because they are created for fellowship with Christ. It is in Christ that the creation discovers its purpose: thus purpose unites creation, salvation and *eschaton*. It is this purpose that distinguishes the Christian notion of 'creation' from the secular term 'nature'. Creation cannot be reconciled with a deist view of first cause; instead, 'creation is part of a narrative of fulfilment for Christians; from our conviction that God redeems all of creation we learn that God, having created

---

[32] *(continued)* universal value. To their sorrow, some of their fellow men refuse to accept the standard. Since they know the standard to be universal the recalcitrance of their fellows is a proof, in their minds, of some defect in the humanity of the non-conformists. Thus a rationalistic age creates a new fanaticism. The non-conformists are figuratively expelled from the human community'. Niebuhr, *Beyond Tragedy* (New York: Scribners 1965) p. 237.

[33] Milbank, *Theology and Social Theory* pp. 5–6; italics original.

[34] Hauerwas and John Berkman, 'A Trinitarian Theology of the Chief End of All Flesh' *In Good Company* pp. 185–197.

all things, wills that all things enjoy their status as God's creatures'.[35] Hauerwas employs a Milbankian view of the priority of peace when he insists that a Christian understanding of creation is derived not just from Genesis 1–2 but also from Romans 8:19–21 and Isaiah 11, two passages that link creation to present suffering and eschatological re-creation.

Eschatology and salvation

In the foregoing discussion of eschatology and creation I have shown how the two are compatible when one sees creation as the nonviolent establishment of harmonious difference. The theological difficulty which remains is whether an emphasis on eschatology plays down and underestimates the significance of the person and work of Christ. Can one continue to maintain the finality of Christ for Christian doctrine and his centrality in Christian ethics, while talking of the ultimate resolution of things and the command to live in the world which will be and is coming to be?

The views that look forward to a future resolution of human aspirations in this world may be termed historicist.[36] Historicist positions put a high value on the notion of history. In this perspective, all teleology is historical teleology. One cannot talk of an 'end' (or a beginning) outside time. All meanings emerge within the process of time itself. The future is the only judge: all human strivings undergo the 'test of time'. For the gradualist, the world is growing from childhood to adulthood, and its problems are largely due to immaturity. The revolutionary is more inclined than the gradualist to hurry up the growth process, but the only force that can do the hurrying is the revolutionaries themselves, since an intervention from outside time and history is excluded.

There are several problems with this perspective. The chief problem is that it does not distinguish between the immature and the evil. If creation is portrayed as incomplete, one comes close to a gnosticism that says creation is bad. If creation is not 'good', but only 'getting better', what would constitute evil? This comes close to an idealism which denies the reality of evil. O'Donovan summarizes the problem neatly: 'The characterization of history as a process replaces the categories of good and evil with those of past and future'.[37] The monopoly of history over all meanings also excludes grace, the definitive action of God. One could say no more about Christ than that he is a representative and an anticipation of the tendency and potential that was already in the world. There is no place for a decisive act, only for a guiding

---

[35] Ibid. p. 193.

[36] Here I am following the use of the term 'historicist' by O'Donovan in his *Resurrection and Moral Order* Chapter 3.

[37] O'Donovan, *Resurrection and Moral Order* p. 64. It is hard to see how such a perspective is sustainable in view of the delay of the *eschaton* noted by the New Testament authors. The fact that evil was still very much around was surely one of the most important reasons why the New Testament was written.

hand. This is an inability to distinguish providence, the teleological ordering of and within the created order, from salvation, the eschatological action from without. Historicism has a place for providence, but not for salvation.[38]

John Howard Yoder offers a definitive description of the 'Constantinian' shift, by which the Church came to see its own best interests coinciding with those of the state. 'Before Constantine, one knew as a fact of everyday experience that there was a believing Christian community but one had to "take it on faith" that God was governing history. After Constantine, one had to believe without seeing that there was a community of believers, within the larger nominally Christian mass, but one knew for a fact that God was in control of history.'[39] One can see the way the 'Constantinian' shift favoured a historicist perspective. The workings of providence and the activity of salvation became difficult to distinguish from one another. A decisive *eschaton* seemed unnecessary, since all that could be wished for was simply more of what already existed. Eschatology lost its transcendent power to criticize historical tendencies and instead underwrote them with a promise of more of the same. A this-worldly eschatology not only favours a 'Constantinian' politics: the two together are intimately connected with a consequentialist ethical method, as O'Donovan, here talking of Western liberal culture, implies:

> To criticize the culture as a whole is unthinkable; one can only speak *for* the culture *against* the culture, as the representative of a new strand in the culture which will fashion its future. To this implausible disguise, then, moral criticism resorts in modern liberal society, presenting itself partly as sociological prediction, partly as threat. The critic must describe the future of the culture in a way that justifies his concerns; and he must show that he speaks for a constituency sufficiently large or sufficiently determined to make his predictions come true![40]

---

[38] Hence the tendency of this kind of eschatology to be more concerned with the incompleteness to be removed than in describing or conceiving of the wonders to come. Such a reticence is appropriate for those who believe in an other-worldly *eschaton*, for such would be by nature inconceivable. The same should not apply for a salvation within time, which should be much more open to conception, but seems not to be. One recalls Oscar Wilde: 'One wonders how long the meek will keep the earth after they inherit it.'

The shortcomings of an ethical gradualist version of eschatology, such as that of Albrecht Ritschl, were caricatured by Richard Niebuhr: 'A God without wrath brought men without sin into a kingdom without judgement through the ministrations of a Christ without a cross' (H.R. Niebuhr, *The Kingdom of God in America* New York: Harper Torchbooks 1959 p. 193).

[39] J.H. Yoder 'The Constantinian Sources of Western Social Ethics' , *The Priestly Kingdom: Social Ethics as Gospel* (Notre Dame, Indiana: University of Notre Dame Press 1984) pp. 135–47 at p. 137.

[40] O'Donovan, ibid. p. 73. O'Donovan observes that protest is the way liberalism pinches itself to find out if it is still alive. Many theologians have asserted a Christological foundation for the significance of protest. O'Donovan, however, suspects 'that here, as with the crowd before the praetorium, what is really happening is the replacement of Christ by Barabbas' (p. 73).

In short, one must be able to show one is master of one's own *eschaton*. What is missing from this approach is both the transcendent quality of the *eschaton* and the perception of grace, in particular Christ, as decisive.[41]

Reinhard Hutter describes the issue at stake as the difference between a Utopian eschatology and a pneumatological eschatology. A Utopian eschatology sees the Church as being in the forefront of efforts to transform society as a whole. This is what O'Donovan calls the 'historicist' view. The alternative, pneumatological eschatology is in the forefront of the action of the Holy Spirit. Thus the Church looks for signs of God's reign in its own practices and encounters. In the pneumatological version, ends and means coalesce; the cross may be the form in which God's reign appears. Success can only be defined in reference to Christ's passion and resurrection.[42]

A more continuous relationship between eschatology and salvation can be established by attending to the context in which the synoptic gospels were written. It is impossible to separate the 'historical Jesus' from the Jesus handed on through the understanding of the early Church. The principal evidence of him is in the transformation he made in the lives of his followers. From the canonical gospels, particularly the synoptics, two related themes emerge. First, Jesus' healing, teaching and miraculous power were focused not so much on himself but on the kingdom of God. Second, Jesus and his followers saw his ministry and passion as decisive. It was not that the first disciples had a mistaken notion of eschatology; rather, they knew, better than Christians today, the decisive effect of the climax of Jesus' ministry. The early Christians

> looked to the end of the world because they were so profoundly convinced that they had already seen the end in the person and work of Jesus Christ. They did not look to the future because they thought the kingdom had not been fulfilled but because they thought it had been fulfilled through the vocation of this man Jesus. ... The kind of nonresistant love characteristic of Jesus' disciples was possible only because they were convinced the kingdom, the end, had in fact come through the life, death and resurrection of Jesus.[43]

It may be that Jesus anticipated that the events of his passion would precipitate the apocalyptic events described in Mark 13 and elsewhere. It may

---

[41] An ironic twist to the this-worldly and future version of eschatology is that it is not necessarily immune from some of the dangers perceived in an other-worldly and future version. This has been demonstrated in the failure of the Marxist rendering of the revolutionary apocalypse. Ruether describes the similarity thus: 'As in Christian history, Marxism begins with the announcement of the apocalyptic day of wrath and the speedy advent of the kingdom of God, but ends in the indefinite prolonging of the era of the Church, which can justify all persecution and suppression of liberty in the name of that final liberation which never comes but to which it is the exclusive gateway.' (Rosemary Radford Ruether, *The Radical Kingdom: The Western Experience of Messianic Hope* New York: Harper and Row 1970 p. 25.)

[42] Reinhard Hutter, 'Ecclesial Ethics, the Church's Vocation, and Paraclesis' *Pro Ecclesia* 2/4 (Fall 1993) 433–34; see also *In Good Company* p. 30.

[43] Hauerwas, 'The Need for an Ending' *The Modern Churchman* 27/3 (1986) pp. 4–5.

also be the case that many of the anticipated events concerned not the cosmic end of the world but the destruction of the Temple in 70 AD. In any case the writers of the New Testament assume that the decisive, all-important event has *already* happened; we are those 'upon whom the end of the ages has come' (1 Corinthians 10:11); we have 'tasted the powers of the age to come' (Hebrews 6:5). It must therefore be a mistake to understand the kingdom as a purely future event. And yet an other-worldly element remains in the abiding expectation of an imminent closure to the story.

The other-worldliness of the kingdom is important in the sense that God's ways differ from human ways. The this-worldliness is affirmed by the fact that the kingdom has already come to this world in Jesus and will return when he does. Yet the fact that the kingdom is a past event clarifies the distinction between whether it is present or future: it can be present and it will be future because it has been in the past. And what it was in the past shows us what it is in the present and what it will be in the future. In short, the kingdom can be present, and can break into the present from another world, because it *has been* decisively present in the past in the career of Jesus. Christians proclaim a future hope and a present community on the basis of a past event.

The theological demands of creation and salvation should therefore profoundly influence the place given to eschatology in Christian ethics. From creation is gained an emphasis on ontology – that which was, is, and will be true before, during, and after the *eschaton*. From salvation is gained what Hauerwas usually calls the Christian narrative – the historical character of Christian convictions, that which cannot be gainsaid by any future *eschaton*. So eschatological ethics are characterized by a rootedness in the ontology of continuing nonviolent creation and particular nonviolent salvation.

Summary

Hauerwas is used to hearing that he is a sectarian, that he is a fideist, and that he lacks a doctrine of creation. In this chapter I have claimed that if he expanded his understanding of eschatology, he could successfully withstand all these criticisms.

Hauerwas could avoid being called a sectarian if he stopped using spatial metaphors (such as 'living in between' Church and world) and conceived of the distinction in terms of time. The traditional language of eschatology has much to offer ethics when it becomes clear that it lends a particular approach to time. The community of the new time, embodied in the resurrection, shares a space with the rest of society but has a different view of the timeful dimension of all its actions.

Eschatology has much to offer Hauerwas in his controversial use of narrative also. Many of the hermeneutical problems associated with postliberal hermeneutics appear very different when attention is paid to the end of the story. While Hauerwas usually addresses such questions by drawing attention to the hermeneutical community, it would help him greatly if he underlined that this community is eschatological in its understanding of revelation.

Eschatology is not a gnostic way of devaluing concrete history and ethical practice, nor is it a way of reducing the stress on the centrality of Christ. If one concentrates on the nonviolent character of creation and the nonviolence of the one who went to the cross, one has a theme – peace – which unites all the stages of the Christian story with the definitive character of the Church.

8

From Tragedy to Irony

In the last chapter I argued that a thorough treatment of eschatology would help Hauerwas make clear to his critics his position on sectarianism, fideism and creation. In this chapter I push further into the exploration of an eschatological ethic consistent with Hauerwas' commitments. This brings my treatment of Hauerwas full circle, for in Chapter 2 I pointed out the link between principles and violence. Here I argue that to embody a truly nonviolent ethic, the Christian community needs to go beyond tragedy. One significant way in which it does so is in the practice of having children.

Beyond tragedy

Tragedy is a theme to which Stanley Hauerwas returns regularly, particularly in the period 1977–83. He makes a number of claims for the way tragedy forms the moral life. Three areas are particularly significant and illustrate the way tragedy applies to a much wider field.

First, in *Truthfulness and Tragedy*, Hauerwas is largely concerned with the importance of tragedy in medicine. The tragic is experienced when a person (perhaps a highly virtuous person) with several responsibilities and obligations, confronted with a single decision having irreversible consequences, finds that these many interests conflict with both his or her own interest and with each other.

> The practice of medicine offers an intense paradigm of the moral life. For the moral task is to continue to do the right, to care for this immediate patient, even when we have no assurance that it will be the successful thing to do. . . . When a culture loses touch with the tragic, . . . we must redescribe our failures in acceptable terms. Yet to do so *ipso facto* traps us in self-deceiving accounts of what we have done.[1]

Hauerwas goes on to argue that policies based on these premises lead to coercion. Medicine teaches that tragic circumstances are 'what the moral life is all about'.[2] In the last essay in the book, 'Medicine as a Tragic Profession', Hauerwas explores these issues in greater detail, and concludes that medicine serves people best when it helps them face up to (rather than cure) the tragic character of their existence.

---

[1] Hauerwas, *Truthfulness and Tragedy* pp. 37–38.
[2] Ibid. p. 115.

Second, in *A Community of Character*, Hauerwas applies the genre of tragedy to the issue of relativism. In doing so he develops his notion of tragedy:

> The conflict of right with right . . . is but a form of a more profound sense of tragedy inherent in living in a divided world. For tragedy consists in the moral necessity of having to risk our lives and the lives of others in order to live faithful to the histories that are the only means we have for knowing and living truthfully.[3]

Hauerwas goes on to maintain that tragedy arises when faithfulness to one's character leads one into situations in which one's 'multiple responsibilities and obligations conflict not only with self-interest, but with each other'. There is no use trying to underestimate or deny the extent of division in the moral world. The tendency of deontological or utilitarian theories is to try to bypass these moral divisions; thus they deny the tragic. This, says Hauerwas, only leads to violence.[4] This brings him to an understanding of the Church as a community where people can keep each other faithful despite the inevitable tragedies each member faces.

Third, Hauerwas considers tragedy in the course of his profound meditation on the spirituality of peaceableness in the last chapter of *The Peaceable Kingdom*. The virtue of patience emerges as the key to enabling Christians to be faithful despite the inevitable tragedies of their lives. This is the point at which the eschatological perspective implicit in his discussion of tragedy comes to the surface:

> Our unwillingness to employ violence to make the world 'better' means that we must often learn to wait. Yet such a waiting must resist the temptation to cynicism, conservatism, or false utopianism that assumes the process of history will result in 'everything coming out all right.' For Christians hope not in the 'processes of history,' but in the God whom we believe has already determined the end of history in the cross and resurrection of Jesus Christ.[5]

Hauerwas goes on to contrast the peace based on conspiracies of lies, with the Church's peace, which unmasks those conspiracies, faces the forces those conspiracies had kept in check, and cares for the casualties.

Hauerwas' arguments for the significance of tragedy are insightful and persuasive. However when it comes to placing them in an eschatological perspective, it begins to appear that tragedy is not quite the right genre. Tragedy has deep associations with Greek notions of fate: fate, in the Greek understanding, is stronger even than the gods. Tragic heroes are often those who transgress the natural moral law. Fate and natural law are notions which sit uncomfortably with Hauerwas' interest in providence and destiny.[6] More

---

[3] Hauerwas, *A Community of Character* p. 106.

[4] Ibid. p. 107. See pp. 18–20 above.

[5] Hauerwas, *The Peaceable Kingdom* p. 145.

[6] 'Communities formed by a truthful narrative must provide the skills to transform fate into destiny'. Hauerwas, *A Community of Character* p. 10.

importantly, the last word in any Christian narrative can never be tragedy since, as Hauerwas himself insists, the last word is Jesus Christ. The Christian narrative claims 'that God has taken the tragic character of our existence into his very life'.[7] Hauerwas himself acknowledges, in the words of Reinhold Niebuhr, that the Christian hope lies 'beyond tragedy'.[8] But where is that?

Hauerwas' insistence on tragedy makes sense when tragedy is used as a way of squaring up to the dilemmas of human existence. His argument for the tragic character of medicine is directed against the tendency of consequentialist reasoning to assume that 'right answers' can be plucked out of the moral whirlpool. The consequentialist tells what we might call a 'comic' story – one with a happy ending, which the action under consideration will aim to bring about. Hauerwas is absolutely right to expose and reject this rendering of the story. But by telling a tragic story Hauerwas comes to share a number of the problems of the deontological approach. He is aware that deontological approaches can become 'a formula for moral callousness and self-righteousness' if the narrative context is ignored.[9] Yet the deontological 'story' is often a tragic story too.

What is missing from Hauerwas' discussion of tragedy is the notion of irony.[10] Irony is the genre which resolves the ambiguities of the notion of tragedy. John Howard Yoder introduces a dimension of irony into Hauerwas' thought by his insistence on luck, surprise and accident, and the way a commitment to nonviolence opens the door to these factors. But Hauerwas still tends to concentrate on martyrdom and the cross, emphasizing the tragic character of Christian faithfulness.

The journey from tragedy to irony may be illustrated by returning to the notion of 'medicine as a tragic profession'. Hauerwas derives this notion from MacIntyre. And indeed it is true: for medicine should teach society the disciplines of tragedy. But the journey from MacIntyre to Hauerwas is the journey from society to the Church. That journey is a journey from tragedy to irony. For what the Church has to say to the profession of medicine is, yes, medicine is not a 'comic' story with a happy ending, but no, medicine is not just a tragic story. It goes beyond tragedy. To say this much is to enter the field of irony.

Irony and eschatology

Ironic ethics

The tenor of an ironic story is one of contrast – contrast between how things appear and how they are, between what participants are aware of and what

---

[7] Ibid. p. 108.
[8] Hauerwas, *The Peaceable Kingdom* p. 148.
[9] Ibid. p. 128.
[10] Irony is not totally absent: Hauerwas uses the word 'irony' three times in his discussion of 'Tragedy and Peaceableness' (ibid. pp. 142–146).

happens in spite of them, between the *status quo* and its increasingly apparent absurdities. The contrasts of the Christian story are between human expectations and God's reality, between human failure and God's victory, between what one supposes to be the end of the story and the final end of the world. The central irony of the Christian story is that it is a human tragedy and a divine comedy. Christians perform that story by affirming the central role of God in the narrative:

> The pure or archetypal ironist is God.... He is the ironist par excellence because he is omniscient, omnipotent, transcendent, absolute, infinite and free.... 'In earthly art, irony has this meaning – conduct similar to God's' (Karl Solger). The archetypal victim of irony is man, seen, *par contra*, as trapped and submerged in time and matter, blind, contingent, limited and unfree – and confidently unaware that this is his predicament.[11]

It becomes clear that irony is a characteristic both of Hauerwas' method and of an eschatological approach to ethics. Hauerwas is constantly chipping away at the self-assurance of those who are confidently unaware of the insecurity or transitoriness or violence of their convictions. He sets up no grand plan, no strategy of the big battalion as a new Babel; instead he engages in hand to hand disputes with those who challenge the pattern of the Christian narrative. A common characteristic of irony is that some people can see something that others cannot. The communion of saints is a perspective that can see the world from a heavenly vantage point. By being part of the communion of saints, the Church shares this ironic perspective.

Meanwhile an eschatological approach is intensely ironic. It truly transforms fate into destiny. It sits in judgement over this time and this world; it mocks all who attempt to thwart its power – by arrogating power to themselves, by trying to evade death, or by behaving as if impervious to judgement. All human efforts to construct an earthly paradise are subsumed in a heaven beyond human imagining. All complacency is undermined when the *eschaton* comes at a time that no one expects. Apparent triumph turns to dust; apparent defeat is exalted. The secrets of all hearts are revealed: neither the sheep nor the goats know quite what to expect. The ethic could best be summarized thus: it is better to fail in a cause that will finally succeed than to succeed in a cause that will finally fail.[12] This is the language of profound irony: beyond tragedy.

When Hauerwas talks at length of the cross and martyrdom, critics such as Oliver O'Donovan complain that his outlook is too bleak. The reason for this bleakness, I suggest, is that Hauerwas takes the ironic perspective for granted, and thus overstresses the tragic dimensions of discipleship. The result is that he labours the human tragedy, and skips the divine comedy. But all the while, the ironic perspective is implicit in what he is saying. This is illustrated by one of the most gruesome stories he tells, that of the Dunkard Brethren.

---

[11] D.C. Muecke, *Irony, the Critical Idiom* (London: Methuen 1970) pp. 37–38.

[12] I owe this expression to Bill Arlow.

Hauerwas quotes U.J. Jones' thoroughly unsympathetic account of the German 'Dunkard' Brethren in Morrison's Cove, Pennsylvania, who refused to take up arms or pay for others to do so during the French, Indian and Revolutionary wars in the eighteenth century. Jones notes that during an Indian raid the Dunkards made no effort at resistance. A handful of Dunkards hid themselves away; 'but by far the most of them stood by and witnessed the butchery of wives and children, merely saying "Gottes wille sei gethan" '. The warriors carried off more than thirty scalps and plenty of plunder. Up to this point this is an extraordinary example of the tragic demands of discipleship implied by Hauerwas. But then there is an ironic twist. Jones apparently misses the significance of his own observation that the Brethren repeated 'Gottes wille sei gethan' so often during the massacre that the Indians thought it was the name of this strange tribe; a fact that came to light when some of the Indians were later captured and enquired whether the 'Gotswilthans' still lived in the Cove.[13] What appeared to be a tragic story turns out to be beyond tragedy. This is at the heart of an eschatological perspective.

In order to gain a different perspective on the way irony is important to Hauerwas' ethics, witness what happens when ethics is conducted without an awareness of irony. Hauerwas exposes this kind of ethics in his essay 'On Surviving Justly: Ethics and Nuclear Disarmament'. The issue here is that one cannot dispense with eschatology: one simply chooses between good eschatology and bad eschatology. In characteristic fashion, Hauerwas shows the absurdity of the survivalist argument.

The survivalist argument concludes that, because nuclear weapons are so destructive, because any nuclear war would probably be a total war, and because the human species may not survive such a war, nuclear war must be excluded at all costs.[14] Humanity, it is said, has no right to endanger a common world based on the biological immortality of our species. This common world is seen as the source of all value: 'there are no ethics apart from service to the human community, and therefore no ethical commandments that can justify the extinction of humanity'.[15] Thus anything that threatens the value of value itself must be immoral. Survival becomes the first principle of ethics.

This argument relies on the human species as the determinant moral factor. But is it so clear that without humanity there will be nothing left of value? This certainly has implications for the relation of humanity to the animal world. The end of survival appears on this view to be so paramount that any means necessary to secure it are presumably legitimate. Such peace

---

[13] See Hauerwas, 'Creation, Contingency and Truthful Nonviolence', Rufus D. Bowman, *Church of the Brethren and War* (Elgin: Brethren Publishing House 1944) pp. 74–75.

[14] Hauerwas, *Against the Nations* pp. 140–146.

[15] Jonathan Schell, *The Fate Of The Earth* (New York: Alfred Knopf, 1982), quoted in Hauerwas, *Against the Nations* p. 142.

at any price is unlikely to be a just peace. Survivalism thus exhibits the shortcomings of an ethic with a weak eschatology. In heavily ironic terms, Hauerwas summarizes the problems involved in the rejection of eschatology on ethical grounds:

> What good is a peace movement that works for peace for the same idolatrous reason that we build bombs – namely, the anxious self-interested protection of our world as it is? ... We do not argue that the bomb is the worst thing humanity can do to itself. We have already done the worst thing we could do when we hung God's Son on a cross. We do not argue that we must do something about the bomb or else we shall obliterate our civilization, because God has already obliterated our civilization in the life, teaching, death and resurrection of Jesus. . . . Our hope is based not on Caesar's missiles or Caesar's treaties but on the name of the Lord who made heaven and earth. People often work for peace out of the same anxieties and perverted views of reality that lead people to build bombs.[16]

The dangers of ironic ethics

If Hauerwas' style is so clearly ironic, and his ethic has such a strong tendency toward eschatology, why are these themes not more thoroughly embraced by his work?

I suspect that the reason may be that irony tends to assume the position of the observer. The archetypal ironic figure is the stranger in a new country, noticing the absurd habits that the locals take for granted. Now in one respect this is very much Hauerwas' position: he is the Christian in a secular world, noticing the absurdities of liberal presuppositions; he also writes as if he is at one remove from denominational differences. Yet in another respect the position of the observer is one that Hauerwas shuns. He shuns it because the kind of ethics he has set himself against is that which assumes it can take the neutral high ground of the disinterested observer. Such an observer has no understanding of the particular narrative and character of those involved in an issue, and thus is in no position to pass judgement – besides which, no such neutral ground exists.

A corresponding criticism of the eschatological perspective on Christian ethics is the danger of gnosticism. If eschatology becomes a secret knowledge concerning events and timings, Christian ethics has lost the perspective on time that I outlined earlier in this chapter. Time has ceased to be a gift, and has become another object to be manipulated. If the *eschaton* is seen as the complete *replacement* of the present order, both creation and salvation are undermined. Such a view prizes the kingdom so highly that it denies our present existence altogether. The result is a gnostic view that assumes that the *telos* of the world is wholly other than its present form, and thus that creation will be set aside in the *eschaton*. The gnostic approach sees the decisive events

---

[16] Hauerwas and Willimon, *Resident Aliens* pp. 89–90.

in salvation not as creation and Christ but as Fall and *eschaton*. The gnostic community separates itself from the world, prizing the secret knowledge which will gain it salvation.

The theologian who has come closest to the ironic approach I am outlining is Wolfhart Pannenberg. The following passage expresses his metaphysical commitment to the 'ontological priority of the future':

> If it is true that only with reference to the *totality* of reality can one speak meaningfully about a revelation of God as the world's Creator and Lord, and that reality (understood as historical) is first constituted as the totality of a single history by the end of all occurrences, then eschatology acquires a constitutive significance not only for the question of the knowledge, but also for that of the reality, of God.[17]

In an important dialogue with Pannenberg, Hauerwas makes explicit his misgivings about what I have called an ironic approach.[18] The issue at stake is whether one can talk meaningfully of the not-yet-existent as if it were the most concrete thing of all. Hauerwas' scepticism here reflects his concern with the particular and contingent: he is, as ever, suspicious of attempts to escape the practical and everyday in search of the timeless and absolute. Hauerwas goes on to criticize Pannenberg for translating the otherness of the kingdom into undefined generalities of justice and love. The heart of Hauerwas' frustration with Pannenberg lies in the latter's resort to abstraction when articulating the ethics of the kingdom. But I believe Hauerwas goes unnecessarily far in criticizing the notion of the 'ontological priority of the future' as an abstraction also. For, as I have already shown, this eschatological perspective does thorough justice to two key elements in Hauerwas' thought: the significance of Jesus as the embodiment of the kingdom, and the perception of the *length* of the Christian story which consequentialist approaches underestimate. The problem with Pannenberg, in my view, is not that he makes metaphysical claims about something that is not yet fully realized – for surely this tension runs through Christian theology, Hauerwas included – but that he does not go far enough towards outlining the particular implications of his eschatological perspective. I have attempted in Chapter 7 to deepen the metaphysical dimensions of Hauerwas' thought by embracing it with Milbank's view of creation; here I am advocating the advantages of Pannenberg's perspective on eschatology.

The Church as satire

While Hauerwas may well have misgivings about irony, I maintain that his concentration on Christian community is the strongest safeguard against

---

[17] Wolfhart Pannenberg, *Basic Questions in Theology* Volume One (London: SCM Press 1971) p. xv.

[18] Hauerwas and Mark Sherwindt, 'The Reality of the Kingdom: An Ecclesial Space for Peace' in Hauerwas, *Against the Nations* pp. 107–121.

them. It is the lives and habits of an actual community that gives eschatology its contemporary concrete embodiment. It is the earthing in the traditions and practices of such a community that both ensures a narrative approach and ties salvation to vocation and thus prevents it becoming other-worldly and world-denying. The existence of an eschatological community, expressing its faithfulness especially in its attitude to time, is the new reality that salvation brings.

One could call the Church, in Hauerwas' ethics, an ironic parody of society, a satire on secularism. In what senses is the Church a satire?

The Church lives among people who care deeply about what they do and weigh carefully the consequences of their actions. There should be no question of the Church not taking the world seriously. But humour, in irony, comes from some characters being able to see something that others cannot. The Christian description of this state is revelation. Revelation is not a secret knowledge, but is embodied in the stories performed by the Christian community. The Christian story amounts to a satire on the story that there is no story.

Like others, Christians believe that their actions in the present are very important; but unlike others, they believe the most important thing has already happened – namely, the life, death and resurrection of Jesus Christ. Like others, Christians believe that their natural environment is of great significance; but unlike others, they describe that environment as creation, and regard its purpose as being fundamentally disclosed in the kingdom embodied in Christ. Like others, Christians want to be successful in their enterprises; but unlike others, they have cause to be patient, assured that their cause will finally succeed. Like others, Christians take steps to avoid violent confrontation; but unlike others, Christians believe that peace is ontologically prior to violence. Christian faith in the sovereignty of God is an ironic statement about all other allegiances.

What makes it legitimate to use the term 'satire', rather than 'irony', is that the Church and the world share a space. The danger of irony is that it can convey a sense of superiority, a sense that the disembodied viewer can see more than the embodied participant. It sits uneasily with Hauerwas' commitment to the historical community. But satire takes place in the company of the satirized. It is the voice of the group who are obliged to borrow their clothes, their time, their space of performance from those who usually 'run the show'.[19] And this is the condition of the Church. Its actions very often look very much like the actions of others; it does not always 'look redeemed'; it can claim no superiority of power or goodness. And yet in the midst of a performance that is so world-like that it is instantly identifiable, lie practices that hint at a story that exposes the emptiness of that world's longings. These are practices such as regular confession and reconciliation, underlining the necessity of forgiveness; baptism; the eucharist, shared in trust as the enactment of the peace between God and his people; politics, the art of articulating

---

[19] See de Certeau's description of tactic, pp. 114–116 above.

difference without violence; peacemaking; facing tragedy; caring for the weak; and maintaining the ability to tell the story. Along with these and other distinctive practices, are the countless things the satirical community do that mirror the actions of others, but are done for such different reasons that they become ironic activities. Among these, having children is one I shall discuss shortly.

Far from the Church having any sense of superiority, it looks ridiculous when it seems to operate in a different time-scale from the world. The story of the Dunkard brethren is one that the world could only see as bizarre.[20] The Church enacts a parallel story to that of secular liberalism, one which satirizes the pretensions of its grander claims. God's ways are different to human ways: and the Church is called to be the place where the difference is performed. The gospels abound in irony and satire – washing the disciples' feet, the crown of thorns, 'but it shall not be so with you', 'he saved others, he cannot save himself', birth in a manger not a palace. The Church is called to embody the ironies of Christian existence, and perform them as satire to the world's story.

Standing in the same place as the world, but in a different time; looking for a time when all shall be well; appearing at times absurd to the secular mind; modelling a parallel way of being society; affirming all the while that God's ways are different to human ways; in all these ways the Church embodies an ironic perspective and tells its ironic story. Charles Pinches expresses beautifully this vocation to imitate the archetypal ironist:

> God is committed to the world, but is not identical with the world; he is *for* the world, but this is not his whole being; he is *prior* to the world; without him, the world could not know itself as world; he would do the world no favour by being absorbed into the world; he serves the world, but has his own integrity and inner life. The Church is the same.[21]

Thus one could describe the Church as an ironic parody of society, a satire on secularism. The Church is the cuckoo in the nest, on others' territory, a resident alien. Hauerwas revels in this approach: he adores to point out to emperors that they have no clothes. The ironist inhabits the same space as the rest of society, but has a perspective that makes some of the nostrums of that society seem absurd. The ironic community makes no claims to superiority or seclusion: it simply operates with a different timescale from the rest of society. For the Church, that is the eschatological perspective.

Having children

I have pointed out that the Church satirizes the society in which it lives by doing many of the same things as non-Christians do but doing them for

---

[20] See p. 168 above.
[21] Charles R. Pinches, 'Hauerwas Represented: A Response to Muray' *Process Studies* 18/2 (1989) p. 99.

different reasons. The practice that Hauerwas returns to most often, that fits this description, is that of having children.[22] Christians and non-Christians alike have children: and perhaps few Christians understand what they are doing as different from what a non-Christian is doing in having children. But, for Hauerwas, having children is not a necessity or simply a 'natural' fact. Instead, it forms and expresses a community's deepest assumptions and convictions about its life, identity and relation to time.

The reasons why Christians have children demonstrate the differences between what they and others take for granted. For example, one of the great injustices of giving birth to a child with a severe mental handicap is often perceived to be that such a child does not and will not turn out as the parents had expected. Yet on a little more reflection it is clear that no child turns out as the parents had expected: the community is not able to control the outcome of any child's life.[23] The question is thus one of how a community receives the unexpected child, what it expects any child to be, and why, in fact, Christians have children at all.

The subject of having children therefore offers an appropriate conclusion to my suggestions for Hauerwas' possible future directions, for it draws attention to his most successful demonstration of the satirical role of the eschatological community. The discussion is a complement to my treatment of Le Chambon-sur-Lignon, another eschatological parody of secular ethics.[24]

The first significant thing about having children is what it says about creation. The Church sees creation, not as nature, but as gift. In his early work, Hauerwas is critical of the emphasis on decision in Christian ethics. One of the fruits of this criticism is a recovery of the significance of everyday habits and practices. Having children is one of a number of practices that are generally taken for granted in Christian communities. In Hauerwas' eyes, ethics is about learning to take the right things for granted, about educating one's habits.

Having children is commonly passed over as an ethical issue because it is perceived as being natural, normal and necessary. These are all suppositions about creation. I have pointed out in Chapter 2 that 'natural' and 'normal' are not the value-free terms they at first appear to be. They may certainly be replaced by the word 'common' (or 'trivial'), but, as I have noted, the most ordinary activities of life are among the most significant. In his essay 'Taking Time for Peace: The Ethical Significance of the Trivial', Hauerwas unites the themes of time, narrative, peace and creation, around the commitment to take care over 'trivial' practices. The first step in a two-step argument is that peace and time are closely related:

> Peace takes time. Put even more strongly, peace creates time by its steadfast refusal to force the other to submit in the name of order. Peace is not a static state but

---

[22] See especially Hauerwas, *Truthfulness and Tragedy* pp. 147–183, *A Community of Character* pp. 155–195.

[23] See Hauerwas, *Truthfulness and Tragedy* pp. 153–154.

[24] See pp. 134–139 above.

an activity which requires constant attention and care. An activity by its very nature takes place over time. In fact, activity creates time, as we know how to characterize duration only by noting that we did this first, and then this second, and so on, until we either got somewhere or accomplished this or that task. So peace is the process through which we make time our own rather than be determined by 'events' over which, it is alleged, we have no control.[25]

The second step is to apply this notion of activity to the practice of having children. Having children emerges as the embodiment of the relationship between time and peace:

> Having children is activity in its most paradigmatic form, as the having of a child is its own meaning. Moreover, having children is our most basic time-full project, not only in the sense that children are time-consuming, but because through children our world quite literally is made timeful. Children bind existence temporally, as through them we are given beginnings, middles and ends. They require us to take time and, as a result, we learn that time is only possible as a form of peace.[26]

Hauerwas goes on to maintain that 'the most radical stance possible for any human is the willingness to have a child in the face of injustice, oppression and tyranny. Having children is the ultimate defeat of all totalitarianisms ... Nothing can be more important for us ... than to go on having children'.

'Taking Time for Peace' is a very important essay because it shows how a practice that affirms creation is also an eschatological practice. Children are not the possession of their parents, as might be the case if the parents' choice were the only factor in their birth; they are not the possession simply of the community, as a strong view of the state might imply; nor are they owned by themselves, as the language of rights suggests. Instead they are the possession of God, called and chosen by him. Parents do not so much choose their children as discover them as gifts that are not simply of their own making. Children are therefore a gift. They are not simply under their parents' control, they are not always what their parents expect or want, the surprises they bring may be ones of pain and suffering rather than joy. As gifts, they do not just supply needs or wants, they create needs, teaching their parents what wants they should have. Children teach their parents how to be: they create in their parents the need to want and love one another. They draw their parents love to them while refusing to be as they wish them to be.

Having children emerges as a practice crucial to helping Christians understand the doctrine of creation in the light of the eschatological ethic. Children teach the Christian community that life is not under its control. The willingness to bear them is an affirmation that time is in safe hands.

---

[25] Hauerwas, 'Taking Time for Peace' *Christian Existence Today* p. 258.

[26] Ibid. p. 262. No one expresses this point better than the character Ian Bedloe in Anne Tyler's novel *Saint Maybe*. See p. 49 above.

The second significant thing about having children is what it says about salvation, and the way salvation is translated into the Christian community as vocation. Christians are called to form the Church – that is, communities which recognize God's sovereignty over all existence and therefore do not need to control the world in order to be secure. Because these communities are not based on fear, they can display the trust and love which God's rule makes possible. Christians and their communities often get it wrong: they often live in fear, particularly fear of the truth; they are often distrustful and sometimes violent. Yet the power of despair and falsehood only illustrates the urgency of truthful, hopeful living. This new, eschatological, community is the crucial demonstration that salvation affirms creation: salvation does not extract humans from time but restores them in a new time.

Having children anchors Christians to historical time. A parent cannot escape the mundanities of existence in the way a single person can.[27] The inter-generational ties of the family teach the community what it means to be historic beings. Being in a family is part of being 'stuck with' a history and a people. If ethics is to be as historical as salvation, it must resist the timeless abstractions of the universal, the abstract and the moment, and take seriously the habits, ordinariness and triviality of family life.

This commitment to historical time is implied by a narrative understanding of revelation. But it also implies an awareness of how things could have been different. The origin of the Christian understanding of having children is itself intimately bound up with historical contingency. The writers of the New Testament did not make marriage and the family the norm for the Christian life: what was required was complete service to the kingdom. The Christian community was expected to grow through the conversion and baptism of outsiders rather than simply through marriage and procreation from within.[28] As the urgency of the imminent *eschaton* receded, the legacy remained: marriage and family had ceased to be a natural or moral necessity and had become a vocation – that is, not the result of choice but the result of being called.

The demand for complete service to the kingdom not only removed the necessity of marriage: it showed that marriage and the family were not objects of loyalty in themselves but were transcended by loyalty to God's rule. Since,

---

[27] Janet Martin Soskice summarizes this parental 'contingency':

> I have been in the past envious and in awe of colleagues (usually bachelors) who spend their holidays living with monks in the Egyptian desert or making long retreats on Mount Athos. They return refreshed and renewed and say things like 'It was wonderful. I was able to read the whole of *The City of God* in the Latin . . . something I've not done for three or four years now.' I then recall my own 'holiday' as entirely taken up with explaining why you can't swim in the river with an infected ear, why two ice creams before lunch is a bad idea, with trips to disgusting public conveniences with children who are 'desperate' . . . (Janet Martin Soskice, 'Love and Attention' in Michael McGee (ed.), *Philosophy, Religion and Spiritual Life* Cambridge: Cambridge University Press 1991 p. 61.)

[28] This is a clear departure from the Old Testament period, with which in other respects the themes of vocation and historical contingency have much in common.

as we have seen, God's sovereignty is not to be understood as abstracted from time, it is the Christian community, the Church, that transcends the family.[29] God's salvation infuses all aspects of humanity, including those – language, interpretation, memory, belief, action, understanding – which are inextricably communal.[30]

Whether one is oneself called to have children or not, no one would be here unless their ancestors and parents had had children. Again, one cannot abstract oneself from contingency. When one talks of inheritance, expectation, change, growth and development, one is using the language of an incipient story. One establishes an identity when one is able to thread together separate events and realities in one's history. Being able to make judgements and give reasons for one's actions is an important part of claiming one's life as something that is one's own.[31] These judgements and reasons are very often retrospective ones: history is lived forwards and understood backwards. This is all the more reason for needing a sense of a narrative that acknowledges truthfully what one has been, yet enables one to go on. For instance, if one treats having children as something that simply happens (or does not happen) to one, one fails to claim one's life and actions as one's own. What is required is a story that places having children in a coherent relation to other events in one's life and does not see one's actions as either determined or random. Without such a story of and for the self one is particularly vulnerable to those who will offer their own ideological rendering of existence. As Hauerwas frequently comments, the ideology of Western liberal democracies is a story which assumes one can live without a story. This leaves communities with children but with no idea why they had them.

The third significant thing about having children is what it says about Christian hope. Hope is the conviction that despite the evidence of misery in the world, God is sovereign, creator and redeemer; though racked with sin, the world and existence are good, and God has given his people the skills to deal with sin, in themselves and others, in a manner that will destroy neither Church

---

[29] This is significant for the issue of children's rights. Parents in a Christian community do not raise their children to conform just to what they, the child's particular parents, think right. The parents are the agents of the community's commitments, memories and understandings. The child is able to appeal to these symbols of significance beyond the family – which apply equally to child and parent – thus guaranteeing the necessary moral and physical space to gain independence from his or her parents. The Church has a role in protecting the child: this is exercised not through the rights of the child, but through the higher loyalty of both the parents and the child. Everyone in the community is responsible for children, though not everyone has children: it is not a matter of protecting individual rights but of learning public duties. In the absence of the Church, the child is likely to turn to its peer group or culture to balance the pull of the family to be a substitute church.

[30] See Kenneson, 'Taking Time for the Trivial' p. 71.

[31] Hauerwas' clearest exposition of this point is in his essay 'Character, Narrative and Growth in the Christian Life' *A Community of Character* Chapter 7. See also pp. 44–48 above.

nor world. In this context, children are a 'promissory note' to present and future generations that the community trusts the Lord who has called them as his people. Having children witnesses to the Church's belief that life is worth living.

Christian hope expresses the relationship between salvation and time. We saw above that salvation involves time and does not bypass temporal human activities and communities. With much wrong that needs righting in the world, having children may appear to be a surrender to the tyranny of time. For having children takes up so much time – time that could be spent on scholarship, creating wealth, alleviating poverty, curing disease, or undermining unjust structures. To the one committed to making the world 'come out right', having children seems an act of despair. To some, having children seems pointless and cruel, since one is bringing them into such an unjust world, and one should not be tied down until the world is made fair and just; to others, the world seems beyond hope, and having children is a self-indulgent form of capitulation to the *status quo*. How, in a world of injustice, can having children be anything other than an admission of failure, a complacent retreat to the 'private' realm, in short, an act of either selfishness or despair?

The answer to this pressing question lies again in the historical view of salvation. Salvation establishes a new people, the eschatological people: and a characteristic of that people is that they live in a new time – an eschatological time. Thus all contemporary society's struggles with time, the greatest enemy, are but another – perhaps the definitive – effort to assert control. Instead, time is a gift. Patience means living in a new time. Just as the kingdom made having children a vocation rather than a necessity, so eschatology makes time, like children, a gift rather than a given. God is sovereign; the kingdom is of God's making; the Christian community can afford to spend time on the ordinary and trivial, since the tyranny of time has been broken, and they trust in a 'new' time, in which their salvation and happiness do not depend on how they 'spend' or 'use' their time.

In this 'new' time, Christians can care for those who cannot make the world healthier, wealthier or wiser. They can comfort one person rather than seek the status of comforting many. They can have time for worship, though the time might have been 'spent' making the world come out 'right'. Such activities, which challenge the prevailing view of time, are eschatological practices. Having children is one of them. Whenever Christian communities engage in such practices, the kingdom breaks in.

Having children is therefore an ironic practice. It seems to be one of the few things in life that is under human control, but it turns out to be the opposite. Having children is a recognition that God is in control. Irony is a characteristic of eschatology, since it contrasts the ways of God, who sees all things, with the ways of his people, who see dimly and respond weakly. An eschatological view of having children makes clear that the activity, the child, and the consequences are nothing like so much one's own as they appear.

Seeing child-rearing as an ironic practice avoids two particular misunderstandings of having children. In the first place, having children is not a direct embodiment of resurrection – as might be understood by saying 'life goes on'. A reductionist view of resurrection is inadequate in the light of an eschatological view. The vital insight is the connection outlined between resurrection and forgiveness. Just as resurrection is an ironic commentary on the limitations of human life, so forgiveness is an ironic statement that human sinfulness does not have the last word.

Neither, in the second place, should child-rearing be understood in gradualist terms. There is no analogy to be drawn between the growth of children to maturity and the moral growth of the world: this leads to replacing the categories of evil and good with those of past and future. If an analogy is to be drawn it is between having children and the relationship of the Church to wider society. Hauerwas describes the idea that one should not impose one's own values on one's children as 'moral cowardice'.[32] Yet failing to influence the world in the same way is not moral cowardice. Is this inconsistent? Perhaps the answer is that Christians share their values with their children not in order to make them faithful, but in order to be faithful themselves. In the same way they act in the world in a certain way (such as nonviolence) not in order to conform the world to them, but because they see that way as the only way to be faithful to the gospel. It is certainly the case that if the Church is to be cohesive as an ironic satire on contemporary society it must have disciplined training and faithful teachers.

The Church learns to deal with time through the way it learns to understand children. The Christian community learns that children are not a natural, normal or necessary 'given' but a gift. Children are a gift to the Church, teaching the practices of peace. Likewise the Church learns to see time not as an enemy to be controlled but as a gift to be enjoyed. Time is not simply a necessary fact of existence: the way Christians respond to time is a witness to their faith in God's sovereignty. To the extent that the Christian community is called to have children, it is given time to do so.

Summary

Eschatology brings a shape to Christian theology and in turn to Christian ethics. By providing an end to the story it shows that the Christian narrative *is* indeed a story, not an endless sequence of events. Since the end is provided from outside, it is not humanity's task to bring this end about. Christian ethics is therefore about acting in accord with the ending that will come about, rather than acting so that a desirable end will come about.

---

[32] In Hauerwas' view parents do no favours to their children by refraining from teaching them 'values' in order that they might later be free to make up their own minds. This is another doomed effort to free children from contingency. More often, it can mask a moral cowardice, since if parents ask their children to believe as they believe, act as they act, and live as they live, they must have the courage to expect themselves to live faithfully. (See Hauerwas' discussion of this in *A Community of Character* p. 166.) If one's values are not good enough for one's children, they are not good enough for oneself. It is less a matter of controlling one's children than of being faithful oneself.

Viewing human existence from the end of the story lends an ironic perspective to Christian ethics. For the ending of any story exposes the folly of those who had acted assuming an alternative conclusion. If one knows how the story is going to end, and that ending is final, one is more likely to live that way in the middle of the story. It is better to fail in a cause that will finally succeed than to succeed in a cause that will finally fail. The danger of an ironic perspective is that it can lead to a sectarian, quietist, detached gnosticism – the possession of a special knowledge that separates one from the world and makes action unnecessary. This is where the narrative is so important: because God has immersed himself in his world through Israel, Christ and the Church, Christians must do the same.

This immersion in the 'triviality' of the world expresses the new time in which Christians live. Because they are not anxious about creating a propitious end to the story, they can spend their time doing things that witness their faith that the story has already been assigned an end. Christians stand out from the world because of the practices they have developed which express their faith in the world's purpose. Meanwhile, many of the practices they do share with the world, they understand in a distinctive way. Having children is such a practice: one that affirms Christians' commitment to the contingencies of life while exhibiting their patience and hope.

Concluding remarks

In this study I have sought to achieve four things. I began by setting Stanley Hauerwas' work in the context of the twentieth-century debate over Christian social ethics in North America. I then outlined Hauerwas' work and the way it has unfolded. In the process I assessed the principal criticisms that his work has attracted. I concluded by suggesting areas which, if explored, would help Hauerwas address his critics.

The two themes of fate and destiny emerged in the introductory chapter. The tradition which Hauerwas inherits has been shaped by Reinhold Niebuhr's sense of the fallenness of social humanity, and by Walter Rauschenbusch's sense of the destiny of the American people. The ethical tradition which Hauerwas in his early years calls 'the standard account' is similarly coloured by its implicit perception of fate and destiny: the tragic fate of the individual whose crises of decision are insoluble in conventional terms, and the limited destiny of the rebellion which claims that 'love is all you need'. Hauerwas finds in the detail of story, particularly through gifted storytellers like Trollope, a display of how a person of character can embody the destiny of their calling amid the givens of their circumstances. Only the Christian story, however, can form a community which treasures, rather than fears, the truth, and can look to its destiny with such hope that it needs no violence to overcome the givens of its existence. Moving beyond Hauerwas, I have argued that the community's hope is shaped by its perception of the end of the Christian story – its notion of what lies on the last page. A true confidence about its destiny enables the Church to face the tragedies of life from an ironic perspective. Rather than cling to a spatial separation from all that might diminish its integrity, the Church is characterized by its relationship to time. Instead of acting to make the world come out right, the Church acts according to the eschatological truth it believes about God. Thus it performs everyday, time-consuming tasks, just like the rest of the world: but for different reasons. It therefore appears to be a satire on society.

The story of the ten bridesmaids in Matthew 25 embodies the eschatological emphasis I am proposing. Whereas the five foolish maidens concentrate their ethic on the moment of crisis, and are found wanting, the five wise maidens perceive that character means concentrating on the time of preparation. They share a space with the foolish maidens; their activities look similar; but they have a different notion of time. They are not called upon to do anything extraordinary when 'that day' comes: they have learned to take the right things for granted, and they do the obvious.

Stanley Hauerwas' work is important because it is pleading with the Church to stay awake. The worship and disciplined practices of the Church form its character, and constant attention to remembering its story prevent its being captivated by false stories. The heart of Christian ethics lies not in the choice of the individual to do the right thing, but in the faithfulness of the Church to the character of God. For if the Church does not perceive its destiny, it will be left to its fate.

Bibliography of the Writings of Stanley Hauerwas

Books

Vision and Virtue: Essays in Christian Ethical Reflection (Notre Dame: University of Notre Dame Press 1974/1981)

Character and the Christian Life: A Study in Theological Ethics (San Antonio: Trinity University Press 1975/1985)

Truthfulness and Tragedy: Further Investigations in Christian Ethics (with Richard Bondi and David Burrell) (Notre Dame: University of Notre Dame Press 1977)

A Community of Character: Toward a Constructive Christian Social Ethic (Notre Dame: University of Notre Dame Press 1981)

The Peaceable Kingdom: A Primer in Christian Ethics (Notre Dame: University of Notre Dame Press 1983; London: SCM Press 1984)

Against the Nations: War and Survival in a Liberal Society (Minneapolis: Winston Seabury Press 1985)

Suffering Presence: Theological Reflections on Medicine, the Mentally Handicapped, and the Church (Edinburgh: T & T Clark 1986)

Christian Existence Today: Essays on Church, World, and Living In Between (Durham, North Carolina: Labyrinth Press 1988)

Resident Aliens: Life in the Christian Colony (with William Willimon) (Nashville: Abingdon 1989)

Naming the Silences: God, Medicine, and the Problem of Suffering (Grand Rapids: Eerdmans 1990)

After Christendom: How the Church is to Behave if Freedom, Justice, and a Christian Nation are Bad Ideas (Nashville: Abingdon 1991)

Preaching to Strangers: Evangelism in Today's World (with William Willimon) (Louisville: Westminster/John Knox 1992)

Unleashing the Scripture: Freeing the Bible from Captivity to America (Nashville: Abingdon 1993)

Dispatches from the Front: Theological Engagements with the Secular (Durham, North Carolina: Duke University Press 1994)

In Good Company: The Church as Polis (Notre Dame: University of Notre Dame Press 1995)

Lord, Teach Us: The Lord's Prayer and the Christian Life (with Scott C. Saye and William Willimon) (Nashville: Abingdon 1996)

Where Resident Aliens Live: Exercises for Christian Practice (with William Willimon) (Nashville: Abingdon 1996)

Christians among the Virtues: Theological Conversations with Ancient and Modern Ethics (with Charles Pinches) (Notre Dame: University of Notre Dame Press 1997)

Wilderness Wanderings: Probing Twentieth-Century Theology and Philosophy (Boulder,
   Colorado: Westview 1997)

Edited Books

*Responsibility for Devalued Persons: Ethical Interactions Between Society, the Family, and the
   Retarded* (Springfield: Charles Thomas Publishers 1982)
Revisions: Changing Perspectives in Moral Philosophy (with Alasdair MacIntyre) (Notre
   Dame: University of Notre Dame Press 1983)
Why Narrative? Readings in Narrative Theology (with L. Gregory Jones) (Grand Rapids:
   Eerdmans 1989)
Schooling Christians: 'Holy Experiments' in American Education (with John Westerhoff)
   (Grand Rapids: Eerdmans 1992)
Theology without Foundations: Religious Practice and the Future of Theological Truth in
   honour of James McClendon (with Nancey Murphy and Mark Nation)
   (Nashville: Abingdon 1994)

Scholarly Articles and Reviews

1969

'The Ethics of Black Power' *Augustana Observer* 67/14 (5 February 1969)

1970

'The Ethics of Population and Pollution' *Engage* 2/19 (1–15 August 1970)
'Politics, Vision, and the Common Good' *Cross Currents* 20/4 (Fall 1970) 399–414
'The Ethics of Population and Pollution' *The Cresset* 23/9 (September 1970)
'The Moral Demands of Disinterest: Should the University be above the Battle?'
   Scholastic 112/9 (13 November 1970)

1971

'The Significance of the Physical' *Scholastic* 112/12 (29 January 1971) 16–19
'Religious Outlooks: A Review of The Logic of Self-Improvement' *The Cresset* 34/4
   (February 1971) 22–23
'Situation Ethics, Moral Notions, and Moral Theology' *Irish Theological Quarterly* 38/3
   (July 1971) 242–257
'Abortion and Normative Ethics' *Cross Currents* 21/4 (Fall 1971) 399–414

1972

'The Future of Christian Social Ethics' in George Divine (ed.), *That They May Live:
   Theological Reflections on the Quality of Life* (Staten Island: Alba House 1972) 123–131
'Democracy as the Quest for Legitimate Authority: A Review of Peter Berger and
   Richard Neuhaus *Movement and Revolution* and Robert Dahl *After the Revolution*'
   The Review of Politics 34/1 (January 1972) 117–124
'The Meaning of Being Human' *Notre Dame Magazine* 1/1 (February 1972) 26–27

'Issues in Ethics: A Review of James Gustafson's *Christian Ethics and the Community*' *Reflection* 69/3 (March 1972) 9–14

'Judgment and the New Morality' *New Blackfriars* 53 (May 1972) 210–221

'The Humanity of the Divine' *The Cresset* 35/8 (June 1972) 16–17

'The Significance of Vision: Toward an Aesthetic Ethic' *Studies in Religion/ Sciences Religieuses* 2/1 (June 1972) 36–48

'Love's Not All You Need' *Cross Currents* 22/3 (Summer/Fall 1972) 225–237

'Theology and the New American Culture: A Problematic Relationship' *Review of Politics* 34/4 (October 1972) 71–91

'Aslan and the New Morality' *Religious Education* 67/6 (November/December 1972) 419–429

'Towards an Ethics of Character' *Theological Studies* 33/4 (December 1972) 698–715

1973

'Review of Ellul's "*Violence*": Reflections from a Christian Perspective' *The American Journal of Jurisprudence* 18 (1973) 206–215

'Abortion: The Agent's Perspective' *The American Ecclesiastical Review* 167/2 (February 1973) 102–120

'Messianic Pacifism' *Worldview* 16/6 (June 1973) 29–33

'The Christian Care of the Retarded' *Theology Today* 30/2 (July 1973) 130–137

'The Self as Story: Religion and Morality from the Agent's Perspective' *Journal of Religious Ethics* 1/1 (October 1973) 73–85

'The Retarded and Criteria for the Human' *Linacre Quarterly* 40/4 (November 1973) 217–222

1974

'Must We Relieve Suffering?' *Paediatric News* 8/3 (March 1974) 54–55

'Self-Deception and Autobiography: Theological and Ethical Reflections on Speer's *Inside the Third Reich*' (with David Burrell) *Journal of Religious Ethics* 2/1 (May 1974) 99–118

'The Moral Limits of Population Control' *Thought* 44 (September 1974) 237–249

'Notes by a Non-Catholic' *Notre Dame Magazine* 3/5 (December 1974) 23–27

1975

'Ethics and Population Policy' (with John Roos) in Virginia Gray and Elihu Bergman (eds.), *Political Issues in US Population Policy* (Lexington: Lexington Books 1975) 189–205

'Natural Law, Tragedy, and Theological Ethics' *American Journal of Jurisprudence* 20 (1975) 1–19

'Education for "Human Scientist" ' *Notre Dame Science Quarterly* 13/2 (January 1975) 9–10

'Changes in Moral Norms: An Ethicist's View' *AD Correspondence* 10/2 (18 January 1975) 2–7

'The Ethicist as Theologian' *Christian Century* 92/15 (23 April 1975) 408–412

'Obligation and Virtue Once More' *Journal of Religious Ethics* 3 (Spring 1975) 27–44

'The Demands and Limits of Care: Ethical Reflections on the Moral Dilemma of Neo-Natal Intensive Care' *American Journal of the Medical Sciences* 269/2 (March/April 1975) 222–236

'Review Essay of Paul Lehmann's *The Transfiguration of Politics: The Presence and Power of Jesus of Nazareth in and over Human Affairs' Worldview* 18/12 (December 1975) 45–48

'Must a Patient Be a "Person" To Be a Patient: Or My Uncle Charlie Is Not Much of a Person, But He Is Still My Uncle Charlie' *Connecticut Medicine* 39/12 (December 1975) 815–817

1976

'Truth and Honor: The University and the Church in a Democratic Age' *Proceeding of the James Montgomery Hester Seminar* (Winston-Salem: Wake Forest University Press 1976) 38–53

'Understanding Homosexuality: The Viewpoint of Ethics' *Pastoral Psychology* 24/3 (Spring 1976) 238–242

'Reflections on the Relation of Morality and Art: A Review Essay of R.W. Beardsmore's *Art and Morality' The Cresset* 39/5 (March 1976) 14–17

'Having and Learning How to Care for Retarded Children: Some Reflections' *Catholic Mind* 74/1302 (April 1976) 24–33

'The Search for the Historical Niebuhr: Review of Merkley's *Reinhold Niebuhr: A Political Account' Review of Politics* 38 (July 1976) 452–454

'Story and Theology' *Religion in Life* 45/3 (Autumn 1976) 339–350

'Memory, Community, and the Reasons for Living: Theological and Ethical Reflections on Suicide and Euthanasia' (with Richard Bondi) *Journal of American Academy of Religion* 44/3 (September 1976) 439–452

'Among the Moved: Reflection's on Speer's *Spandau' Worldview* 19/10 (October 1976) 47–49

1977

'The Family: Theological and Ethical Reflections' in Van Kussrow and Richard Baepler (eds.), *Changing American Lifestyles* (Valparaiso: University of Valparaiso Press 1977) 111–119

'Selecting Children to Live or Die: An Ethical Analysis of the Debate Between Dr Lorber and Dr Freeman on the Treatment of Meningomyelocele' in Denis Horon and David Mall (eds.), *Death, Dying and Euthanasia* (Washington DC: University Publications of America 1977) 228–249

'Medicine as a Tragic Profession' in David Smith (ed.), *No Rush to Judgment: Essays on Medical Ethics* (Bloomington, Indiana: Poynter Center Publication 1977) 93–128

'From System to Story: An Alternative Pattern for Rationality in Ethics' (with David Burrell) in M. Tristram Engelhardt and Dan Callahan (eds.), *Knowledge, Value and Belief* II (New York: Hastings Center 1977) 111–152

'Rights, Duties, and Experimentation on Children: A Critical Response to Worsfold and Bartholomew' *Research Involving Children: Appendix* (Washington DC: National Commission for Protection of Human Subjects of Biomedical and Behavioral Research, Department of Health, Education and Welfare Publication No. (Os) 77-0005, 1977) 5 1–24

'Community and Diversity: The Tyranny of Normality' *National Apostolate for the Mentally Retarded* 8/1–2 (Spring/Summer 1977) 20–23

'Learning to See Red Wheelbarrows: On Vision and Relativism' *Journal of the American Academy of Religion* 45/2 (June 1977) 644–655

'Love and Marriage: A Wedding Sermon' *The Cresset* 40/8 (June 1977) 20–21

'Virginity and the Virgin: A Review Article of Warner's *Alone of All Her Sex*' *Medical Tribune* (22 June 1977) 35–41

'The Politics of Charity' *Interpretation* 31/3 (July 1977) 251–262

1978

'Care' in *Encyclopedia of Bioethics* I (New York: Free Press 1978) 145–150

'The Moral Value of the Family' *Working Paper Series: Center for the Study of American Catholicism* (Notre Dame: University of Notre Dame 1978) 1–24

' "Daring Prayer" A Review' *Princeton Seminary Bulletin* 51/1 (New Series 1978) 50–51

'Autobiography and Politics: Review Essay of Campbell's *Brother to a Dragonfly* and Coffin's *Once to Every Man*' *Worldview* 21/4 (April 1978) 49–51

'A Failure in Communication: Ethics and the Early Church: Review Essay of Sanders *Ethics in the New Testament* and Osborn *Ethical Patterns in Early Christian Thought*' *Interpretation* 32/2 (April 1978) 196–200

'Sex and Politics: Bertrand Russell and "Human Sexuality" ' *Christian Century* 95/14 (19 April 1978) 417–422

' "*The Wing-Footed Wanderer*": A Review' *Journal of Religion* 58/3 (July 1978) 332–333

'Ethical Issues in the Use of Human Subjects' *Linacre Quarterly* 45/3 (August 1978) 249–257

'Can Ethics Be Theological?' *Hastings Center Report* 8/5 (October 1978) 47–49

'Irrepressible Ethicist: An Interview' *Leabhrach* (Autumn 1978) 4–5

'Religious Concepts of Brain Death and Associated Problems' *Annals of the New York Academy of Sciences* 315 (17 November 1978) 329–338

'Letter to the Editor: On Liberalism and Virtue' *Commonweal* 105/24 (8 December 1978) 790, 799

'Hope Faces Power: Thomas More and the King of England' (with Thomas Shaffer) *Soundings* 61/4 (Winter 1978)

'Jesus: The Story of the Kingdom' *Theology Digest* 26/4 (Winter 1978) 303–324

1979

'Theological Reflections on *In Vitro* Fertilization' *Research Involving Human In Vitro Fertilization and Embryo Transfer: Report of Ethics Advisory Board of Department of Health, Education and Welfare* (Washington: Department of Health, Education and Welfare Publication 1979) 5 1–20

'Reflections on Suffering, Death, and Medicine' *Ethics in Science and Medicine* 6 (1979) 229–237

'Ethics and Ascetical Theology' *Anglican Theological Review* 61/1 (January 1979) 87–98

'On the Ethics of War and Peace: Review Essay of Walzer's *Just and Unjust Wars* and Durnbaugh's *On Earth Peace*' *Review of Politics* 41/1 (January 1979) 147–153

'Review of Norton's *Personal Destinies*' *Worldview* 22/1–2 (January/February 1979) 52–55

'A Classic Restatement: Review Essay of Stob's *Ethical Reflections: Essays on Moral Themes*' *Reformed Journal* 29/3 (March 1979) 25–26

'Capital Punishment: It's a Rite of Vengeance' *Notre Dame Magazine* 8/4 (October 1979) 67–68

'Editorial' *Journal of Medicine and Philosophy* 4/4 (December 1979) 345–346

'Death and Moral Principles: Review of Devine *The Ethics of Homicide* and Kohl *Infanticide and the Value of Life*' *National Catholic Reporter* (14 December 1979) 14

1980

'Character, Narrative, and Growth in the Christian Life' in J. Fowler (ed.), *Toward Moral and Religious Maturity* (Morristown: Silver Burdett Company 1980) 442–484

'Sex in Public: Towards a Christian Ethic of Sex' in Kelley M.L. Brigman (ed.), *Focus on Human Sexuality* (Milledgeville Georgia: Georgia College Publications 1980) 108–131

'Abortion: Why the Arguments Fail' *Hospital Progress* (January 1980) 38–49

'Forgiveness and Political Community' *Worldview* 23/1–2 (January/February 1980) 15–16

'Protestants and the Pope' *Commonweal* 107/3 (15 February 1980) 80–85

'The Church in a Divided World: The Interpretative Power of the Christian Story' *Journal of Religious Ethics* 8/1 (Spring 1980) 55–82

'Learning Morality from Handicapped Children' *Hastings Center Report* 10/5 (October 1980) 45–46

'The Freedom of a Guilty Conscience' *Notre Dame Magazine* 9/4 (October 1980) 67–68

'The Moral Authority of Scripture: The Politics and Ethics of Remembering' *Interpretation* 34/4 (October 1980) 356–370

'The Holocaust and the Duty to Forgive' *Sh'ma* 10/198 (3 October 1980) 137–139

Forgiveness and Forgetting' *Sh'ma* 11/202 (28 November 1980) 12, 15–16

1981

'Abortion: Once Again' in Thomas Hilgers, Dennis Horan and David Mall (eds.), *New Perspectives on Human Abortion* (Frederick: University Publications of America 1981) 420–439

'Rational Suicide and Reasons for Living' in Marc Basson (ed.), *Rights and Responsibilities in Modern Medicine* (New York: Alan R. Liss Inc. 1981) 185–199

'Jews and Christians Among the Nations: The Social Significance of the Holocaust' *Cross Currents* 31/1 (Spring 1981) 15–34

'The Significance of "Other" ' (with Bonita Raine) *Catechist* 14/7 (April 1981) 15, 20, 21

'Rev Falwell and Dr King' *Notre Dame Magazine* 10/2 (May 1981) 28–29

'A Tale of Two Stories: On Being a Christian and a Texan: A Theological Entertainment' *Perkins Journal* 34/4 (Summer 1981) 1–15

'Don't Let Them Eat Cake: Reflections on Luck, Justice and Poor People' *Notre Dame Magazine* 10/5 (December 1981) 24–25

1982

'Authority and the Profession of Medicine' in George Agich (ed.), *Responsibility in Health Care* (Dordrecht: D. Reidel 1982) 83–104

'Self-Sacrifice as Demonic: A Theological Response to Jonestown' in Ken Levi (ed.), *Violence and Religious Commitment* (University Park, Pennsylvania: Pennsylvania State University Press 1982) 152–162, 189–191

'The Retarded, Society, and the Family: The Dilemma of Care' in *idem* (ed.), *Responsibility for Devalued Persons: Ethical Interactions Between Society, the Family, and the Retarded* (Springfield: Charles Thomas Publishers 1982) 42–65

'Critics' Choices: Religious Book Week' *Commonweal* 109/4 (26 February 1982) 123–124

'The Demands of a Truthful Story: Ethics and the Pastoral Task' *Chicago Studies* 21/1 (Spring 1982) 59–71

'The Kingdom of God: An Ecclesial Space for Peace' (with Mark Sherwindt) *Word and World* 2/2 (Spring 1982) 127–136

'Review of Alasdair MacIntyre's "After Virtue" ' (with Paul Wadell) *The Thomist* 46/2 (April 1982) 313–321

'Christianity and Democracy: A Response' *Center Journal* 1/3 (Summer 1982) 42–51

'The Gesture of a Truthful Story: The Church and "Religious Education" ' *Encounter* 43/4 (Autumn 1982) 319–329

'Work and Co-Creation: A Remarkably Bad Idea' *This World* 3 (Fall 1982) 89–102

'God the Measurer: A Review of Gustafson's "Ethics from a Theocentric Perspective" ' *Journal of Religion* 62/4 (October 1982) 402–411

'Disciplined Seeing: Imagination and the Moral Life' (with Philip Foubert) *New Catholic World* 225:1350 (November/December 1982) 250–253

1983

'On Keeping Theological Ethics Theological' in *idem* (ed.), *Revisions: Changing Perspectives in Moral Philosophy* (with Alasdair MacIntyre) (Notre Dame: University of Notre Dame Press 1983) 16–42

'On Living Between the Times' *Valparaiso University Law Review* 17/1 (1983) 55–61

'Language, Experience, and the Life Well-Lived: A Review of the Work of Donald Evans' (with Richard Bondi) *Religious Studies Review* 9/1 (January 1983) 33–37

'Constancy and Forgiveness: The Novel as a School for Virtue' *Notre Dame English Journal* 15/3 (Summer 1983) 23–54

'A Gun in the Home' *The Neighbourhood News* 13/8 (22 July 1983) 5

'Ethical Elitist: Interview with Stanley Hauerwas' *Review of Books and Religion* 12/1 (Mid-September 1983) 4

'Eliminating People who Suffer?' *Stauros Notebook* 2/5 (September/October 1983) 1–4

'Casuistry as a Narrative Art' *Interpretation* 37/4 (October 1983) 377–388

'What Can the State Ask?' *Christianity and Crisis* 43/19 (November 1983) 458–459

'Eschatology and Nuclear Disarmament' *The NICM Journal* 8/1 (Winter 1983) 7–17

'On Surviving Justly: An Ethical Analysis of Nuclear Disarmament' *Center Journal* (Winter 1983) 123–152

1984

'Marginalizing the Retarded' in Flavian Dougherty (ed.), *The Deprived, The Disabled, and the Fullness of Life* (Wilmington, Delaware: Michael Glazier 1984) 67–105

'Marriage and the Family' *Quaker Religious Thought* 56/20:2 (Spring 1984) 4–24

'Why the Truth Demands Truthfulness: An Imperious Engagement with Hartt' *Journal of the American Academy of Religion* 52/1 (Spring 1984) 141–147

1985

'Characterizing Perfection: Second Thoughts on Character and Sanctification' in Theodore Runyon (ed.), *Wesleyan Theology Today: A Bicentennial Theological Consultation* (Nashville: Kingswood 1985) 251–263

'On Medicine and Virtue: A Response' in Earl Shelp (ed.), *Virtue and Medicine* (Dordrecht: D. Reidel 1985) 347–355

'Salvation and Health: Why Medicine Needs the Church' in Earl Shelp (ed.), *Theology and Bioethics* (Dordrecht: D. Reidel 1985) 205–224

'Embarrassed by God's Presence' (with William Willimon) *The Christian Century* 102/4 (30 January 1985) 98–100

'Seeking a Clear Alternative to Liberalism: A Review of Lindbeck's "The Nature of Doctrine" ' (with L. Gregory Jones) *Books and Religion* 13/1 (January/February 1985) 7

'Review Essay of "Christianity, Social Tolerance and Homosexuality" by John Boswell' *St Lukes Journal* 28/2 (March 1985) 228–232

'The Family as a School for Character?' *Religious Education* 80/2 (Spring 1985) 272–286

'Time and History in Theological Ethics: The Work of James Gustafson' *Journal of Religious Ethics* 13/1 (Spring 1985) 3–21

'Pacifism: Some Philosophical Considerations' *Faith and Philosophy* 2/2 (April 1985) 99–105

'Peacemaking' *The Furrow* 36/10 (October 1985) 605–612

'In Praise of Gossip: The Moral Casuistry of Life' *Books and Religion* 13:8–9 (November/December 1985) 5, 23

'Medical Care for the Poor: Finite Resources, Infinite Need (with Larry Churchill and Harmon Smith) *Health Progress* 66/10 (December 1985) 32–35

'The Faithful Are Not Always Effective' *Gospel Herald* 77/52 (25 December 1985) 903

1986

'A Christian Critique of Christian America' *Recovering Moral Virtues: Christian Life Commission Seminar Proceedings 1986* (Publication of the Christian Life Commission of the Southern Baptist Convention 1986) 8–17

'Foreword' to Duane Friesen, *Christian Peacemaking and International Conflict: A Realist Passivist Perspective* (Scottdale: Herald 1986) 11–12

'Foreword' to Warren Groff, *God's Story – And Ours* (Elgin, Illinois: Brethren 1986)

'Virtue' in Kenneth Vaux (ed.), *Powers that Make Us Human* (Urbana: University of Illinois Press 1986) 117–140

'The Need for an Ending' *The Modern Churchman* 27/3 (1986) 3–7

'Review of Robin Lovin's "Christian Faith and Public Choices: The Social Ethics of Barth, Brunner and Bonhoeffer" *Journal of Religion* 66/1 (January 1986) 87–88

'Clerical Character: Reflecting on Ministerial Morality' *Word and World* 6/2 (Spring 1986) 181–193

'Taking Time for Peace' *Religion and Intellectual Life* 3/3 (Spring 1986) 87–100

'Review of James Turner Johnson's "Can Modern War Be Just?" ' (with L. Gregory Jones) *Theology Today* 42/1 (April 1986) 104–106

'Should Christians Talk So Much About Justice?' *Books and Religion* 14:5 & 6 (May/June 1986) 5, 14–16

'How Christian Universities Contribute to the Corruption of Youth: Church and University in a Confused Age' *Katallagete* 9/3 (Summer 1986) 21–28

'A Pacifist Response to "In Defense of Creation" ' *The Asbury Theological Journal* 41/2 (Fall 1986) 5–14

'Some Theological Reflections on Gutierrez' Use of "Liberation" as a Theological Concept' *Modern Theology* 3/1 (October 1986) 67–76

'A Christian Critique of Christian America' *The Cresset* 50/1 (November 1986) 5–16

'From Conduct to Character: A Guide to Sexual Adventure' (with Allen Verhey) *Reformed Journal* 36/11 (November 1986) 12–16

1987

'The Church as God's New Language' in Garrett Green (ed.), *Scriptural Authority and Narrative Interpretation* (Philadelphia: Fortress 1987) 179–198

'Catholicism and Ethics: A Reply to the Editorial Entitled "Sobering Thoughts" ' *North Carolina Medical Journal* 48/2 (February 1987) 67–68

'On the "Right" to be Tribal' *Christian Scholars Review* 16/3 (March 1987) 238–241

'Will the Real Sectarian Stand Up?' *Theology Today* 44/1 (April 1987) 87–94

'The Gospel's Radical Alternative: A Peace the World Cannot Give' (with Michael Cartwright) *The Other Side* 23/6 (July/August 1987) 22–27, 45

'On Learning Simplicity in an Ambiguous Age' *Katallagete* 10/1–3 (Fall 1987) 43–46

'Critics' Choices for Christmas: Books I Would Recommend Anyone to Read' *Commonweal* 114/21 (4 December 1987) 708–709

1988

'Epilogue: A Pacifist Response to the Bishops' in Paul Ramsey, *Speak Up for Just War or Pacifism: A Critique of the United Methodist Bishops' Pastoral Letter 'In Defense of Creation'* (University Park: The Pennsylvania State University Press 1988) 149–182

'On God: Ethics and the Power to Act in History' in Willard Swartley (ed.), *Essays on Peace Theology and Witness* (Elkhart, Indiana: Institute of Mennonite Studies 1988)

'On Honor: By Way of a Comparison of Barth and Trollope' in Nigel Biggar (ed.), *Reckoning with Barth: Essays in Commemoration of a Centenary of Karl Barth's Birth* (London: Mowbray 1988)

'Reconciling the Practice of Reason: Casuistry in a Christian Context' Baruch Brody (ed.), *Moral Theory and Moral Judgements in Medical Ethics* (Dordrecht: Kluwer 1988) 135–156

'The Ministry of a Congregation: Rethinking Christian Ethics for a Church-Centred Seminary' in Joseph Hough Jr and Barbara Wheeler (eds.), *Beyond Clericalism: The Congregation as a Focus for Theological Education* (Atlanta: Scholars 1988) 119–136

'The Morality of Teaching' in A. Leigh DeNeff, Crauford Godwin and Ellen Stern McCrate (eds.), *The Academic's Handbook* (Durham, North Carolina: Duke University Press 1988) 19–28

'The Sermon on the Mount: Just War and the Quest for Peace' *Concilium* 195 (Edinburgh: T & T Clark 1988) 36–43

'Faith and the Republic: A Francis Lewis Law Center Conversation Between Stanley Hauerwas, Sanford Levinson, and Mark Tushnet' *Washington and Lee Law Review* 45/2 (Spring 1988) 467–534

'God, Medicine, and the Problems of Evil' *The Reformed Journal* 38/4 (April 1988) 16–22

'Hating Mothers as the Way to Peace' *Journal for Preachers* (Pentecost 1988) 17–21

'On Being Professionally a Friend: Review of "Faith and the Professions" by Thomas Shaffer' *Christian Legal Society Quarterly* 9/2 (Summer 1988) 24–26

'Paul Ramsey Remembered' *This World* 22 (Summer 1988) 20–22

'The Grace to Live Contingently' *Reformed Journal* 38/7 (July 1988) 9–11

'On Developing Hopeful Virtues' *Christian Scholars Review* 18:2 (December 1988) 107–117

'Flights in Foundationalism, or Things Aren't As Bad As They Seem: A Review of Jeffrey Stout's *Ethics After Babel*' *Soundings* 71/4 (Winter 1988) 683–699

1989

'Foreword' to Paul Wadell, Friendship and the Moral Life (Notre Dame: University of Notre Dame Press 1989) ix–xii

On Being Placed by John Milbank: A Response in Kenneth Surin (ed.), *Christ, Ethics and Tragedy: Essays in Honour of Donald MacKinnon* (Cambridge: Cambridge University Press 1989) 197–201

'On Being Dispossessed: Or, This Is a Hell of a Way to Get Some Place' *Reformed Journal* 39/1 (January 1989) 14–16

'What About the Church?' (with William Willimon) *Christian Century* 106/9 (1–8 February 1989) 111, 128

'Ministry as More than a Helping Profession (with William Willimon) *Christian Century* 106/4 (15 March 1989) 282–284

'What Could Methodists Tell John Tower?' (with Will Willimon) *Reformed Journal* 39/5 (May 1989) 5–6

'Interpreting the Bible as a Political Act' (with Steve Long) *Religion and Intellectual Life* 6/3–4 (Spring/Summer 1989) 134–142

'Freedom of Religion: A Subtle Temptation' *Soundings* 72/2–3 (Summer/Fall 1989) 317–340

'Can Aristotle be a Liberal? Nussbaum on Luck' *Soundings* 72/4 (Winter 1989) 675–691

1990

'God, Medicine, and the Problems of Evil' in Richard Neuhaus (ed.), *Guaranteeing the Good Life: Medicine and the Return of Eugenics* (Grand Rapids: Eerdmans 1990) 213–228

'Die Kirche: in Einer Zerrissenen Welt und Die Deutungskraft der Christlichen' in Hans Grulrich (ed.), *Evangelische Ethik* (Munich: Chr Kaiser Verlag 1990) 338–381

'Pacifism: A Form of Politics' in Michael Cromartie (ed.), *Peace Betrayed? Essays on Pacifism and Politics* (Washington: Ethics and Public Policy Center 1990) 133–142

'Preface' to Hazel Morgan, *Through Peter's Eyes* (London: Arthur James 1990) 7–9

'The Limits of Medicine' in Paul Homer and Martha Holstein (eds.), *A Good Old Age? The Paradox of Setting Limits* (New York: Simon and Schuster 1990) 120–139

'On the Production and Reproduction of the Saints: A Sermon' *Reformed Journal* 40/2 (February 1990) 12–13

'Testament of Friends: How My Mind Has Changed' *Christian Century* 107/7 (28 February 1990) 212–216

'The Importance of Being Catholic: A Protestant View' *First Things* 1/1 (March 1990) 21–30

'Peculiar People' (with William Willimon) *Christianity Today* (5 March 1990) 16–19

'Happiness, the Life of Virtue, and Friendship: Theological Reflections on Aristotelian Themes' *Asbury Theological Journal* 45/1 (Spring 1990) 5–48

'A Response to Quinn: Athens May Be a Long Way from Jerusalem, but Prussia is Even Further' *Asbury Theological Journal* 45/1 (Spring 1990) 59–64

'The Limits of Care: Burnout as an Ecclesial Issue' (with William Willimon) *Word and World* 10/3 (Summer 1990) 247–256

1991

'Abortion: Theologically Understood' (Ephrata, Pennsylvania: Task Force of United Methodists on Abortion and Sexuality 1991) 1–20

'Honor at the Center' *First Things* 10 (February 1991) 26–31

'Christianity and War' *Seasons: An Inner-Faith Family Journal* 10/2 (Summer 1991) 5–6

'Pacifism, Just War and the Gulf: An Exchange with Richard John Neuhaus' *First Things* 13 (May 1991) 39–42

'Christianity: It's Not a Religion, it's an Adventure' *US Catholic* 56/6 (June 1991) 6–13

'Beyond "Political Correctness," Left or Right' *New Oxford Review* 58/8 (October 1991) 9–11

'Why Resident Aliens Struck a Chord' *Missiology* 19/4 (October 1991) 419–429

'Discipleship as a Craft, Church as a Discipline Community' *Christian Century* 108/27 (2 October 1991) 881–884

'Some Words in *New York Magazine*' *Unitarian Universalist Christian* 46/3–4 (Fall/Winter 1991) 68–69

'Of Grit and Grace' *Reformed Journal* 40/9 (November 1991) 10–13

'If It Were Up To Me: Critics' Choice' *Salt* 11/10 (November/December 1991) 26–27

'The Politics of Community: Review of *The Good Society*' *The Independent Weekly* 9/51 (18 December 1991) 36

1992

'Ethics, Christian' in Donald Musser and Joseph Price (eds.), *New Handbook of Christian Theology* (Nashville: Abingdon 1992) 160–167

'Outside the Church there is No Salvation: Salvation as Politics' in A. W. Musschenga, B. Voorzanga and A. Soeteman (eds.), *Morality, World View, and Law: The Idea of a Universal Morality and Its Critics* (Assen, The Netherlands: Van Gorcum 1992) 9–25

'Whose "Just" War? Which Peace?' in David DeCosse (ed.), *But Was It Just?* (New York: Doubleday 1992) 83–106

'A Communitarian Lament: A Review of *The Good Society* by Robert Bellah *First Things* 19 (January 1992) 45–46

'Encyclicals are an Extraordinary Witness' *Compass* 9/6 (January/February 1992) 64

'Whose Conscience? Whose Emotion? Review of Sidney Callahan's "In Good Conscience: Reason, Emotion and Moral Decision-Making" ' *Hastings Center Report* 22/1 (January/February 1992) 48–49

'The Eyes Have It' *Second Opinion* 17/4 (April 1992) 41–43

'The Chief End of All Flesh' (with John Berkman) *Theology Today* 49/2 (July 1992) 196–208

'An Interview: Stanley Hauerwas' *& straightaway* 3/1 (Summer 1992) 1–6

'The Church and/as God's Nonviolent Imagination' (with Philip D. Kenneson) *Pro Ecclesia* 1/1 (Fall 1992) 76–88

'The Irony of American Christianity: Reinhold Niebuhr on Church and State' (with Michael Broadway) *Insights: A Journal of the Faculty of Austin Seminary* 108 (Fall 1992) 33–46

'The Kingship of Christ: Why Freedom of "Belief" is not Enough' (with Michael Baxter) *De Paul Law Review* 42/1 (Fall 1992) 107–127

'Why Truthfulness Requires Forgiveness: Commencement Address for Graduates of a College of the Church of the Second Chance' *Cross Currents* 42/3 (Fall 1992) 378–387

'An Interview with Stanley Hauerwas' *Cokesbury Good Books Catalog* (Fall/Winter 1992/3) 2–3

'The Sources of Charles Taylor' (with David Matzko) *Religious Studies Review* 18/4 (October 1992) 286–289

'A Nonviolent Proposal for Christian Participation in the Culture Wars' *Soundings* 75/4 (Winter 1992) 477–492

'A Sermon on the Sermon on the Mount' *St Mark's Review* 150 (Winter 1992) 29–31

'In Praise of *Centesimus Annus*' *Theology* 95/768 (November/December 1992) 416–432

1993

'A Meditation on Developing Hopeful Virtues' in Peter Ochs (ed.), *The Return to Scripture in Judaism and Christianity: Essays in Post-Critical Scripture Interpretation* (New York: Paulist 1993) 308–324

'Foreword' to Paul Ramsey, with Steve Long, *Basic Christian Ethics* (Louisville: Westminster/John Knox 1993)

'Review of *A Gentle Touch: From a Theology of Handicap to a Theology of Human Being* by David Pailin' *Studies in Christian Ethics* 6/2 (1993) 99–100

'Living the Proclaimed Reign of God: A Sermon on the Sermon on the Mount' *Interpretation* 47/2 (April 1993) 152–157

'Who is the "We"?' *Sojourners* 22/3 (April 1993) 15

'Christian Practice and the Practice of Law in a Church without Foundations' *Mercer Law Review* 44/3 (Spring 1993) 743–751

'Christian Soldiers' *Charlotte Observer* (31 May 1993)

'*The Door* Interviews William Willimon and Stanley Hauerwas' *The Door* 129 (May/June 1993) 6–11

'Political Righteousness' *Perspectives* 8/6 (June 1993) 8–9

'The Difference of Virtue and the Difference it Makes: Courage Exemplified' *Modern Theology* 9/3 (July 1993) 249–264

'When the Politics of Jesus Makes a Difference' *Christian Century* 110/28 (13 October 1993) 982–987

'*Veritatis Splendor*: A Comment' *Commonweal* 120/18 (22 October 1993) 16–18
'Why I am Neither a Communitarian Nor a Medical Ethicist' in 'The Birth of Bioethics Special Supplement' ed. A.R. Jonsen *Hastings Center Report* 23/6 (November/December 1993) S9–S10

1994

'Like Those Who Dream: A Sermon' in Donald McKim, *The Bible in Theology and Preaching: How Preachers Use Scripture* (Nashville: Abingdon 1994) 134–136
'The Church's One Foundation is Jesus Christ Her Lord: Or, In a World Without Foundations, All We Have is the Church' in *idem* (ed.), *Theology Without Foundations: Religious Practice and the Future of Theological Truth* (with Nancey Murphy and Mark Nation) (Nashville: Abingdon 1994) 143–162
'To Be or Not To Be a Bricoleur' *Koinonia* 4/1 (1994) 109
'*Splendor of Truth*: A Symposium' *First Things* 39 (January 1994) 21–23
'Jews and the Eucharist' *Perspectives* 9/3 (March 1994) 14–15
'A Homage to Mary and the University Called Notre Dame' *The South Atlantic Quarterly* 3 (Summer 1994) 717–726
'Whose Church? Which Future? Whither the Anabaptist Vision?' *Brethren Life and Thought* 39/3 (Summer 1994) 141–152
'Jacques Ellul, Courage, and the Christian Imagination' *The Ellul Forum* 13 (July 1994) 4
'Missing from the Curriculum: Review of George Marsden's *The Soul of the American University*' *Commonweal* 121/16 (23 September 1994) 19–20
'Practice Preaching' *Journal for Preachers* 18/1 (Advent 1994) 21–24

1995

'Creation as Apocalyptic: A Homage to William Stringfellow' (with Jefferson Powell) *Radical Christian and Exemplary Lawyer* ed. Andrew McThenia Jr (Grand Rapids: Eerdmans 1995) 31–39
'Geschichte als Schicksal, Wie in Amerika ans der "Rechtfertigung aus Glauben" Anthropologie und Geschichte wurde' in Michael Beintker, Ernstpeter Maurer, Heinrich Stoevessandt, Hans G. Ulrich (eds.), *Rechtfertigung und Erfahrung*, (Gutersloher: Chr. Kaiser 1995) 269–286
'Killing Compassion' in Jean Bethke Elshtain and J. Timothy Cloyd (eds.), *Politics in the Human Body* (Vanderbilt University Press 1995) 197–210
'Niebuhr, Reinhold' *Concise Encyclopaedia of Preaching* ed. William Willimon and Richard Lischer (Louisville: Westminster/John Knox 1995) 347–350
'The Church and Mentally Handicapped Persons: The Continuing Challenge to the Imagination' in Marilyn E. Bishop (ed.), *Religion and Disability: Essays in Scripture, Theology and Ethics* (Kansas City: Sheed and Ward 1995) 46–64
'Virtue and Character' in *Encyclopaedia of Bioethics* (Revised Edition) Volume 5 (New York: MacMillan Library Reference 1995) 2525–2532
'Domesticating the Spirit: Eldin Villafane's *The Liberating Spirit: Toward An Hispanic American Pentecostal Social Ethic*' (with Brett Webb-Mitchell) *Journal of Pentecostal Theology* 7 (1995) 5–10
'The Radical Edge of Baptism' (with Brett Webb-Mitchell) *Reformed Liturgy and Music* 29/2 (1995) 71–73

'What Could It Mean for the Church to be the Body of Christ: A Question Without a Clear Answer' *Scottish Journal of Theology* 48/1 (1995) 1–21

'Knowing How to Go On When You Do Not Know Where You Are Going: A Response to John Cobb' *Theology Today* 51/4 (January 1995) 563–569

'Standing on the Shoulders of Murderers: The End of Sacrifice' *Preaching: A Professional Journal for Preachers* 10/5 (March/April 1995) 40, 42

'Remembering Martin Luther King Jr Remembering: A Response to Christopher Beem' *Journal of Religious Ethics* 23/1 (Spring 1995) 135–148

'Story Telling: A Response to "Mennonites on Hauerwas" ' *The Conrad Grebel Review* 13/2 (Spring 1995) 166–173

'Preaching As Though We Had Enemies' *First Things* 53 (May 1995) 45–49

'Creation, Contingency, and Truthful Nonviolence: Reflections on John Milbank's *Theology and Social Theory*' *Faith and Freedom* 4/2 (Coogee, New South Wales June 1995) 12–17

'Truthful Difference: An Interview with Stanley Hauerwas' *Faith and Freedom* 4/3 (September 1995) 13–16

1996

'Agency: Going Forward by Looking Back' in Lisa Sowle and James Childress (eds.), *Christian Ethics: Problems and Prospects* (in honour of James Gustafson) (Cleveland: Pilgrim 1996) 185–195

'Foreword' to Bonnie Shullenberger, *A Time to Be Born* (Cambridge Massachussets: Cowley 1996) xi–xiii

'How Christian Ethics Became Medical Ethics: The Case of Paul Ramsey' in Allen Verhey (ed.), *Religion and Medical Ethics: Looking Back, Looking Forward* (Grand Rapids: Eerdmans 1996) 61–80

'Murdochian Muddles: Can We Get Through Them If God Does Not Exist?' in Maria Antonaccio and William Schweiker (eds.), *Iris Murdoch and the Search for Human Goodness* (Chicago: University of Chicago Press 1996) 190–208

'Resurrection, the Holocaust, and Forgiveness: A Sermon for Eastertime' in Howard Clark Kee and Irvin J. Borowsky (eds.), *Removing Anti-Semitism from the Pulpit* (Philadelphia and New York: American Interfaith Institute and Continuum 1996) 113–120

'The Church's Think-Tank: An Interview with Stanley Hauerwas about the Role of the Seminary' *The 1996 Seminary and Graduate School Handbook* (Evanston: Berry 1996) 15–21

'The God that Failed: The Pathos of Medicine in Modernity' in Hilary Regan, Rod Horsfield and Gabriel McMullen (eds.), *Beyond Mere Health: Theology and Healthcare in a Secular Society* (Adelaide: Open Book 1996) 80–102

'The Liturgical Shape of the Christian Life: Teaching Christian Ethics As Worship' in David F. Ford and Dennis L. Stamps (eds.), *Essentials of Christian Community: Essays for Daniel W. Hardy* (Edinburgh: T & T Clark 1996) 35–48

'Unthinking Necessity: Response to Patterson's "Dressing the Wounds of the People" ' in Hilary Regan, Rod Horsfield and Gabriel McMullen (eds.), *Beyond Mere Health: Theology and Healthcare in a Secular Society* (Adelaide: Open Book 1996) 242–245

'Why Christian Ethics is Such a Bad Idea' in ibid. 64–79

'Review of *Violence Unveiled: Humanity at the Crossroads* by Gil Bailie' *Modern Theology* 12/1 (January 1996)

'Christian Schooling: Or, Making Students Dysfunctional' *Prism* 3/2 (January/February 1996) 22–25

'Embodied Memory' *Journal for Preachers* 19/3 (Easter 1996) 20–24

'Your Kingdom Come ...' (with William Willimon) *Sojourners* 25/3 (May/June 1996) 30–33

'Reading Yoder Down Under' *Faith and Freedom* 5/1–2 (June 1996) 39–41

'Christian Virtues Exemplified: On Developing Hopeful Virtues' (with Charles Pinches) *Pro Ecclesia* 5/3 (Summer 1996) 334–348

'Practicing Patience: How Christians Should Be Sick' (with Charles Pinches) *Christian Bioethics* 2/2 (August 1996) 202–221

'Reformation is Sin' *Perspectives* 11/8 (October 1996) 10–11

'For Dappled Things: Commencement Address for PhD Ceremony, Duke University 1996' *Duke Dialogue* (4 October 1996 Faculty Forum 8/1) 1, 3, 4

'Worship is Evangelism' *Circuit Rider* 20/10 (December/January 1996–97) 6–7

1997

'Foreword' to Philip Kenneson and James L. Street, *Selling Out the Church: The Dangers of Church Marketing* (Nashville: Abingdon 1997) 11–14

'Not All Peace Is Peace: Why Christians Cannot Make Peace with Engelhardt's Peace' in Brendan P. Minogue with Gabriel Palmer-Fernandez and James E. Reagen (eds.), *Reading Engelhardt: Essays on the Thought of H. Tristram Engelhardt Jr* (Dordrecht: Kluwer 1997) 31–44

'On Doctrine and Ethics' in Colin Gunton (ed.), *The Cambridge Companion to Christian Doctrine* (Cambridge: Cambridge University Press 1997) 21–40

'Timeful Friends: Living with the Handicapped' in Th. A. Boer, R. Seldenrijk, J. Stolk (eds.) *Zinvolle zorgvergverlening: Wat maakt zoorgen voor mensen met een verstandelijke handicap zinvol?* (Utrecht, The Netherlands: Vereniging's Heeren Loo 1997) 15–31

'Failure of Communication *or* A Case of Uncomprehending Feminism: A Response to Gloria Albrecht' *Scottish Journal of Theology* 50/2 (1997) 228–239

'Review of *Moral Actions and Christian Ethics* by Jean Porter' *The Journal of Religion* 77/1 (January 1997) 172–173

'The Sanctified Body: Why Perfection Does Not Require a "Self"' *The Aldersgate* 3/1 (February/March 1997) 1–8

'Christians in the Hands of Flaccid Secularists: Theology and "Moral Inquiry" in the Modern University' *The Cresset* 60/5 (Easter 1997) 5–13

'Review of *Soul and Society: The Making and Renewal of Social Christianity* by Gary Dorrien' *Modern Theology* 13/3 (July 1997) 418–421

'Virtue, Description, and Friendship: A Thought Experiment in Catholic Moral Theology' *Irish Theological Quarterly* 62/2–3 (1996–7) 170–184

'Cloning the Christian Body' (with Joel Shuman) in Ronald Cole-Turner (ed.), *Human Cloning: Religious Responses* (Louisville: Westminster/John Knox Press 1997) 58–65

General Bibliography

Robert Adams, *The Virtue of Faith and Other Issues in Philosophical Theology* (Oxford: Oxford University Press 1987)

Gloria Albrecht, *The Character of our Communities: Toward an Ethic of Liberation for the Church* (Nashville: Abingdon 1995)

—'Review, *In Good Company: The Church as Polis*' *Scottish Journal of Theology* 50/2 (1997) 218–227

Aristotle *Metaphysics*

—*Nicomachaean Ethics*

Erich Auerbach, *Mimesis: The Representation of Reality in Western Literature* (Princeton: Princeton University Press 1953)

Karl Barth, *Dogmatics in Outline* translated by G.T. Thomson (London: SCM 1949)

R. Bellah et al. eds., *Habits of the Heart* (University of California Press 1985)

—*The Good Society* (Knopf 1991)

Frithjof Bergmann, *On Being Free* (Notre Dame: University of Notre Dame Press 1977)

Pierre Bolle (ed.), *Le Plateau Vivarais-Lignon: Accueil et Résistance 1939–1944* (Le Chambon-sur-Lignon: Société d'Histoire de la Montagne 1992)

Rufus D. Bowman, *Church of the Brethren and War* (Elgin: Brethren Publishing House 1944)

Walter Brueggemann, *The Bible and the Postmodern Imagination: Texts under Negotiation* (London: SCM 1993)

Donald Capps, *Deadly Sins and Saving Virtues* (Philadelphia: Fortress Press 1987)

Michael G. Cartwright, *Practices, Politics and Performance: Toward a Communal Hermeneutic for Christian Ethics* (PhD dissertation, Duke University 1988)

—(ed.), *The Royal Priesthood: Essays Ecclesiological and Ecumenical* (Grand Rapids: Eerdmans 1994) 359–373

Stanley Cavell, *Must We Mean What We Say?* (Cambridge: Cambridge University Press 1969)

Brevard Childs 'The Canonical Approach and the "New Yale Theology" ' in *The New Testament as Canon: An Introduction* (Philadelphia: Fortress Press 1984) 541–546

Gary L. Comstock, 'Two Types of Narrative Theology' *Journal of the American Academy of Religion* 55/4 (Winter 1987) 687–717

Stephen Crites 'The Narrative Quality of Experience' *Journal of the American Academy of Religion* 39/3 (1971) 291–311

—'Myth, Story, History' in Tony Stoneburger (ed.), *Parable, Myth and Language* (Cambridge, Mass: Church Society for College Work 1968)

Michel de Certeau, *The Practice of Everyday Life* translated by Stephen Rendall (Berkeley: University of California Press 1988)

Craig Dykstra, *Vision and Character* (Paulist Press 1981)

David Fergusson, 'Another Way of Reading Stanley Hauerwas?' *Scottish Journal of Theology* 50/2 1997 242–9

Thomas Finger, *Christian Theology: An Eschatological Approach* (Nashville: Nelson 1985)

Joseph Fletcher, *Situation Ethics* (Philadelphia: Westminster 1966)

David F. Ford, 'The Best Apologetics is Good Systematics: A Proposal about the Place of Narrative in Christian Systematic Theology' *Anglican Theological Review* 67/3 (July 1985) 232–254

—(ed.), *The Modern Theologians* (Oxford: Blackwell 1997[2])

Hans Frei, *The Eclipse of Biblical Narrative: A Study in Eighteenth and Nineteenth Century Hermeneutics* (New Haven and London: Yale University Press 1974)

—*The Identity of Jesus Christ* (Philadelphia: Fortress 1975)

'The "Literal Reading" of Biblical Narrative in the Christian Tradition: Does it Stretch or Will it Break?' in Frank McConnell (ed.), *The Bible and the Narrative Tradition* (New York: Oxford University Press 1986) 36–77

Duane Friesen, 'Normative Factors in Troeltsch's Typology of Religious Association' *Journal of Religious Ethics* 3/2 (Fall 1975) 271–283

Michael Goldberg, 'God, Action and Narrative: *Which* Narrative? *Which* Action? *Which* God?' *Journal of Religion* 68/1 (January 1988) 39–56

Ronald Grimes, 'Of Words the Speaker, of Deeds the Doer' *Journal of Religion* 66 (1986) 1–17

James Gustafson, *Can Ethics Be Christian?* (Chicago: University of Chicago Press 1975)

—*Ethics from a Theocentric Perspective* Volume I *Theology and Ethics* (Chicago: University of Chicago Press 1981), Volume II *Ethics and Theology* (Chicago: University of Chicago Press 1984)

—'The Sectarian Temptation: Reflections on Theology, Church and the University' *Proceedings of the Catholic Theological Society* 40 (1985) 83–94

Philip Hallie, *Lest Innocent Blood Be Shed: The Story of the Village of Le Chambon-sur-Lignon and How Goodness Happened There* (London: Michael Joseph 1979)

Julian Hartt, 'Theological Investment in Story: Some Comments on Recent Developments and Some Proposals,' *Journal of the American Academy of Religion* 52 (1984) 117–130

A.E. Harvey, *Jesus and the Constraints of History* (London: Duckworth 1982)

Eilert Herms, 'Virtue: A Neglected Concept in Protestant Ethics' *Scottish Journal of Theology* 35/6 (1982) 481–95

George Hunsinger, *How to Read Karl Barth: The Shape of his Theology* (New York: Oxford University Press 1991)

L. Gregory Jones, 'Alasdair MacIntyre on Narrative, Community and the Moral Life' *Modern Theology* 4/1 (1987) 53–69

David Kelsey, *The Uses of Scripture in Recent Theology* (Philadelphia: Fortress 1975)

Philip Kenneson, 'Taking Time for the Trivial: Reflections on Yet Another Book from Hauerwas' *Asbury Theological Journal* 45 (Spring 1990) 65–74

Nicholas Lash, *Theology on the Way to Emmaus* (London: SCM 1986)

Paul Lauritzen, 'Is "Narrative" Really a Panacea? The Use of "Narrative" in Metz and Hauerwas' *Journal of Religion* (1987) 322–339

James W. McClendon Jr, *Ethics: Systematic Theology Volume One* (Nashville: Abingdon 1986)

—*Biography as Theology* (Philadelphia: Trinity Press 1990[2])

Alasdair MacIntyre, *After Virtue: A Study in Moral Theory* (London: Duckworth 1984)

—'Why is the Search for the Foundation of Ethics so Frustrating?' *Hastings Center Report* 9/4 (1979) 15–30

—*Three Rival Versions of Moral Enquiry* (London: Duckworth 1990)

See Gilbert Meilaender, *The Theory and Practice of Virtue* (Notre Dame: University of Notre Dame Press 1984)

'The Place of Ethics in the Theological Task', *Currents in Theology and Mission* 6 (1979) 190–205

Mary Midgely, *Beast and Man: The Roots of Human Nature* (Ithaca NY: Cornell University Press 1978)

John Milbank, *Theology and Social Theory: Beyond Secular Reason* (Oxford: Blackwell 1990)

—*The Word Made Strange: Theology, Language, Culture* (Oxford: Blackwell 1997)

Wilson Miscamble, 'Sectarian Passivism?' *Theology Today* 44 (April 1987) 69–77

D.C. Muecke, *Irony, the Critical Idiom* (London: Methuen 1970)

Leslie A. Muray, 'Confessional Postmodernism and the Process-Relational Vision' *Process Studies* 18/2 (1989) 83–94

Iris Murdoch, *The Sovereignty of Good Over Other Concepts* (Cambridge: Cambridge University Press 1967)

Paul Nelson, *Narrative and Morality: A Theological Enquiry* (Philadelphia: Pennsylvania State Press 1987)

Richard Neuhaus (ed.), *Virtue – Public and Private* (Grand Rapids: Eerdmans 1986)

H. Richard Niebuhr, *Christ and Culture* (New York: Harper and Row 1951)

—*Ernst Troeltsch's Philosophy of Religion* (New Haven: Yale University Dissertation 1924)

—*The Responsible Self* (New York: Harper and Row 1963)

—*The Meaning of Revelation* (New York: Macmillan 1941)

—*The Purpose of the Church and its Ministry* (New York: Harper and Row 1956)

—'The Responsibility of the Church for Society' K.S. Latourette (ed.), *The Gospel, the Church and the World* (New York: Harper and Row 1946)

—*The Kingdom of God in America* (New York: Harper Torchbooks 1959)

Reinhold Niebuhr, *An Interpretation of Christian Ethics* (New York: Meridian Books, Living Age Edition 1956)

—*Moral Man and Immoral Society* (New York and London: Scribner's 1932)

—*Beyond Tragedy* (New York: Scribners 1965)

Timothy O'Connell, *Principles for a Catholic Morality* (New York: Seabury 1978)

Oliver O'Donovan, *Resurrection and Moral Order: An Outline for Evangelical Ethics* (Grand Rapids: Eerdmans 1994[2])

Thomas Ogletree, 'Character and Narrative: Stanley Hauerwas' Studies of the Christian Life' *Religious Studies Review* 6/1 (January 1980) 25–30

Gene Outka, 'Character, Vision, and Narrative' *Religious Studies Review* 6/2 (April 1980) 110–118

D.Z. Phillips, 'Wittgenstein's Full Stop' in Irving Block (ed.), *Perspectives on the Philosophy of Wittgenstein* (Cambridge: MIT Press) 179–200

Michael J. Quirk, 'Beyond Sectarianism?' *Theology Today* 44 (April 1987) 78–87

Wolfhart Pannenberg, *Basic Questions in Theology* Volume I (London: SCM 1971)

Charles R. Pinches, 'Hauerwas Represented: A Response to Muray' *Process Studies* 18/2 (1989) 95–101

Edmund Pincoffs, 'Quandary Ethics' *Mind* 80 (1971) 552–571

Paul Ramsey, *The Just War: Force and Political Responsibility* (New York: Scribner's 1968)

Arne Rasmusson, *The Church as Polis: From Political Theology to Theological Politics as Exemplified by Jurgen Moltmann and Stanley Hauerwas* (Notre Dame: University of Notre Dame Press 1994)

Walter Rauschenbusch, *A Theology for the Social Gospel* (Nashville: Abingdon Press 1945)

J. Wesley Robbins, 'On the Role of Vision in Morality' *Journal of the American Academy of Religion* 45 (1977) 623–641

Rosemary Radford Ruether, *The Radical Kingdom: The Western Experience of Messianic Hope* (New York: Harper and Row 1970)

Jonathan Schell, *The Fate Of The Earth* (New York: Alfred Knopf, 1982),

Irfan Shahid, *The Martyrs of Najran: New Documents* (Brussels: Société des Bollandistes 1971)

Robert Sokolowski, *The God of Faith and Reason: Foundations of Christian Theology* (Notre Dame: University of Notre Dame Press 1982)

Janet Martin Soskice, 'Love and Attention' in Michael McGee (ed.), *Philosophy, Religion and Spiritual Life* (Cambridge: Cambridge University Press 1991) 59–72

Jeffrey Stout, *Ethics after Babel: The Languages of Morals and their Discontents* (Boston: Beacon 1988)

Ronald Thiemann, *Revelation and Theology: The Gospel as Narrated Promise* (South Bend: University of Notre Dame Press 1985)

Terrence W. Tilley, 'Incommensurability, Intertextuality and Fideism' *Modern Theology* 5/2 (January 1989) 87–111

Iain Torrance in 'They Speak to Us across the Centuries: 2. Cyprian' *The Expository Times* 108/12 (September 1997) 356–9

Thomas Tracy, *God, Action and Embodiment* (Grand Rapids: Eerdmans 1984)

Gregory Trianosky, 'What is Virtue Ethics All About?' *American Philosophical Quarterly* 27/4 (Oct 1990) 335–44

André Trocmé, *Jesus and the Nonviolent Revolution* (Scottdale: Herald 1973)

Ernst Troeltsch, *The Social Teachings of the Christian Churches* (New York: Macmillan 1931)

Mark I. Wallace, *The Second Naïveté: Barth, Ricoeur and the New Yale Theology* (Macon GA: Mercer University Press 1990)

J. Denny Weaver, 'Atonement for the NonConstantinian Church' *Modern Theology* 6 (July 1990) 307–323

William Werpehowski, 'Ad Hoc Apologetics' *The Journal of Religion* 66 (1986) 282–301

Lee Yearley, 'Recent Work on Virtue' *Religious Studies Review* 16/1 (1990) 1–9

John Howard Yoder, 'Reinhold Niebuhr and Christian Pacifism' *Mennonite Quarterly Review* 29/2 (April 1955) 101–17

—*The Christian Witness to the State* (Newton: Faith and Life Press 1964)

—'A People in the World: Theological Interpretation' in James Leo Garrett Jr (ed.), *The Concept of the Believers' Church* (Scottdale: Herald 1969) 252–283

—*The Original Revolution* (Scottdale, Pennsylvania: Herald Press 1971)

—'Living the Disarmed Life' *A Matter of Faith: A Study Guide for Churches on the Nuclear Arms Race* (Washington DC: Sojourners 1981) 40–3

—*The Politics of Jesus: Vicit Agnus Noster* (Grand Rapids: Eerdmans 1972/1994)

—*Christian Attitudes to War, Peace, and Revolution: A Companion to Bainton* (Elkhart Indiana: Goshen 1983)

—*The Priestly Kingdom: Social Ethics as Gospel* (Notre Dame: University of Notre Dame Press 1984)

—*Nevertheless: Varieties of Religious Pacifism* (Scottdale Pennsylvania: Herald 1992)

—*What Would You Do?* (Scottdale: Herald 1992)

—'How H. Richard Niebuhr Reasons: A Critique of *Christ and Culture*' in Glen H. Stassen, Diane M. Yeager, and John Howard Yoder (eds.), *Authentic Transformation: A New Vision of Christ and Culture* (Nashville: Abingdon 1995)

Name Index

Subject Index